CW01676741

CULTURAL SNIPING

Cultural Sniping brings together a wide range of Jo Spence's photographs and writings for the first time. Her work is characterized by its challenging and oppositional stance, coloured by a spirit of exploration and playfulness. This invigorating combination is reflected in the images and texts in this book, which tackle complex issues of gender, class, health and the body, and their impact on her understanding of personal history and the construction of identity.

Included here are images from Spence's early work in documentary photography and from her pioneering phototherapy projects, explored in collaboration with other photographers. The book reproduces work from her *Return to Nature* and *Death Rituals* series, in which she tries to come to terms with the reality of death. Jo Spence's commitment to engaging with personal experience, political understanding and critical theory makes her writing and photography a vital contribution to our understanding of the politics of representation.

Jo Spence was one of Britain's pioneering photographers. Born of working-class parents living in South Woodford, she worked for many years as a studio photographer. Her political concerns led her to documentary photography and she was a founder member of the Photography Workshop. Her life changed at 46 when she began a degree at the Polytechnic of Central London (now the University of Westminster) in the theory and practice of photography, and with the discovery of her breast cancer. Despite this, and through her struggle to find ways to tackle cancer and to share the experience with others, she developed new ways of using photography and new ways of living that affected her critical approach to a range of photographic projects. Jo Spence published and exhibited widely during her career, and her radical and innovative work has influenced a generation of practitioners and students of photography. She died in 1992.

FRONTISPIECE: Jo Spence/Rosy Martin/design Ann Braydon, 1986
Jo Spence Photographer – Calling Card

JO SPENCE PHOTOGRAPHER

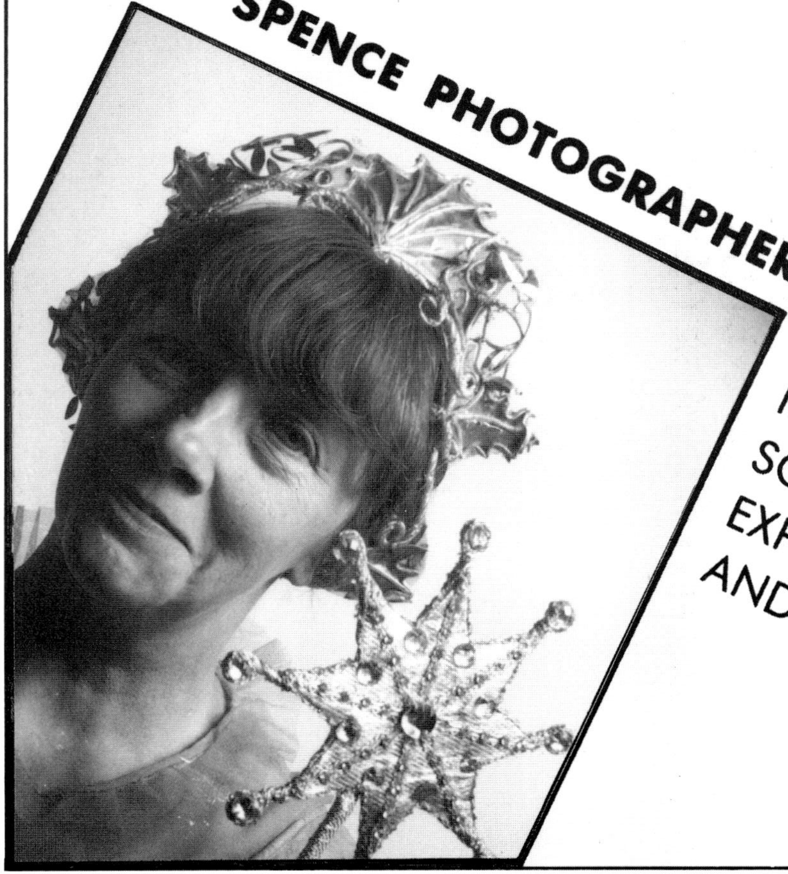

AVAILABLE FOR
DIVORCES, FUNERALS,
ILLNESS, SOCIAL INJUSTICE,
SCENES OF DOMESTIC VIOLENCE,
EXPLORATIONS OF SEXUALITY
AND ANY JOYFUL EVENTS

CULTURAL SNIPING

THE ART OF TRANSGRESSION

by Jo Spence

literary editing by Jo Stanley
picture editing by David Hevey
foreword by Annette Kuhn

ROUTLEDGE

London and New York

COMEDIA

Series editor:
David Morley

First published 1995
by Routledge
11 New Fetter Lane, London EC4P 4EE

Simultaneously published in the USA and Canada
by Routledge
29 West 35th Street, New York, NY 10001

Typeset in Sabon by Solidus (Bristol) Limited
Printed and bound in Great Britain by
Butler & Tanner Ltd., London and Frome

British Library Cataloguing in Publication Data
A catalogue record for this book is available from the British Library

Library of Congress Cataloguing in Publication Data
A catalogue record for this book has been requested

ISBN 0–415–08883–6
0–415–08884–4 (pbk)

Dedicated to my lovely David Roberts –
my husband and best friend

Affirming the highest acknowledgement to Terry Dennett
for his love and solidarity over many years

CONTENTS

PART ONE: CLASS, REALISM AND BEYOND

PART TWO:
A CRISIS OF REPRESENTATION: HEALTH AND BODIES

PART THREE:
IDENTITY, PHOTOGRAPHY, THERAPY

ILLUSTRATIONS

ABOUT THOSE DIRECTLY INVOLVED IN THIS BOOK

David Hevey is a disabled photographer, writer and broadcaster. His book, *The Creatures Time Forgot*, is published by Routledge. He has just had a baby boy, Liam Christie.

Annette Kuhn, for many years a freelance writer, lecturer and critic, now teaches film and television studies at the University of Glasgow. *Family Secrets*, her book of memory work, has recently been published by Verso.

Jo Stanley is a feminist and socialist who organizes, does life history work in the community, lectures, reviews and agitates. A writer of fiction and non-fiction, her current book is a history of women pirates, *Bold in Her Breeches* (London, Pandora, 1995).

Jo Spence was a photographer/educator who wrote, taught, exhibited, energized, organized and photographed politically from the early 1970s, particularly as a founding member of Photography Workshop. Born in 1934, she spent most of her life in Wembley and Islington, London. She started off her photographic career doing portraits in a studio and now influences generations of cultural workers and students internationally with her pioneering and radical practice including phototherapy and family album work. She died in June 1992.

ACKNOWLEDGEMENTS

ACKNOWLEDGEMENTS AND INFLUENCES FROM JO SPENCE

First I want to thank my family: my brother Michael Clode, Lisa and Kimble and Jo. Next, my adopted sisters: Margaret Munyard (and her lovely daughter Rosie), Joan Solomon and Sophie O'Neil (deceased). And my mum and dad.

Second, there are many groups that have supported me. These include: my older women's co-counselling peer group – Astra, Rosy Martin and Judith Gair; my post-education working-class women's group – Valerie Walkerdine, Helen Lucey, Joan Solomon, Jo Stanley and Pam Trevithick; the Polysnappers group – Charlotte Brinkley, Mary Ann Kennedy and Jane Munroe; the old Hackney Flashers photography group.

Thanks also to Bill Brandt, Ros Coward, Ute Eskilden, Jan Zita Grover, David Hevey, Stuart Hood, Bushy Kelly, Keith Kennedy, Patti Levey, Erik Linssen, John Maltby, Alison Marchant, Rosy Martin, Alice Miller, Susan Buck-Morss, Dennis Potter, Jay Ruby, Angelo Schwarz, Allan Sekula and Sally Stein, Seth Siegelaub, Abigail Solomon-Godeau, Yana Stajno, Simon Watney, Judy Weiser and John Willett.

I wish to acknowledge my appreciation for the British Film Institute Education Department as it was from the mid-1970s onwards, particularly David Lusted, Sue Isherwood, Jim Cook. From the BFI Production Department in the early 1980s I'd like to thank in particular Peter Sainsbury, Terence Davies and Rose English.

For their work with me over the years, I thank the following galleries: Camerawork, especially for all their efforts on behalf of the Jo Spence health fund show; Cockpit Gallery cultural studies department, especially Martin Lister; Cambridge Darkroom Gallery; Bristol Watershed.

I'm grateful for the support of The Space Between Group – Di Dosser, Pru Clements; Format – Maggie Murray, Brenda Prince; Ten-8 collective and John Taylor in particular; Photo-fusion; The Photo Co-op; Women Artists Slide Library; *Spare Rib*; and the *Feminist Arts Newsletter*.

Last but very much not least, I thank Bert Hogenkamp, Stanley Foreman and Ruth and Eddie Frow for their friendships and support as colleagues over the years; David Evans for sharing his work on John Heartfield with me and helping with *Photography/Politics: One*; Liz Heron for her backing over many years, particularly during the difficult days following my sacking from *Camerawork* magazine.

There are many more people I want to thank but I'm too ill to think of them at present. I hope they know how much I appreciate them anyway.

Jo Spence June 1992

THANKS FROM THE EDITOR

I'd like to thank Terry Dennett and David Hevey for all their work on the pictures, and for their support; Dave Morley for encouraging advice on ways to tackle such a mammoth editing job and David Roberts for practical backing and affection. Rosy Martin, Margaret Munyard and Joan Solomon were wonderful in helping me create the chronology, context notes and bibliography.

For company, interest, incisiveness (and sometimes cake) I thank Assuntina Cardillo-Zallo, Norma Clarke, Anna Davin, Helen Lucey, Cathy Porter, Valerie Walkerdine. For sane approaches when I thought the task impossible, Dorothy Badrick, and Susan Schenkel for writing *Giving Away Success – Why Women Get Stuck and What to Do About It* (Harper Perennial, New York, 1991).

In particular, I'm grateful to Dominic Sweetman. Without his love, buoyant tactics and generosity over facilities, this book would have been a much more painful process.

At Routledge, editors Rebecca Barden and Moira Taylor managed to be friendly and open despite all the pressures on them.

Above all, I thank Jo Spence for writing work that was always instructive to read and reread, and for being the inspiring and obnoxious mate/collaborator she once was.

Jo Stanley

ACKNOWLEDGE-MENTS

We gratefully thank the following for giving their permission to reprint articles by Jo Spence:

Artpaper: for 'The artist and illness: cultural burn-out/holistic health!', 1991.
Camerawork: for 'The politics of photography', 1976, and 'The unpolitical photograph?', 1978.
Comedia: for 'Ten years of Photography Workshop', 1984.
Family Welfare Newspaper: for 'Getting Better', 1982.
Feminist Arts News: for 'Class confusion or cultural solidarity?', 1991.
Ikon Gallery: for 'The daughter's gaze: blaming, shaming, renaming and letting go', 1990.
Photography Workshop: for 'What did you do in the war, mummy? Class and gender in the images of women', 1979.
Practice: for 'Could do better ... towards a personal and political theatre of the self', 1990.
Screen: for 'An *Omnibus* dossier', 1983, and 'Remodelling photo-history', 1983.
Views: for 'Identity and cultural production', 1990.

EDITOR'S PREFACE

Photographer, writer, educator, Jo Spence put fifty-eight articles together just before she died in June 1992. She handed them over to me in a Tesco bag at the Marie Curie hospice, Hampstead, relieved and pleased that at last they had a publisher – Routledge – and that the full scale of her work was going to be visible to all. I was selected as literary editor because we were friends and Jo knew that as a writer and life history worker I was doing with words something of what she was doing with pictures. I had already collected and bound most of the writings she'd given me since our friendship began in the mid-1980s.

This anthology is brutally reduced from the original fat and definitive volume Jo dreamt of; she would have hated that – and the editor. She was so prolific that her collected articles and writings, let alone her pictures, could make three volumes. Jo knew before she died that 180,000 words would have to be edited down to 70,000 words. Cutting such valuable material has been a difficult job, not least because my respect for her grew the more I reread her work. At one point, almost any omissions felt like a ludicrous waste. At the time of her death, a lot of people needed this book to be a complete summary of her efforts. Instead, we've had to accept that it is just one small collection – and that there can and will be more.

The criteria for excising at least twenty items include whether they are easily available elsewhere, for example in Jo's picture autobiography *Putting Myself in the Picture* (London, Camden Press, 1986) and in other Routledge books. I have also reduced the length of some articles on the grounds that they were repetitive or that aspects of them were inappropriate to this short book, for example several pages narrating John Heartfield's life and work. Cuts are indicated by ellipsis points (. . .). The sections and sequences are as Jo suggested.

The chronology and contextualizing notes have been compiled posthumously and will contain inaccuracies. It's been instructive for me as a historian to see that even within six months of someone's death, much information is lost. We don't know about all her TV programmes, for example. And of course everyone has a different version of what were significant events in her life. Although her book lists have been checked as far as possible, sometimes precise details and confirmation cannot be found. I apologize in advance for any wild-goose chases caused by this.

All the articles Jo wrote, unexpurgated, are available through the Jo Spence

Memorial Archive, based at 152 Upper Street, London N1 1RA, telephone: 0171 359 9064. A full chronology, personal documents and her photographs, in the form of several loanable exhibitions, are also located there.

Jo Stanley, Upper Holloway, December 1992

INTRODUCTION

We need to be subjects of history, even if we cannot totally stop being objects of history. And to be subjects, we need unquestionably to claim history critically. As active participants and real subjects, we can make history only when we are continually critical of our very lives.[1]

The front cover of Jo Spence's 'political, personal and photographic autobiography', *Putting Myself in the Picture*, bears five photographs of the author. Four are colour portraits showing a middle-aged woman wearing no makeup, a school blouse under a pullover, and a series of not easily readable facial expressions. These pictures (from a phototherapy session conducted in collaboration with Rosy Martin in the mid-1980s) are overlaid on an older, fainter, monochrome image: a photo from Jo Spence's family album, taken when she was an 11-year-old evacuee, 'looking like a refugee'.[2]

On its own this grainy image of a schoolgirl might evoke responses which, even if tinged with pain, are commonly enough associated with the family photograph ('We [evacuees] felt the adults had abandoned us'[3]). But the juxtaposition of the more recent photographs may jolt the viewer into a very different response: shock. This assemblage of images puts publicly into the picture a child's feelings of loss as remembered and relived forty years on. It thus refuses to allow memory to keep to its proper, safe place in an imagined and closed-off past – or at most in a present inner life shared, if at all, only with one's closest intimates.

If there is a thread which runs through all of Jo Spence's work, it is surely this capacity to challenge the boundaries between inner and outer, private and public, personal and political; and in so doing to 'make strange' the distinctions which pervade our culture and shape the ways we think about ourselves and our lives. Jo Spence's chosen theatre of operations was photography and, increasingly after about 1980, her own body (itself a battleground, always imaged in a political and social context) as figured in photographs. In its totality, the achievement of the work is an apparently paradoxical one. In using 'personal' materials – photographs, memories, body – as a site of cultural intervention, it succeeds in challenging taken-for-granted assumptions concerning the public as against the private. But also, and perhaps in the end more significantly, it taps into a rich vein of collective memory and feeling.

This may be universal in the sense that everyone has a past upon which she can reflect, and most of us can use photographs in a variety of ways to aid this process. But perhaps of greater political importance is the fact that Jo Spence's work brings to light and subjects to scrutiny the memories and the fantasies of a social class, a gender group, a particular generation – people whose inner lives are commonly dismissed as insignificant, impoverished, even non-existent; and shows us how these permeate our more immediately felt day-to-day lives as children, workers, parents, lovers.

When the exhibition 'Beyond the Family Album' opened in London's Hayward Gallery in 1979, it had exactly this impact upon many of those who saw it, myself included. In themselves, the images on display – all from Jo Spence's own archive – seemed conspicuous for their very ordinariness: in nature, content and ordering, they were remarkably similar to my own family album (and presumably also to a lot of other people's). But in aggregate the work felt utterly out of the ordinary. In the first place, these 'commonplace' photographs were mounted on the walls of one of our foremost art museums; and in the second, the images and their meanings were quite transmuted by what the artist had done with them. Captions, running in two series, tell a story of a life. This is set against another story, one concealed more than revealed by the photographs: a story of sickness, anger, struggle.

But far from stopping with the conclusion that the family album masks essential truths about our pasts, the exhibit in the end foregrounds the *processual* quality of its own project: 'there is no peeling away of layers to reveal a "real" self, just a constant reworking process. I realize that I am a process'.[4] Besides offering a 'how-to' guide, the institutional seal of approval implicit in the public exhibition of such work may embolden the viewer, give her courage to look afresh at her own family photographs. The beauty of this sort of memory work is that anyone who possesses a family album can do it, if she wants to.

But if, in the gallery context at least, the very accessibility of the family album project might provoke (as it certainly did in some quarters) a certain discomfort, how are we to respond to the taboo-breaking quality of much of Jo Spence's later work? This work – notably in phototherapy and, more obviously perhaps, on health in general and conventional and 'alternative' cancer treatments in particular – once again questions the limits of the 'personal'. But it also lays siege to our preconceptions about what is acceptable in photographic (and indeed in other visual) representations of the human body, specifically in this instance of a female, sick and ageing body. For this body categorically refuses to portray itself in the only culturally endorsed mode available, as victim.

The voyeuristic gaze – combining fascination and non-involvement –

solicited by such a great deal of contemporary public photography is impossible here; and there is little room either for retreat into narcissistic identification. The phototherapy images in particular seem so intensely personal: how can a moment captured in a therapy session speak to an outsider? And yet how narrowly personal *are* the meanings available from these images? In looking at a portrait of a woman of 50 dressed in a fairy costume,[5] do I, the viewer, acknowledge the little girl within my own adult self? Do I laugh at the silliness of such a fantasy? Or do I mourn its loss, grieved by the gulf that separates a childhood self for whom everything seemed possible from a grown woman who has learned to settle for so much less? And if so, how much has this to do with limitations on my horizons imposed by class and gender, and how much with sharing in a more universally felt sense of loss?

The questions are uncomfortable, and not just because the images make strange the conventions of photographic representation. For the force with which they insist on bringing together past and present, inner and outer, private and public, is quite impossible to contain within any safe nostalgic retreat that we might choose to label memory. A minefield, indeed.

Jo Spence characterizes the 'Family Album' exhibition as a first step in investigating her own family and class background, and what it means to be a woman: 'The cross-fertilization between class and sexuality has informed all my work since this period.'[6] In fact, while it is undeniably feminist, questions around social class weave themselves through all of Jo Spence's work, articulating themselves diversely, and in varying degrees openly, at different times and in different contexts. In her later work (see, for example, the 1991 'Cultural Sniper' interview, Chapter 24 of this volume) there is a very explicit return to the issues of class politics and photography which had been at the core of the work up till 1979 (when the anthology *Photography/Politics: One* was published) and which had remained central in all of Spence's collaborations with Terry Dennett. By 1991, however, questions around class are nuanced by concerns with the psyche, with the inner life and fantasy; by concerns raised in 1980s feminist thinking on representation and sexual difference and, more importantly perhaps, by Spence's own less overtly theorized work on the family album and in phototherapy.

The significance of this later work is that, unlike a good deal of feminist politics and feminist theory, it does not shrink from addressing differences *between* women, notably differences of social class. Refusing a-priori theorizing, and again drawing on 'personal' material – images, memories – as a starting point, the writings of Jo Spence's last years break through to a characteristically angry and humorous revelation of the inner drama of class difference. In the process it suggests how, for upwardly socially mobile women of working-class origin, our class formation remains deeply inscribed in our inner worlds, and continues to shape our opportunities and inform our outward lives.

How will Jo Spence's work be remembered? It seems impossible to put a label on it: it refuses to be confined within any of the numerous 'isms' that describe cultural tendencies and movements. This is not because the work is one-off, too individual or idiosyncratic to find a place within a broader cultural or sociocultural context, however. On the contrary: it is rather that questions of form, style, even of content, are not particularly relevant within its sphere of operation. What matters here is that images and their meanings (and indeed theories about the meanings of images) are, precisely, subsumed to their *uses* – to praxis, to what we do now and what we might do in the future with our photographs, as we explore our past and present lives in the quest to find ways of changing things.

But this work does nevertheless have parallels within other cultural practices. Examples which spring most immediately to mind include the educational activities of Paulo Freire, and John Heartfield's photo-montage. In the 1960s, Freire pioneered a fresh approach to adult literacy in his native Brazil. This was grounded in the practice of 'conscientization': the educational process – non-hierarchical and participatory – involved an awakening of consciousness on the part of students, a development of a critical and questioning attitude towards their own lives and the world around them. Working in 1930s Germany, John Heartfield used familiar photographic images in a practice of montage which at once denaturalized the 'reality-effect' of photography and exposed the power relations underlying the outward façade of Nazism.[7]

Freire's and Heartfield's practices, both progressive in intent, are very different; and both are obviously very much of their own time and place. But they are united by the broadly serviceable conviction that an awakening of critical consciousness among those who lack power is a crucial step in the process of democratization. In this sense, both are in the business of education, if we take education to mean an activity involving dialogue, reflection and awareness that touches the heart as well as the mind. And both build a praxis with tools and materials that are readily to hand: the reflections of peasants and workers on their own lives, the common currency of photographic images.

In content as well as in context, Jo Spence's work is different yet again. It is infused, for example, by the new understandings of the relation between the personal and the political brought forth in the second wave of feminism. And more specifically, it is marked by its social, cultural and institutional conditions of existence, notably the rise and decline during the 1970s and 1980s of publicly funded 'community arts' projects in Britain, and the dismantling of the British welfare state. And yet, in drawing on what is available or readily observable in our everyday lives, it shares with Freire's and Heartfield's practices a commitment not only to accessibility but also to an appropriation and transformation of the raw material of the commonplace in the building of critical consciousness, in the practice of education in its best sense. Above all, in common with its counterparts, Jo Spence's work is driven by anger at injustice, by abundant compassion, and by a relentless yearning for personal, political and social change.

To ask how this work will be remembered is perhaps to assume that the artist's death in some way draws a line under it. Far from it: as long as its social and psychical conditions remain in place, so will the need for social change and for the subversive impulse that lies behind its 'cultural sniping'. Jo Spence's work has touched the lives of many 'ordinary' people, not least because it embodies and makes accessible the tools of its own practice: it offers us, in other words, the means of carrying on the work, of doing it for ourselves. Here, the use value of the photographic image lies not in its place in any art historical movement or category. It lies in its potential for active and imaginative deployment in the quest for personal/political change. Evading the deadening categorization, the work of Jo Spence continues to point beyond itself and towards a multitude of possible future uses.

Annette Kuhn, Haworth, West Yorkshire, April 1993

NOTES

1 Paulo Freire, *The Politics of Education: Culture, Power and Liberation*, London, Macmillan, 1985, p. 199.
2 Jo Spence, *Putting Myself in the Picture: a Political, Personal and Photographic Autobiography*, London, Camden Press, 1986, p. 86.
3 ibid.
4 ibid., p. 97.
5 'Double Exposure – the Minefield of Memory', exhibition by Rosy Martin and Jo Spence, Photographers' Gallery, London, 1987.
6 Spence, op. cit., p. 82.
7 Paulo Freire, *Pedagogy of the Oppressed*, Harmondsworth, Penguin, 1972; Heartfield's work is discussed in Chapter 5 of the present volume.

CHRONOLOGY OF JO SPENCE'S LIFE

1934 Joan Clode born 15 June to parents in South Woodford, Essex. Later brought up in Kingsbury, London.

1940 Evacuated to Cornwall, then Derbyshire.

1948 Finished state school at 13. Began two-year course at private secretarial school.

1951–62 Began career as shorthand typist, then Girl Friday to commercial photographer. Freelance evening work as printer.

1962–4 Printer/assistant to Canadian advertising photographer Walter Curtin.

1964 Married Keith Holland and became a farm secretary in Brockwood Park, Hampshire.

1966 Went to live with disc jockey Neil Spence in Ireland. Changed her name by deed poll to his.

1967–74 Set up Joanna Spence Associates, a portrait and wedding photograph studio in Hampstead. Began relationship with David Phillips.

Political and educational photography work started

1970–3 Did projects with Children's Rights Workshop, London.

1973 Began relationship with Terry Dennett.

1974 With Terry Dennett, co-founded Photography Workshop, which later combined its programme with the Half Moon Gallery to form Half Moon Photography Workshop and the innovative magazine *Camerawork*.

1976 Sacked from Half Moon Photography Workshop.

1977 Refounded Photography Workshop with Terry Dennett and David Phillips. Project groups initiated during this period included the Faces Group, the Camberwell Beauties, the Hackney Flashers and the Photography/Politics: One Group. Working at British Film Institute as full-time secretary.

1979 Socialist feminist exhibitions by Hackney Flashers: 'Women and Work in Hackney' and 'Who's Holding the Baby?' Started BA in Film and Photographic Arts at Polytechnic of Central London (now the University of

Westminster). Made and exhibited 'Beyond the Family Album', Hayward Gallery, London. Photography Workshop created a small mobile exhibition 'What Did You Do in the War, Mummy?', and Jo began to give talks on 'Images of Women'.

1982 Graduated from PCL with first-class honours. Made and exhibited 'Family, Fantasy, Photography' with Polysnappers. Participated in *Omnibus* TV programme.

Work on identity, subjectivity, mental and physical health became her focus

1982 Moved briefly to Nottingham. At a routine check-up discovered she had breast cancer. Decided to have simple lumpectomy followed by Gerson therapy and Chinese herbs, refusing mastectomy and radiotherapy. Began treatment with Yana Stajno and David Lurie.

1983 Stabilized her breast cancer, although it recurred eighteen months after the lumpectomy. Began co-counselling course run by Peter Clark where she met Rosy Martin and began working with her on connections between photography and therapy, evolving their own practice of phototherapy. Split up with Terry Dennett but agreed to collaborate on Photography Workshop and other projects as usual. Exhibition created: 'The Picture of Health?' with Jessica Evans, Rosy Martin, Maggie Murray, Yana Stajno.

1984 Organized mega fiftieth fancy-dress women-only birthday party, on the theme of *Cinderella*, at which she dressed as fairy godmother. Met David Roberts at Neuro-Linguistic Programming course in May, started to co-counsel with him in June, and moved into his Wembley home in October. September. Wrote first article – together with Rosy Martin – on the practice of phototherapy. Became the adopted sister of Margaret Munyard, and subsequently of Joan Solomon, in a 'family' of her own making.

1985 Health improved sufficiently to put together a large retrospective show 'Review of Work: 1950–1985, Jo Spence', Camerawork Gallery, then touring nationally. It was the first time Jo's phototherapy work had been exhibited. The phototherapy section of the show emerged as a separate exhibition, 'The Phototherapy Road Show', with Rosy Martin.

1986 *Arena* TV programme on *Cinderella* broadcast, 21 January. Exhibited in touring exhibition co-produced with Rosy Martin: 'Don't Say Cheese, Say Lesbian'. In December, *Putting Myself in the Picture* – her first book – launched.

1987 February. 'Double Exposure – The Minefield of Memory', exhibition by Rosy Martin and Jo Spence, Photographers' Gallery, then touring.

March. *Putting Ourselves in the Picture – the Work of Jo Spence* broadcast on BBC *Arena*, 20 March.

April. Gave keynote speech at first National Conference of Photography. Was so distressed by her reception that she decided to give up that kind of photography and move into phototherapy.

July. Exhibition at Photographers' Gallery: 'Body Politics'.

September. Exhibitions at Photographers' Gallery: 'Transforming the Suit – What Do Lesbians Look Like?' by Rosy Martin and Jo Spence; 'Tales my Father Never Taught Me', by Jo Spence and David Roberts.

1988 Was instrumental in getting John Healy's first novel *The Grass Arena* published and started working with him on writing and agenting his second work. Began difficult short relationship with Healy over the summer which ended in November. *Opening up the Family Album*, series designed by Jo Spence and directed by Nina Killgren, broadcast on C4, 9–30 August.

1989 'Great Expectations', exhibition by Rosy Martin and Jo Spence at Islington Libraries. *Tip of the Iceberg* TV programme broadcast. Left BFI and worked as freelance lecturer, writer, facilitator. Became involved with the Educated Working-Class Women's Group following Women's Therapy Centre workshop with Pam Trevithick on working-class women.

1990 Glasgow's New Gallery said it would name a room the Jo Spence Room.

September–December. National tour of Australia and US with exhibition 'Jo Spence – Collaborative Works'. It left Jo so exhausted that it became clear she was seriously ill.

Xmas Eve. Leukaemia and the return of breast cancer confirmed. New round of searching for treatment began – recorded photographically as usual. Jo Spence health fund set up, received international response.

1991 Made *Video Diary* for BBC with brother Michael Clode.

July. Exhibited as part of 'Missing Persons/Damaged Lives', Leeds City Art Gallery, then touring.

Autumn. Exhibited as part of 'A Daughter's View', Watershed Gallery, Bristol.

1992 Increasingly ill and unable to work. Documented that process.

13 May. Wearing scarlet kaftan, married David Roberts at Brent Town Hall.

18 May. Admitted to Marie Curie Hospice, Hampstead.

24 June. Died in hospice.

2 July. Funeral at Golders Green crematorium.

1994 'Jo Spence: Matters of Concern: Collaborative Images 1982–1992', Festival Hall, London, then touring.

Jo Spence Memorial Archive set up. Terry continued to disseminate her work (see exhibition list on p. 237).
Increased international interest in her practice.

Forthcoming

Large international retrospective exhibition in process of being organized for the late 1990s. Anthology jointly co-edited with Joan Solomon, *What Can a Woman Do With a Camera?*, (London, Scarlet Press, 1995). Exhibition 'The Final Project', with Terry Dennett, in progress. *Class Shame* – book with Terry Dennett commissioned by Working Press. 'In Memoriam' – exhibition in preparation. 'Freedom' – exhibition in preparation.

It needs to be said that these are only the major evidences and exigencies of twenty-hour days full of writing diary and articles, photographing, facilitating workshops, reading, debating, talking, planning, networking and therapy. Jo worked with active cancer in her breast from 1984.

PART ONE

CLASS, REALISM AND BEYOND

1 · THE POLITICS OF PHOTOGRAPHY

This was originally published in the first edition of the radical British journal *Camerawork* in 1976, and later republished in the *British Journal of Photography* and other magazines. It was Jo's contribution to the extended discussions taking place within Photography Workshop on the nature of British photography as it then was, and on the urgent need for new thinking and a more radical political approach to documentary photography.

Every day photographers produce countless images, most of which will never be seen by a mass audience. However, those that are seen, in newspapers, magazines and on high-street hoardings, play an important part in our lives. With their messages – both explicit and hidden – they help to shape our concepts of what is real and what is normal. They give us information about the sort of sex roles we are expected to play in society, contribute to our image of ourselves, to our expectations and to our fantasies.

Television, cinema and all visual media echo the same ideology. Continually repeated visual images, in time, become part of our stored experience. Images help us to believe that people are innately aggressive, intelligent, loving or lowly – according to their sex or race, or to the idea being sold to us. . . .

It is important to look at the context from which these images spring and at the background of the people who produce them.

CURRENT TRENDS IN COMMERCIAL PHOTOGRAPHY

Photographic colleges, as part of their policy of trying to professionalize photography, are still tightening up their entrance qualifications. They do this in liaison with the official bodies representing photographers. Once through the initial vetting, students then live and work for several years in the rarefied atmosphere of colleges in which there are no realistic deadlines or cares about the cost of materials and equipment, and in which they are in isolation from the feelings and needs of the majority of people whom they will use as subject matter. Here they learn to pass more examinations.

They are then released in great numbers onto the very competitive job market where the only bodies likely to be interested in their qualifications will be industry and government establishments. The remainder then chase the few other jobs available, become freelances, set up their own businesses, or find some entirely different way to earn a living. Commercial photography is a competitive rat race entirely geared to servicing the needs of contemporary consumer society.

Alongside this, photographic technology advances rapidly, with faster-acting materials and more expensive time-saving equipment. At the same time, though, materials not considered commercially viable by manufacturers are slashed from catalogues and disappear for ever. Photographers themselves are caught in the trap of improving their techniques, whilst at the same time the content of their pictures becomes more stereotyped, transiently fashionable, semi-pornographic or obtuse. Sophisticated courses have even been devised to train photographers how better to exploit a situation in order to get people to relate more easily to the intrusive camera, thus becoming more easily turned into objects.

SOCIAL REALISM

Concurrent with commercial photography is the race to be more socially realistic in our picture making. More and more we are assailed with aesthetically cropped pictures of corpses, gun fights, starving children or the so-called important members of our society. With rare exceptions such photo-journalism is seldom set in any meaningful social or political perspective. More often than not it is an unjustifiably voyeuristic and one-sided account of the stark situation in which many people are forced to live – or a superficial treatment of the joys and sorrows of celebrity life.

Photo-journalists are employed mostly by magazines and newspapers, and they are tightly controlled by a very few companies and publishing houses. Work is often edited beyond recognition or used out of context. Printed in the mass press, or alongside the hi-fi and sherry adverts in the colour supplements, this imagery eventually becomes just another commodity for us to thumb through in our search for distraction or for the 'truth'.

Other photographers, interested in the problems of poverty and oppression, work for charities. There are now over 400 national bodies dealing solely with children; some of them now employ quite sophisticated techniques to attract our attention and make us feel guilty. Using international advertising agencies we are sold the illustrated saga of the under-privileged and those suffering from the 'cycle of deprivation' (or could we call it the cycle of exploitation?). . . .

SOME ALTERNATIVES

Groups like Report and the Alternate News Service have now formed in order to service political newspapers, magazines and community presses. They concentrate on industrial and community action, showing solidarity among people, unlike the mass press which often depicts only the struggle of the individual. Other collectives have formed to record life in the neighbourhoods of working people, whilst others are recording social conditions and inequalities. Linked to statistics, or used in juxtaposition with glossy advertising myths or official documents, or alongside interviews with the people depicted, individual or national issues can be highlighted in order to reveal the lack of understanding of the planners and decision-makers who shape our destinies. Such work is also used away from galleries, in high streets, public meeting places and in education, as a mirror to show events considered 'un-newsworthy' by the national press.

Other photographers, because of their disillusionment with the highly competitive job market, and because of a genuine identification with the need for social change, have gravitated towards alternative magazines and books. These cover a wide variety of issues ranging from community action, anti-psychiatry and radical social work to feminism and children's rights. Such work has deeper political perspectives but it reaches a more limited audience. Generally there is very little financial reward from it, these photographers often having to supplement their income with other types of work.

Community photography

The most recent break with traditional fields has been the use of photography as a *tool* by community activists, already a well-established practice in North America. Several photographers (singly or in groups) have now managed to obtain short-term grants or funds for the setting up of photographic units within community, neighbourhood or youth projects. Here photography can be explained to and used by lay people. This is done by starting with simple cameras or video, and then gradually working through to the more technically advanced

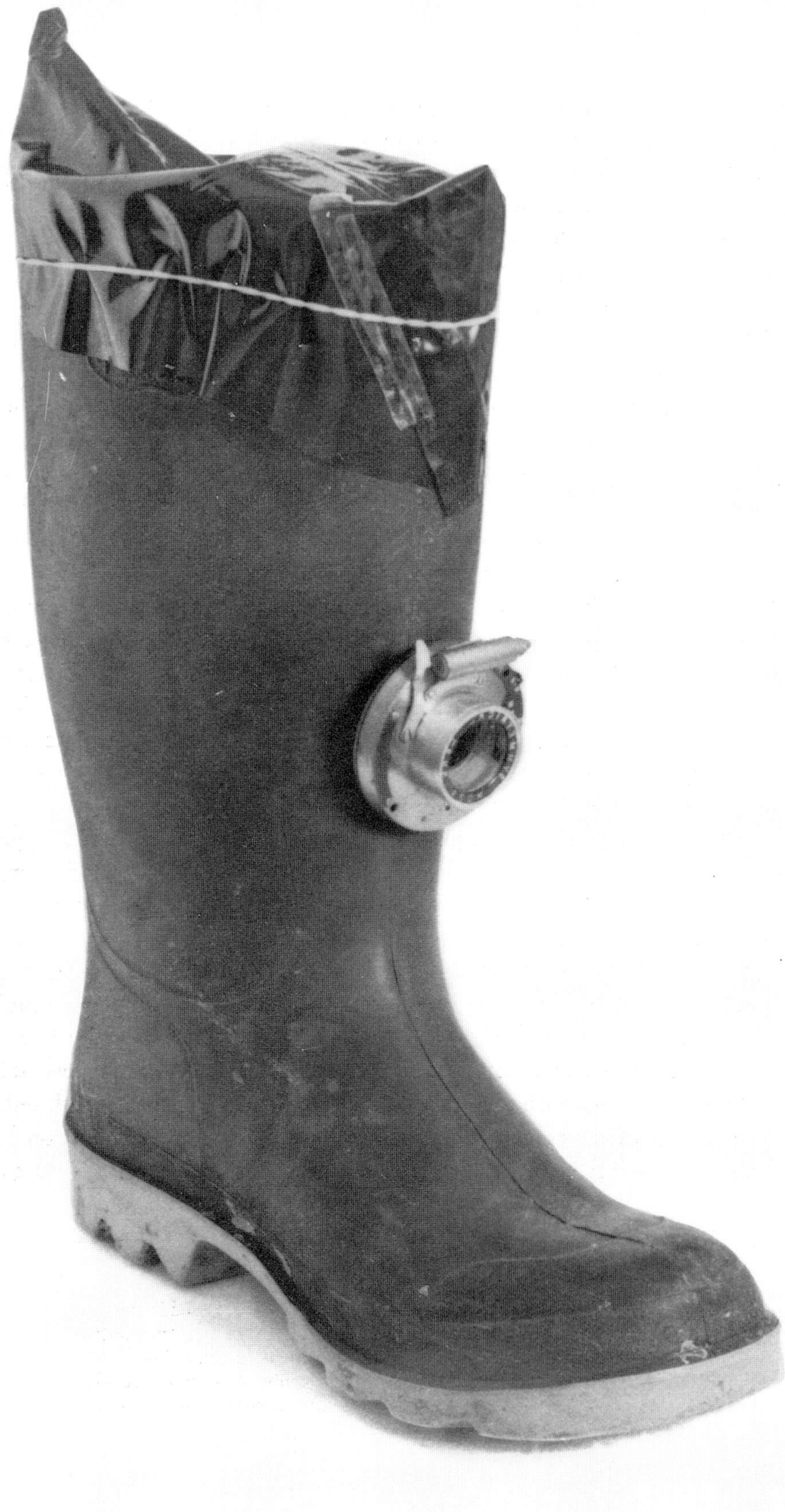

equipment, linked to darkroom and printing skills. This puts photography into the hands of a lot of people who will eventually be able to dispense with the experts. This move has provoked some reaction from those who have fought for years to gain for photography the status of a profession, elevating it ... out of the grasp of the majority of people.... Such policy is entirely in keeping with our hierarchical class society. The middle class mystifies and refines knowledge; at the same time it manages to rationalize its activity by convincing us that this is all in the interests of progress and economic growth. Photography as a tool is far removed from such attitudes because it negates elitism.

Community photographers are encouraging people to photograph each other, friends and family, then their social environment. This provides immediate feedback for discussion, provides aids for storytelling and reading, and makes it possible to look at the world differently. People can discover how to relate to themselves and to others more positively when armed with images of themselves – images which counteract the stereotypes usually seen in the mass media.

The main objective here is to enable people to achieve some degree of autonomy in their own lives and to be able to express themselves more easily, thus gaining solidarity with each other. It also helps to some extent to demystify the media and to make the relationship much less of a one-way affair. This is a far cry from the passive and abject individual problems of those depicted in charity appeals. Basically, though, they could be the same people – just totally different approaches. Agitators or objects of pity: which to choose?

What long-term results community activists can achieve with photography still remains to be seen. Funds and grants are hard to get (and much competed for) and are always given conditionally. Some photographers have already been threatened with the withdrawal of their funds because they have supposedly gone too far. Hopefully people in their own neighbourhoods are not already so alienated from themselves and from each other that they will adopt techniques of dishonesty or exaggeration in their picture making. Those who have their roots in a neighbourhood cannot afford to photograph people as mere 'things'. They still have to live with each other after the pictures have been produced.

This has of course been a problem for photographers for a long time; however involved they are, they still have to gain the confidence of their subject

1 Terry Dennett/Photography Workshop, 1975
Welliflex Camera
One of a series of home-made cameras that evolved in the Children's Photo Workshops run by Terry Dennett at the South Island Workshop, Lambeth. The project was continued with the help of Jo Spence, as part of the Photography Workshop Mobile Photo Darkroom Project, carried out on adventure playgrounds.

matter in order to get their pictures (be they paid models or the unsuspecting general public). Then, having gained their objective, they can go back to their clients, potential markets or private collections, more often than not closing the door on the lives of those with whom they were temporarily involved.

Common sense might tell us that this is often due to lack of time. Is it as simple as that? Or is it part of our demarcation of personal life and professional life?

2 · THE UNPOLITICAL PHOTOGRAPH?

(with Terry Dennett)

Jointly written by Terry Dennett and Jo Spence while they were members of the founding editorial group of *Camerawork*, this appeared in *Camerawork*, no. 7, 1978, pp. 6–8. It was a response to a letter by Roger Mayne in *Camerawork*, no. 6 which criticized Jo's interview with photographer Robert Goldman in *Camerawork*, no. 3, July 1976. This article was one of many attempts by Jo and Terry to introduce a discussion on class into the magazine and into the projects of the Half Moon Photography Workshop. Terry sees interventions such as this as the eventual cause of their exclusion from the workshop and of Jo's sacking from it.

The problem of being able to distinguish between a 'working-class' or a 'middle-class' photographer doesn't seem to us to be of primary importance. Rather, it might be useful to ask how their photographs are decoded and used by *various audiences*. What we mean by this will become clearer when we have looked at some of the problems involved in producing and using images.

The argument that photographers should decide whether to spend their time taking photographs or going into politics is confusing. We believe that photographers are *already* in politics. This is because the images we make carry ideological messages which, cumulatively, help to shape people's ideas, values and attitudes. If we are shown enough pictures of women's bodies, or packets of Daz, then we could probably conclude that society has a value for such imagery. Equally, if we *don't* see certain aspects of society then we could conclude that their omission (if we even notice it) is because they are of no importance. In this respect photographers cannot be anything but political. What Roger Mayne really seems to be asking is 'What is the *class* nature of a photograph?'[1] As this is so often forgotten or glossed over today, it is this particular question to which we would like to address ourselves.

THE NEUTRAL WORLD?

There seems to be a widespread assumption among photographers that their work is somehow 'neutral' or apolitical, that politics is something that goes on in Parliament or the White House. How do we convince them that they are mistaken? We have approached the problem by listing various stages at which manipulation or bias can occur in the production of photographs. Bearing in mind the fact that only a minute proportion of work ever reaches a wide audience because of the choosing of photographers by potential buyers, publishers, galleries or grant-funding bodies, the following will all have a bearing on the final photographs, and then the way they are received and decoded:

1. the photographer's consciousness (i.e. philosophical understanding) and thence use of the camera;
2. the photographer's darkroom practice;
3. the editorial process of choosing from a range of pictures (both as done *by* the photographer and as done *to* her/him – you can't evaluate anyone by their published work alone);
4. the juxtaposition of different pictures during layout;
5. the addition of text;
6. a consideration of the context in which it appears (i.e. what else appears alongside it?);
7. the form that it takes (i.e. is it in a newspaper, on a gallery wall, in a family album, in a school reading book?).

This last point raises a whole range of questions that also need to be asked. For example, is the image:

1. for public or private consumption (i.e. to be looked at in the street, transmitted to the home, stood on the piano)?
2. for distribution as part of mass media, by government bodies, through 'alternate' or minority channels?
3. free, inexpensive, easily accessible or exclusive?
4. aimed at a particular group (e.g. army recruits, managers, mums)?
5. aimed at a particular social or economic class?

It is also important to consider how much access photographers are allowed to specific areas of public life (for example, schools, factories and courts are all 'private property'). Also, how much censorship is exercised at the individual, group or class level,[2] or by the state? Another essential factor is the question of who owns or controls the means of production and reproduction of an image (i.e. do they have a vested interest, either financially or ideologically, in propagating or omitting certain images and not others?). Not least of all, we must consider at what historical and economic point in time the picture was taken and how this can contribute to various interpretations.

Finally, it is crucial to raise the question of the beholder. What bias does the viewer/reader inflect in the viewing of the picture or in the reading of the text (language is also ideologically biased and can be understood in many ways)? What might be the possible responses of a person who is not part of the social, sexual or racial groups an image is explicitly directed at?

All photographs are message carriers, either between members of the same social class who share common codes, or between differing classes and cultures. In our society most of the 'messages' received by the working class are mediated via the middle class. Clearly, most of these messages are class-biased (as well as being biased in other ways), and they conceal or distort the relationships of working-class people with all other classes, and often with each other. Sometimes these messages are so distorted that they need the medium of fantasy, as in the cartoon. This contributes to the general lack of information about the true nature of social and economic relationships (what Marxists call 'false consciousness'). However, in order to begin to answer Mayne's question of how we distinguish between working-class and middle-class photographers we need first to discuss some of the terminology which is required and then to find a context in which to apply it.

CLASS EXPERIENCES

In most social and economic relations there is a basic antagonism between those who have the *power* to make decisions and have them carried out, linked to those who have the *authority* to carry out such decisions – and those who have *neither the power nor the authority*. The term 'working class' is usually taken to mean people who have no means of production and who earn their living by selling their labour power to others. As a generic term it is perhaps misleading (there are now many definitions of it) because within the working class itself there are many hierarchies of power and earning capacity, as well as sexual and racial oppression.

WHERE DO IDEAS COME FROM?

Are they God-given or mystical? No. They have their roots in the day-to-day world which has shaped us since birth. Western society has gone through various historical and economic developments, including patriarchy, capitalism and imperialism, each moulding our attitudes, values and laws with its respective ideologies of sex, class and race oppression. Such oppression – which is still with us – is not simply a matter of class discrimination between some groups, or sex or race discrimination between others. It is a mixture of all three, the balance of which is constantly shifting, at both the individual and group levels. However, we believe that the fundamental oppression still remains a matter of one's class.

If we take these structures as a starting point, any understanding or *teaching* of photography should be extended to examine our social and economic history. We can then look at our own preconceptions with regard to other complexities such as 'human nature', language, science, psychology, culture and art. Depending on our ultimate 'world view' and where we think we as photographers fit into all this, and which social group/s we identify with, so will this influence how we proceed to document the world and show (or hide) these structures and relationships in our photographs.

PROFESSIONAL AND CLASS CODES

All image makers (and photographers are no exception) must codify 'reality' in a number of ways, at both the shooting and the production stages of their work. Their own class, sex, age and race are factors which are usually ignored and yet are crucial when one is concerned to understand more clearly the problems of viewing, selecting and evaluating a potential subject for a photograph. Such factors will influence, however unconsciously, the technological, aesthetic and ideological choices that have to be made for the actual taking of a picture and the subsequent processes it undergoes.

The dominant codes that pervade all stages of the process, and which combine to form the biased view of the world that helps to maintain the status quo, are becoming more and more part of the learned professional practice within colleges, universities and professional institutions. Professionalism encourages the use of 'codes of conduct' and 'standards of excellence' which are not seen by the participants as being political. In the main these are not perpetuated by coercion but by professional consent and can become more extreme according to the political climate. Thus we learn to police ourselves.

And, as photography slowly becomes more professionalized, so it is being seen as the delegated task of some 'photographers' or 'artists' to record the lives of working-class people. It is important to ask what is the class nature of the relationships between these people and those they photograph. Particularly in view of the fact that most working-class people *already* own cameras themselves and could easily record more aspects of their own lives if encouraged to see beyond the lucrative smokescreen of Kodak technology and the consumer ethic. Mass photography has never been regarded at any time as an important documentary form (although it is often seen as such once the material has become 'historical'). Having said that, it must be reaffirmed that because someone may be sympathetic to, or may belong to, the working class, or may be critical of the ruling class, it does not necessarily follow that he or she will have a coherent political critique of social and economic relationships. Such a person's photography will tend to reflect this.

LOOKING AT PICTURES

In examining documentary photographs of working-class life we have found that emphasis has usually been placed upon *social customs* and *conditions* (disaster, deprivation, 'deviation', celebration, tradition). What has been most ignored has been the labour process (activity around the 'point of production') – the real world that millions of us wake up to every day of our lives. A world which is apparently invisible if one is to judge from the images seen in the media and in most photographic magazines or galleries. Photography conveys a great deal of information to us, but instead of clarifying class roles it mystifies, universalizing and generalizing situations so that social and economic contradictions and boundaries are blurred or disappear entirely. All forms of labour and production are totally misrepresented. For instance, in publications aimed at a mass working-class audience the emphasis of work is usually upon the *untypical* (entertainers, politicians, sportspeople, stars) as the important workers in our society. Industrial or manual workers seldom appear. Conversely, in publications aimed at middle- and upper-class audiences, workers often appear (as they also do in specialist journals) where their true function – to produce wealth for others and to be controlled – is only too apparent.

In trying to analyse and compare what particular photographers or artists are doing in their work there is no reason to use esoteric or maverick approaches. It is far more important to try to arrive at a broad set of assumptions and to use a common language which is scientifically based. This could most usefully be the language and methodology of dialectical and historical materialism.[3] Working in this manner we could then move on from the limitations and ambiguity of such subjective words as 'excellent', 'fine', 'sensitive', 'strong', etc., and discuss the growth and development of a photographer's work, class values and aesthetics. This has been quite normal for some time in areas of study such as film and literary criticism. In short, we need to be able to use the language of an Eisenstein, a Brecht or Benjamin.

PHOTOGRAPHY – CRITICAL OR PROGRESSIVE?

We believe that it is possible to learn a great deal about photographers' views by looking at the ways in which they represent (both in pictures and text) activity at such critical junctures as the point of production. . . .

Once we as photographers become aware of the contradictory nature of most social and economic relationships then we can ask the following of our photographs of working-class people: do they indicate a struggling class or an apathetic one? Do they show unity or conflict between different classes? Do they show people as objects or as subjects? Do our pictures heighten the awareness of the working class's *own* strength and value as a group? Do the pictures form part of a 'narrative' in which previously unseen or unrecognized elements of *working-class experience* are discernible (as opposed to the more universal 'human' experience concentrated on by most photographers)? Does a photograph falsely glamorize for ideological or economic reasons? Do we show a realistic image of our own class and the capitalist class?

Most important of all, it is not only what *we* the makers of images think, but also how the message is received and acted upon by our audience. There will be differing class responses to many ideas which are represented, and most especially to the type of illustrations [that Photography Workshop displays].

Finally, the 'boring' 'religion of Marxism' that Mayne writes about (dialectical and historical materialism) is in no way dull or mystical, but is the highest development within the fields of philosophy and aesthetics. Its use will mean the questioning of all our assumptions about the making and using of photographs. For photographers today who are interested in trying to help bring about social change it will mean a struggle to expose and throw off the dominant ideology and try to find more critical forms of representation. (This may even mean, in some instances, moving away from photography and into photomontage and conceptual work.) For those who use this method there is a coincidence of form and content in their work; no separation between photography and politics, or between theory and practice. It means positive action. Unlike Roger Mayne, we believe that the world *is* knowable and can be changed, for the better.

3 · WHAT DID YOU DO IN THE WAR, MUMMY?

Class and gender in the images of women

This appeared in Photography Workshop's innovative annual *Photography/Politics: One*, 1979, which Jo co-edited with Terry Dennett, David Evans and John Myers. A slightly different version, 'What do people do all day?', appeared in *Screen Education*, no. 29, Winter 1978/9. The article was a result of Jo's admiration for the work initiated by Stuart Hall at the Centre for Contemporary Cultural Studies, Birmingham, and was heavily illustrated with *Picture Post* advertisements. It was part of her contribution to Photography Workshop's study of social life in the Second World War as seen through the media. In keeping with Jo's practice of making multiple uses of any work, where appropriate, it was also presented as part of a small laminated exhibition of the same name and became one of the themes of her 'Images of Women' talks.

Much of the current work on images of women has been based on two concepts:

1 that there is a binary opposition within systems of signification in which what is present is definable only in relation to what is absent:[1] thus 'woman' is signified in relation to 'man' or 'feminine' in relation to 'masculine';
2 that we decode images by looking at what is present in the image itself, trying to locate its various 'signs and meanings'; a process of selective remembering

> and selective forgetting. This decoding process usually obscures from us the fact that we are looking not at real things, but at socially and culturally constructed and learned concepts (or formulations), which may or may not have a basis in reality. . . .

Such approaches have sometimes undervalued the ways in which the meaning of an image is also determined by the historical and institutional context of its production and reception.[2] More importantly, they may also concentrate solely on the binary opposition of woman/man at the expense of other possible oppositions, notably that of labour/capital. Usually the woman's 'symbolic lack' (of the phallus) and her exclusion from the patriarchal order have been stressed; but I would like to ask if the concept of 'woman as sign' can also illuminate her place in the 'symbolic order' of capitalism. In other words I want to broaden the question of decoding images of women to take into account not just the symbolic sexual lack, but also the exploitation of women's labour power under capitalism.

In this reformulation it may help to 'map out' some possible approaches.

1 The *personal*. As an example, I have examined myself as a system of signification which can be recorded. This makes 'me' the *mediator* as well as the *subject* of the information. This work has enabled me to start to deconstruct my own 'image', and then start the work of reconstruction within a wider understanding of theories of visual representation. A photographic record of some of this work is available in the Arts Council of Great Britain catalogue for the 1979 show 'Three Perspectives on Photography' held at the Hayward Gallery.
2 The *empirical*. I monitored representations of women, aimed at a broadly 'popular' audience, between 1972 and 1978. Thousands of images from women's and family magazines, from popular newspapers, children's books and comics, cartoons, street hoardings, greetings cards, wrappers, film posters, and wherever else they could be found, were put onto 35mm colour slides. These were sorted and categorized on a light box which then made it possible to track ephemeral or random images, as well as trace visual links and study areas of constant repetition and overlap. This way it was possible to arrive at some preliminary conclusions about the very limited 'narratives' set up for women, and the ways in which 'femininity' was constructed through representation.
3 The *specific*. It is possible to discover some of the many differently inflected significations of one basic stereotype by examining in depth particular representations of women. By doing this with the contemporary image of the

'secretary' (office worker), it becomes obvious that stereotypes are not *universal* but differ markedly depending on the context in which they are used, and the type of (class) audience; e.g. the stereotype offered to women in women's magazines is totally different from that offered to, say, business men in trade magazines.

4 The *historical*. A comparison with a historical conjuncture (like the Second World War) in which typical representations of women differ considerably from today's dominant stereotypes, can suggest some of the ways in which images are affected by economic and political changes. It also makes clear that stereotypes are not necessarily *fixed* but emerge and disappear when the news or advertising 'agendas' change in response to the needs of industry or the state, or to changed legislation.

It is the historical approach that I concentrate on here, but that work needs to be placed back in the context of the results of the empirical and specific studies which are in *Screen Education*, no. 29. Hopefully this work will be useful to illuminate the difference in visual representations between periods when women are needed as *labour* (as in wartime) and as *consumers* (as now, in a time of a crisis of capital), and how this shift can be studied for its 'ideological effect'.

WOMEN, WORK AND WAR

This 'case study' comes out of some more general research which has included looking at the illustrated news magazine *Picture Post* from its inception in October 1938 through to 1947. This research has revealed some dramatic shifts in the ways that women were represented there during that period of time. . . .

The idea of women as an integral part of the industrial and agricultural workforce (as well as the armed forces), concurrent with their 'jobs' as wives and mothers, was taken up and expanded upon by *Picture Post*. The old ideas about women did not disappear though. The need for 'beauty' had been a running thread in early *Picture Post* editorials, and in February 1941 a 'woman's editor', Anne Scott-James, was appointed. Her job was to provide articles of 'interest to women', dealing with 'fashion, beauty, decoration, sewing and knitting, cooking, gardening, ideas for comfort ... stressing the words beauty and comfort'. The ideas of women as domestic and narcissistic were therefore only displaced from the separate features on women at work. Women's 'sexuality' or 'glamour' were hived off into other features on the world of fashion, or show business, and these features continued to use the more traditional images of women displaying themselves.

The advertisers in *Picture Post* also took up the theme of 'women at war' with amazing rapidity, often using news-type photographs or 'realist' drawings. Before long, specific *class* stereotypes emerged, e.g. the industrial worker, the land girl, the bus conductress. Advertisements soon showed women doing two jobs, and filled out the little 'human details' that were often too trivial for news and feature stories. Products were offered which would enable women to function better as 'working mothers', keeping their health, safety and strength up to scratch, and to do the washing and cooking more quickly. Women were seen as the mainstay of the family and the 'home front' at a time when everything else was chaos. The products and services offered were usually aimed at very real and immediate needs, rather than at some fantasy future.

Particularly of value to me in this research has been Stuart Hall's work on *Picture Post*, in which he comments on the 'limitations of the news photograph':

> Its [*Picture Post*'s] 'social eye' was a clear lens. But its 'political' eye was far less decisive. It pinpointed exploitation, misery and social abuse, but always in a language which defined these as 'problems' to be tackled and remedied with energy and goodwill: it was instinctively reformist – in both a good (humanist) and bad (humanist) sense. It never found a way . . . of relating the *surface images* of these problems to their structural foundations[3] (my emphasis). . . .

Another aspect of visual representation which should be mentioned is that with the onset of war the *depiction* of extremes in social and economic inequality became less pronounced, and in the news, features and advertisements *women of all classes were shown working together*. This is important to note because the repertoire of signs connoting class (or class power) is far more limited than those connoting gender. Class relations are structured and, therefore, in visual terms, 'absent'; they were, in Hall's terms, beyond the scope of *Picture Post*'s 'political' eye. A class identity is – like sexuality – constructed through a system of representation. In the case of *Picture Post*, the identity produced was social democratic, stressing consensus and coexistence rather than oppression and struggle. Although quite clearly these wartime images of women could in no way be considered 'sexist', the continual use of the term 'woman', with the concentration on gender similarities (i.e. not only were all women now alike, but also women could now do men's work), masked the very real social and economic class *differences* which existed between women, and which continue to exist.

Although the research from which these examples are drawn is still incomplete, it is possible at this stage to see that there were clear differences between representations of the same stereotype. I would relate this to the general distinction between the *point of production* (the *labour* visually represented and written about in the 'serious' news and feature articles), and the *point of consumption* represented by the advertisements. A study of the various images of the industrial worker will give an indication of some of the shifts of visual rhetoric between news and various types of advertisement.

Such images do suggest quite clearly that industrial and state needs for changes in the social division of labour had some effect on the types of images of women that were produced during the war. This also seems to be borne out by what happened when the war ended. Just as the 'new' and 'positive' images emerged when women were desperately needed in the labour force, so the idea of 'two jobs' soon collapsed back into 'one job' when women were encouraged to re-enter the domestic sphere during the massive task of the re-employment of demobbed labour. This is epitomized in a Milk of Magnesia advert which shows a mother saying 'I'm clocking in at home'.

Of course the war was a 'special case' – the historical and socioeconomic determinants of particular stereotypes are seldom so blatant. But it does underline the potential usefulness of the binary opposition of labour/capital in analysing images. This 'historical' work is offered to indicate an approach to *encoding practice*, as there is no simple way of understanding the potential range of 'readings' available to *Picture Post*'s original audience, whose 'readings' were informed by their own historically specific class and gender positions.

It is important to emphasize that we need to understand the ideological process by which a class identity is constructed, especially as this construction is not necessarily the same as our *actual* class location in the capitalist relations of production and reproduction. This becomes a crucial issue for working-class women who are scarcely visible within visual representation (except in a negative sense) and are continually forced to locate themselves as 'women' rather than as members of a class, with specific class interests.

4 · PROJECT ON IDENTITY

This was prepared in the late 1970s, when Jo was working at the Half Moon Photography Workshop and thinking extensively about her role as educator of adults. It was intended as a project guide for B.Ed. students at Bulmershe College, Berkshire. Written at a time when Women's Liberation Movement debates on women's identity were just entering mainstream education, this was an early signalling of her later interest in encouraging women to explore their self-image through photographs.

This is a short-term project on identity, resulting from my view that most of the teenagers with whom I worked had a very fixed view of their visual identity, their sex roles and their class expectations.
Over the course of eight two-hour sessions we covered the following areas:

- how the different sexes are depicted in media (children's books, comics, advertisements, etc.)
- how students first reacted to the camera
- how they looked when observed by an unseen photographer on outside visits
- how they thought they would ideally like to look
- how they reacted directly to the camera
- various assumed identities, chosen at random
- forward or backward projections of their own lives
- fantasy projections
- how they looked when interacting with others
- how somebody else made them up (just faces)

- how somebody else saw and described them
- how they would look in advertisements.

The starting point for all this was a slide show of images of children from advertisements. Juxtaposing male and female images alongside each other, it was immediately apparent that the media give a specific and different treatment according to sex. This was the starting point for many discussions, and easily led into a comparison of depiction of adults in advertisements, whether such depictions were accurate or not, why such images occurred, etc.

One factor which emerged from this project was that girls who had a low self-image (i.e. they didn't match up to the media's depicted perfection in beauty) rarely took seriously the sessions in which makeup was involved – preferring to turn themselves into vampires, fun figures. The girls who were traditionally pretty (and who had a high self-image visually) invariably 'improved' upon their looks in these sessions.

It was always remarkable to see how differently students behaved when they had assumed a new identity, with more confidence or daring. Very often the students with lower visual self-image blossomed in these sessions.

The use of makeup, splitting up into pairs or small groups, always brought about an enormous degree of friendly interaction. Usually groups consisted of either boys or girls. This was not intentional but was the random result of the schools which sent us groups. On occasions when both sexes worked together there was always much more tension, and less inclination towards self-revelation, because we were discussing issues which we came to conclude were very much part of the self-erected sexual images already created. . . .

Many of the students compiled small books about themselves and their families or friends, usually adopting either a narrative or a question-and-answer format (i.e. a series of provocative questions had to be answered with images of some sort – either with pictures taken by other students, from family albums, from photo machines, from media images, or with drawings). The emphasis was at all times on visual and not verbal depiction, expression or decoding. In the questions we were able to raise issues like 'who is the most powerful person?', 'who is the poorest person?', mixed with questions like 'which part of you could you do without?' or 'this is somebody I really like to be with'. (A lot of advice about this form of 'Id-kit' was given to me by Keith Kennedy who was at the Middlesex Polytechnic Teacher Training College.)

Another project which was quite useful was to make visual histories of ourselves (we, the tutors, participated at all sessions). Starting from the earliest photograph available (from family albums, mums, grandmothers), we constructed visual lifelines. These were stuck on sugar paper in concertina form so that they could be opened out across the room and thus give a time progression. This enabled students to see that they had started somewhere, had gone through various phases, changing all the time, and were in a state of dynamic progression. This made it realistically possible to be speculative about the future. It raised the notion of choice (versus the fatalism expressed by many students). It also provided an ideal way for us as tutors to demystify ourselves. We were able to show that we too had passed through a variety of phases, made drastic changes in our lives, made mistakes and decisions, and were still moving (hopefully!).

The areas into which we moved were never planned, but just evolved from session to session, based on the needs of the group. Outside visits to workplaces were interspersed with indoor sessions around media, makeup, equal pay, work conditions, expectations, fantasies....

Students who were initially reticent about being photographed were offered the opportunity to be photographers. When they saw the results they produced (with 35mm reflex camera, electronic computer flash and colour transparency material) they wanted to be on the opposite side of the camera as well.

We used colour transparencies because it was found that students enjoyed watching slide shows in which they featured; also it was always easier to talk spontaneously when they were all looking at a screen in a semi-darkened room, with no tutor facing them. Some students who had a particularly low self-concept asked constantly to see pictures of themselves. (Many students asked for colour prints to be made, which we were able to do at low cost.) We never used other media (except for one use of video in which boys enacted role reversals for a glorious two hours). The photography was never a major feature of any sessions, just a method of recording and then discussing 'reality'. Students were able to see that on different occasions they looked totally different, that their moods differed, that they acted differently when made up. They were also able to work in a group, which, when viewing individual images of students, helped group integration because in the friendly discussion of faces nobody was ever rejected by the group....

This project was only short term, in isolation from any other form of study, as it was part of a supplementary schooling project for fifth and sixth formers. It took place at Street Aid at 36 Earlham Street, London WC1, where I was temporarily employed to teach women's studies. It could have been a starting point for many other integrated projects, linked to drama, producing poetry, literacy materials, social history documentation, etc.

If anybody is interested to discuss these ideas further or would like a similar project set up I would be pleased to cooperate.

5 · THE SIGN AS A SITE OF CLASS STRUGGLE

Reflections on the work of John Heartfield

This is my very abridged version of Jo's long article which was more biographical and less skewed towards women's experience. It appeared in *Block*, 1982, a British critical media magazine. An amended version of the original was published in *Photography/ Politics: Two* in 1986. Heartfield, with his emphasis on the political use of photographs, was one of Jo's strongest influences.

In this article I concentrate on the period from 1922 to 1932 in which John Heartfield worked in Weimar Germany (and later in Prague). This for me is of central importance, not only as an extended example of a uniquely high level of integration between cultural and political struggle on the Left in an advanced capitalist country, but also because one of the means considered important by the two major contending class powers (communists and fascists) was the agitational and/or propagandistic use of photography and film, although often their aesthetic modes differed greatly, as did their methods of publication and distribution.

I want to deal with particular aspects of Heartfield's work and to approach them within the historical specificity of political struggles of his period. I shall avoid, therefore, the approach which elevates him to a privileged position as an individual artist. I also want to look at two examples of his work where questions of the representation of 'women' can be seen in relation to issues of class struggle and anti-fascist strategies. In looking at his work retrospectively I am aware that we cannot merely extrapolate from it and apply such knowledge to today's problems and struggles. It is important, however, that certain modes of *organization* and thinking are re-examined, particularly in relation to ongoing theoretical debates in cinema and photography. . . .

One of the most important aspects of Heartfield's work is his dialectical method of representation. By this I mean not only his technique of reassembling photos and texts in order to communicate new political understandings, but also the way in which his work was embedded in certain specific modes of information dissemination very different from those typical of the Fine Arts. . . .

THE METHOD OF PHOTO-MONTAGE

Heartfield was part of a movement which helped develop the technique of photo-montage (later taken up and extended by advertising), a signifying practice which, in his case, emphasized the social *and* economic nature of the world through a sign system of images and words gathered from diverse sources. By using these culturally coded elements (either those already existing and available drawn from a variety of sources, or those which had to be previsualized and staged with the help of long-suffering photographers and retouchers who have now been forgotten), Heartfield was able to construct visual scenarios in which easily recognizable (and previously apparently disparate) elements could take on ambiguous or new meanings by being juxtaposed in non-naturalistic ways (but not in illogical or random ways). Then, taking key phrases from the speeches of Nazi leaders (i.e. words which already had political currency), or details of crucial events, Heartfield would reposition them as one or more elements within his overall construction so that in relation to the visual signs, they would set up a new field of meanings which could cause rifts in the previously naturalized structures of meaning which had underpinned the words and images in their original use. Changes of perception could then begin to make the viewer conscious of the previously obscure political processes and facts of Nazi capitalism. Thus it could become possible to identify not only the centres of power, but also whose *frames of reference* were being used to define and represent reality. In this way Heartfield could eventually cause the viewer to contemplate the reality which lay *outside* the text, in the light of their own (often repressed) class knowledge, whilst continuing to be informed by the underlying historical-materialist method of meaning production within the text.

Sometimes Heartfield took preposterous leaps into theatrical irony and parody, punning and playing with the double meanings of words and images as do picture postcards and jokes, so that his final captioning of the overall montage could then anchor down any lingering ambiguities, turning the original key phrases inside out to reveal their literal meanings. This method of working relates aesthetic method to political *intent*, and calls into question our view of both aesthetic and political reality which, although fetishized by *my* removal of it from *its* historical specificity, still offers the possibility for us now to grasp the method of his work, in spite of language barriers. The political system which he foregrounds and criticizes so virulently – a hierarchical class society in which people were oppressed and killed because of their political beliefs, race, 'unusual' sexual habits, or 'abnormal' minds or bodies, a society which became explicitly and systematically fascist in 1933 when the Nazi Party attained political power – was once a horrifying historical reality. Heartfield's photo-montages were produced with great rapidity and urgency in response to that reality. Their purpose was to demystify the monumental myths of the Nazis as fast as the Nazis generated them.

THE QUESTION OF WOMEN IN HEARTFIELD'S WORK

We need to take account of the violently opposing methods of signification between fascists and communists, who, however, belonged to the same 'sign community', each wielding their own ideological apparatuses, until eventually one group maintained domination because it was able to take complete command of the repressive state apparatuses.

Heartfield as 'proletarian artist' must be located within the events preceding the Second World War. It was a period of intensive and bloody militant class struggle both inside Germany and elsewhere, a time of wide-scale working-class poverty, unemployment and inflation. From the fascist point of view a militaristic nationalism had developed which should be seen against the global socioeconomic politics of German capitalists (late on the scene to seize colonies) struggling once again for world markets. This gave rise to intensive class struggle, interpenetrated with the racist and anti-feminist politics which rose up from the late 1920s. One important aspect of Heartfield's work which seems to have been neglected by critics (and which I feel might illuminate a discussion of ideology) is the extent to which, as a committed communist, the question of women in a class society was tackled by him.

'Woman' and 'class' are not seemingly or easily compatible within signifying systems, for whilst indices of 'gender' work on a system of visible differences which are flexible but have certain parameters, the visual indices which indicate 'class' are much more idiosyncratic and not necessarily in any relationship at all to an actual class position (which is usually defined either at the 'point of production' and/or at the 'point of consumption'). Heartfield had to differentiate iconographically between women of different classes so that he could allow working women to *identify* with the 'working' women in his photomontages. At the same time he had to encourage them to be critical of the concept of the 'bourgeois' woman, isolated and alienated at home, often with servants, whose well-being, family life and possessions were assured via the income of her husband, but who was nonetheless oppressed, *though not exploited* in the ways in which her working sisters were. So Heartfield had to use different levels of signification from the iconic to the symbolic within the same representation.[1] (Photos of real individuals were used as types who represented particular social groups.) A female viewer can identify with an iconic representation of a woman because they are the same sex, but, on the other hand, a tension may well arise in a working woman who realizes that in class terms she does not match up to the depicted female.

As we shall see shortly, Heartfield depicts in one montage an individual female who in turn stands for a particular group of aspiring-to-be or already affluent bourgeois women, but simultaneously he addresses other women (working-class women) whose class would lead them to identify with the plight of an unemployed male also shown in the montage.[2] Here the relation of gender, race and class to one another is crucial because at a point, say in feminist or racial struggles for equality, within signification there is less emphasis on apparent class differences, whilst within the context of *class* struggle, women generally would need to be clearly class-differentiated because of their differing positions in the hierarchy of wage earners and power.

Critics as perceptive as John Berger have accused Heartfield of being too acquiescent to the German Communist Party, thereby undermining his essential individuality as artist.[3] However, it is surprising how often we can see that Heartfield, prophetically, made the correct analysis of the political situation, especially when we consider that the catastrophic defeat of the German working class in 1933, the part played by Stalin and the horrors of the purges in the Soviet Union, made a clear analysis of the future situation very difficult. We can see with hindsight that, as Tim Mason has said:

> In the years 1928–32, when all round him in the party and in world communism was confusion, intrigue, self-deception and catastrophe, he kept on, undistracted, producing the bitterly critical and marvellous eloquent photo-montages against political reaction and Nazism. This was his way of being a communist . . . because as George Grosz once put it, he had learned to hate well.[4]

Heartfield was enraged by the brute force of fascism yet he never lost sight of its class character. Of particular interest to me is his treatment of aspects of women's struggles, bearing in mind again that women do not occupy the same class position as their respective menfolk, because of the additional division of labour in the family. The problem of how to represent the 'bourgeois woman' in a class society was, I feel, handled most illuminatingly in his montage entitled *The Highest (or Finest) Products of Capitalism.*

Herein we see two people: a man of medium stature dressed in a drab suit; he has an 'intelligent' face and wears glasses which convey a certain class and racial ambiguity (perhaps he is a Jew). Possibly we are invited to identify with the situation rather than the man because we cannot tell much about his character from his face or clothes. Around his neck is a placard saying 'I'll take any work'. The man has his hands in his pockets and looks resigned but slightly defiant. Behind him to the left is a bride in a beautiful, expensive lacy white gown. She is raised up on a plinth or steps; she holds a bouquet, her lips are set firm, unsmiling, her gaze is introverted. One gets the impression she is not human but a dummy in a shop window. The unemployed man stands on her dress which tumbles down to the bottom of the image. Thus they are bound together – but perhaps not permanently? (Could we possibly envisage this as a photo from a family album?) The montage is organized around a series of oppositions, namely dark/light, male/female, working class/middle class, plain dress/elaborate dress, deprivation/luxury. The difference of sex or gender is thus overlaid with a class or wealth difference.

A text accompanying the picture informs us that the gown cost $10,000 and that there are 20 million out of work. Here Heartfield is exaggerating, and anticipating incredibly high levels of inflation and unemployment. We are now in the realm of contradiction expressed through irony. The irony is reinforced by the title – *The Finest Products of Capitalism* – which draws our attention to the fact that two products are for sale in the shop window: the gown and the worker's labour power. Those with capital can buy either. The presence of the worker also indicates that the expensive commodity – the gown – has a relationship to the labour force of Weimar, capitalist Germany. In this way, Heartfield defetishizes the commodity by reminding us that we cannot look at only one aspect of the contradiction between capital and labour. He suggests, even in such a simple montage, the complex economic and social relationships which make up the class-divided German state. (Other aspects are dealt with in other montages; one cannot expect a single montage to deal with everything.) He manages to shift our perception to a rational level so that we can perceive anew the elements which are so crucially interconnected and yet which are usually avoided within representation. Labour as commodity is privileged and literally foregrounded, particularly that reserve army of labour which is so often forgotten or callously discarded, and linked via the gown to other commodities which are generally, as separate elements, disengaged from the process of production which brought them into existence.

Looking again at the bride, we may reflect that in many cultures women at the time of their marriages are treated as commodities. In one sense she is the universal ideal towards which women conventionally aspire; Heartfield undermines this dimension by exposing the economic relationship. The bride is a kind of dream-symbol: the epitome of expensive virginity, a fairy princess of mythology. But also the starting point of the good bourgeois German family, in a state which requires women to produce healthy children so that they in their turn can become 'the finest products of capitalism'.

The transfixed female viewer standing in front of this image is reminded, though, that such romantic dreams rest upon the realities of unemployment and inflation, the complexities of which lie outside the montage. Clearly she ('I') cannot effect an identification if the cost is so great. Here we encounter the rupturing process of Heartfield's work. Perhaps she should abandon her dreams and stay in her (actual) class and join with others in struggle. In this way, it could be argued, Heartfield demythologizes the fetishized woman. The viewer's thoughts are set in motion by the juxtaposed visual and verbal elements as she seeks to resolve the enigma they present. This enigma cannot, however, be solved within representation because its solution lies outside the montage in the world of political action and struggle. Drawing on Brecht's theory of distanciation, Stephen Heath views Heartfield as calling 'commonsense' beliefs into question by restructuring signs in such a way that he 'punctuates "representation" with "formulation", a process Brecht refers to as "literarization"'. This then is not 'a "form" but a mode of analysis, the very mode of understanding of dialectical materialism . . . where the spectator is placed in a critical position'.[5]

In sharp contrast to the romantic image of the bride is the montage showing a pregnant, non-bourgeois woman with a dead boy soldier behind her. She represents all mothers with sons who might die in wars. The multiple texts of the original montage read: 'Forced deliverer of human material. You mothers, let your children live' (Brecht); whilst the caption underneath states: 'Have courage, the state needs unemployed people and soldiers.' Here woman is represented in her role as biological producer: she produces and reproduces the human species. Man is represented in his traditional role as warrior, as defender of the tribe, the family, the nation. Unlike the joyous pregnant woman familiar to us from advertising, however, Heartfield's woman is anxious and unlovely. Her direct, fearful gaze towards the viewer is quite unsettling. Similarly, in place of the proud, brave soldier of the recruiting poster, Heartfield shows us the corpse which is the inevitable product of war. In this montage the reproductive function of woman seems to take precedence over her class identity, but at the same time that very identity reminds us that the vast mass of the army are recruited from workers and peasants. Implicit, but unmentioned, is the issue of abortion: the montage, which was produced in 1930, refers to the struggles around the notorious paragraph 218 on abortion legislation in Weimar Germany.

Heartfield's way of forcing us back and forth, shifting us across the signs, across the intertextuality of his work, causes a process of demythologization to take place which, eventually, leads to a confrontation with historical reality. It is Heartfield's grasp of the complex, material interrelationships of the class society in which he lived, signalled in and across so many of his montages, which enables his work to unhinge the ideology of the dominant forms of representation. Heartfield uses, and simultaneously challenges, the dominant forms of representation, and yet, through the use of identifiable iconographic elements of class, he still attempts to include 'us' – assuming that we recognize ourselves as belonging to the class addressed – in the history they eventually refer to. That history is the world of class struggle, a world which also helped to produce the reading subject. Thus if the montage 'speaks' to us as members of a class, then we can respond by using such pictorial representations to pose questions to the reality external to the montage and to other representations.

It has not been my intention to privilege these two images of Heartfield's above all the others he produced, but to cite them as examples of works which, if examined within their historical specificity, within cultural and political struggle, opposed the dominant modes of signification. As Voloshinov has pointed out, the sign is a site of ideological and class struggle. Heartfield understood this fact. Nothing has changed in this respect, consequently this is one aspect of his work which is relevant to today.

CONTEMPORARY PRACTICE?

And now, in the mid-1980s, what kind of signifying practices would we consider to be 'most suitable' in relation to the range of different cultural and political struggles at present in full flow? How do we situate ourselves as photographers, artists or cultural workers without any central coherent cultural or political points of focus? Across that vast range of 'audiences' for photography, each with their different 'needs', 'identities', alliances and beliefs, how can we begin a new mapping process which moves away from endlessly repeating the inherited stereotypes of poverty and class on one side of a critical fence, 'positive' images in the middle ground, and erudite 'deconstructions' of patriarchy, shuttling back and forth in international galleries and journals, on the other?

Even though ideology may be a system of representation, political power still depends, in the final analysis, on who controls the repressive apparatuses of the state. In the end – as in Nazi Germany and in other revolutions – you cannot separate them out from one another, though sometimes one is more hidden than the other.

6 · THOUGHTS ON THE PROCESS OF EXHIBITION SELECTION

This was published in the 'Open Photography' catalogue of the Midland Group, 1982, the exhibition where Jo had her first experience of being a 'selector'.

The business of passing across from being a photographic exhibitor to being a selector is indeed most strange. Rigid criteria applied in producing and selecting one's own work become transformed when one is caught up as part of the gallery apparatus, alongside others who attempt to chart photography. In accepting the responsibility of becoming a selector, I was aware of no specific constraints, no list of dos and don'ts to start out from, yet clearly as selectors we should not be seen as people entirely free to make real decisions about what to hang in any show, or as merely working from 'personal' preference. Such decisions have already partly been made through the understanding of the ground rules by those who entered their work, from which we then made our choices. Second, through forms of self-censorship we can quickly learn to navigate the network of structuring relationships when we enter the gallery system. And this two-way traffic, in asking for or conferring status or value upon work, comes not only through the validation of those working as selectors, organizers, managers and administrators within the gallery system, or from funding bodies, it also comes from an existent (though invisible) hierarchy of artists or photographers who have already jumped across a series of hurdles on their way to institutional, commercial or critical acclaim. These hurdles prescribe a certain obligatory competitiveness between artists for whichever few sites are on offer; open shows are perhaps introductory hurdles for work, which can thereby reach a wider audience. So, it must be said, the mapping of an open show, where all-comers can apparently offer their work for pleasure and scrutiny, is a very particular kind of democracy – one in which certain 'voices' can be heard more clearly than perhaps others. And real problems arise when those who are producing work for very different reasons (for example social action or political photography groups, who are not necessarily looking for critical acclaim, or seeking to politicize the gallery system itself) find their work (now bereft of its context and currency) hanging randomly alongside work which is engaged in very different forms of struggle.

Interestingly, though this year's three selectors were ostensibly very different from each other, it soon became apparent to me that we in fact shared a common matrix of cultural expectations in the situation in which we found ourselves, although individually no doubt these would be articulated very differently. Looking at the entries, it began to feel rather like Christmas as I moved from one unwrapped pile of pictures to the next. And, like Christmas, it became apparent that there were many dutiful offerings and only occasionally did any of us catch a glimpse of something which excitingly called the whole ritual into question. The show we eventually chose represents some very different philosophies within a network of possibilities, which intersect here in order to give an indication of both the harmonics and polemics emerging within British photography at the moment. Put another way, for me there is a rather top-heavy mixture of those works which naturalize and render invisible as *practice* the history of photography, rather than those which have tried to foreground or denaturalize aspects of visual representation in a more 'thinking' way.

The organizers of 'Open Photography 1982' have, quite rightly, stated as their aim that they wished to provide a platform for 'as great a variety of new photography as possible'. In the event, though, it seemed that the invitation had not been fully engaged with. In a way, the idea of an 'open' show is an anachronism – for many photographers seem quite content to repeat the pleasurably familiar and predictable closed circuit of, for example, endless petrol stations, fairgrounds, bicycles, flowers, empty landscapes; only a few offered a form of practice which attempted to give *critical* pleasure, or even – more simply – to introduce a jarring or questioning text with their pictures. Such adventurous work as could be included in the selection, if hung for maximum effect, could perhaps indicate future possibilities for next year's entrants and selectors.

In a recent issue of *Artefact* (news-sheet of East Midlands Arts) there was mention that major revenue clients of EMA, such as the Midland Group, should be further encouraged in their attempts at what is called 'outreach work'. This would mean a more substantial attempt to move work out of the gallery to smaller venues, supported by workshops, lectures and demonstrations. But part of this policy should surely also be to encourage a wider and more politicized flow of artefacts into the galleries in the first place so that the work of those presently engaged in different types of cultural as well as political struggle could be engaged with. The question of open shows is politically very important and such sites (among others) should not be left to become perpetually similar.

Finally, I must add, the voices of those involved in sexual and labour politics, anti-fascists and anti-racists, as well as those in the peace movement are still very faint within the general day-to-day world of the gallery system in this country, which somehow still manages to avoid any sustained engagement with these political and economic issues. Aptly, Tony Benn commented recently in his Guardian Lecture 'Television in democracy' (reprinted in the *Guardian*, 28 July 1982) that 'the characteristic of a democracy is that people have the ultimate power to destroy their governments without bloodshed'. How do we begin to apply such definitions to the gallery system?

7 · FAIRY TALES AND PHOTOGRAPHY

These extracts are a small part of Jo's unpublished BA thesis at the Polytechnic of Central London, 1982. It's the first reference to key ideas developed in her later phototherapy work with Rosy Martin, including magical interventions by fairy godmothers and princes, and the exclusion of the 'ugly' Other. Her *Cinderella* research was used in the *Arena* TV programme on 21 January 1986, much edited. Her diary and *Putting Myself in the Picture* show how long-lived and strong was her anger with the final broadcast version.

My current study of fairy stories has come about because I felt dissatisfied with the ways in which I previously worked. These somehow seemed to assume on the part of the audience a total rationality in regard to the photographs offered – which would then allow them to feel free to take up a more critical position in relation to their own lives. Clearly this is not the case – people are just not open to straightforward logic.... Much more work needs to be done on the actual processes whereby photographs actually work on us, not so much *what* they mean but *how* they mean it....

I want to take as my focus the illusion of romantic love – particularly in fairy stories.... It is the *concept* which is so important in the maintenance of western culture, rather than its ability to fulfil any of its promises in a material way. Research among postgraduate field workers and youth club workers in England has shown that for most working-class girls the myth of romance is deeply embedded in their idea of their own conscious femininity. Whilst this is hardly a startling revelation, it does become an important point to consider in relation to any theory of class. For those women who are systematically discriminated against (and I was one of them) it is hardly surprising that part of the female utopian imagination is the hope that somebody will come along and take them away from all that. . . .

Quite obviously, love is important in all our lives, but it is actually a class-defined love. . . . No direct appeal to class consciousness is possible without taking account of the symbolic world which constructs for us the dominant and apparently universal categories of feminine and masculine. . . .

In my own work, particularly around the concept of 'motherhood', I found it necessary to seek further for reasons for the persistence of the importance given both ideologically and materially to the heterosexual, white, nuclear, sexually divided family. This is especially so, as a recent government census in Britain revealed that only 5 per cent of the population at that time were actually living within the ideal family of a father at work, mother at home and two young children. However, in media analysis this is the image of the family which is constantly found.

This persistent image somehow led me to a study of fairy stories and their origins, settling finally on the story of Cinderella. This is known in Britain as a rags-to-riches story. The possibility of rising from humble beginnings, providing we can display the right moral and physical characteristics, allowing us to take up our rightful place as heroines and brides alongside our betters, is full of timeless appeal.

However, I found very unsatisfactory a simple study of the story as it now stands in Britain. It seemed a straightforward enough story which is repeated year in and year out, read to children on their parents' knees, revered in primary schools and for ever embalmed as part of the Walt Disney legacy. But a closer study revealed that it is widely acknowledged to be the oldest and most popular story in the world. When I started to look I was amazed to find that some thousand or so variants have already been traced. . . .

It is one of the six basic story types which have been found within structural analysis – with the basic, simple formula of:
lack
intervention of outside agent
restoration of lack

Cinderella shows:
lack of love and material comfort
intervention of magic
restoration of love from prince.

The story initially offers us the familiar scenario of a family conflict – she wants to go out dancing and be beautifully dressed and meet boys, rather than be stuck at home with her ugly and jealous sisters and her wicked stepmother.

The transformation is startling and final: the boy she meets just happens to be a rich young Prince Charming who chases her and offers her a life of ease and luxury. We are hardly likely to ask the question of where his money comes from, or who will do the housework in future. Nor can we identify in any way with her sisters or mother whom we must banish to some never-never land in our imagination because perhaps we secretly fear we might be like them. . . .

The version which children can read to themselves was the starting point for my final study of *Cinderella*, as it teaches a basic vocabulary of words. Finally I made this up into a twin-track slide show which I could use for teaching purposes to show how I had analysed it in juxtaposition with photography.

I concentrated on the way in which young female children are encouraged (through their mothers) to be obsessed, competitively, with appearance. I moved into looking at various symbols such as the crown and the shoe, and took up themes such as dancing and housework, before looking at love and marriage. It also became clear from this study that any kind of active sexuality is totally absent from such stories – it's expressed only through romantic love and the kiss.

What began to be interesting from my broader study was that in each cultural form I examined there were different stresses and points of emphasis. For example, I saw four different pantomime versions last Christmas where the tradition is that the ugly sisters are rather grotesque men and the butt of everyone's humour. There is also an 'Everyman' character who desperately loves Cinderella but who is in the end supplanted by the prince.

The same story took on different class dimensions as different aspects were emphasized or de-emphasized, depending on the historical context which produced it or the audience it was addressed to. However, across all the versions the same basic plot emerged: the resolution of family and economic conflict for women through notions of personal transformation and recognition of true worth following proof of their moral and physical ability to take up a higher class position within marriage.

It is only when we draw away from the versions which have come through to us so continuously in western culture that we can think to re-examine some of the versions which could not gain popular appeal because they were never allowed to appear in print, or on stage or screen. I am not suggesting that such exclusion was blanket and deliberate, but that once the dominant versions had moved into the 'cultural funnel', a further process of refinement has gone on, rather than a standing back and rethinking. We need to ask why the dominant versions of fairy stories are so popular before we can ask 'what function do they serve?' Certainly we can infer from them that family life is universal, timeless and unchanging, and that history is to do with royal families and their progeny.

Of particular value to my study has been the work of Jack Zipes, who has written on radical theories of folk and fairy tales.[1] Originally folk tales were part of an oral tradition used by ordinary people to express their perceptions of the social order and nature. . . .

However, folk tales gradually began to be appropriated and changed by aristocratic and bourgeois writers from the sixteenth century onwards. As publishing expanded, so fairy tales – with the emphasis on particular magical forms of transformation – began to emerge as a literary genre. These began to show – and perhaps reinforce – the changes in values and conflicts in a transition from feudalism to early capitalism. In this shift, essential differences occurred, for example shifts from collective to selective representations, from public ownership to private ownership, and a fundamental move from retelling and reworking to the reading of fixed texts. More importantly, illustrations began to be added.

To move briefly back into the emergence of photography, here we appear to have had a different kind of development. With the advent of the box camera and the mass manufacture in 1899 of roll film, photography was apparently a medium whereby ordinary people could once again tell their stories to themselves – this time without even the intervention of the generalized storytellers. Yet even a cursory glance will indicate the limitations on just which stories it was possible to tell. The camera was and still is used mostly around family life, for holidays, rituals and celebrations. . . .

As such, photography was obviously not seen (except by politicized photographers, for example in the Worker Photographer movement) as a tool for showing or exploring other versions of everyday life – for example as the site of other pleasures, or as the site of conflict, either within the family or in neighbourhood life or work life. Additionally, through forms of self-censorship, or actual legislation, certain 'amateur' photographs were never taken (in industry, in prisons, courts and other state institutions, for instance). . . . Various branches of a developing professionalization could now, in a new form, within a culture and mass printing industry, turn other people's experience into marketable products or artefacts through which only very specific and limited forms of storytelling would take place. This continues to be a major part of the image industry today. . . . The major stories of formation of state and professional institutions of capital are still not being told, except in highly laundered forms. . . .

In England, learning to read is an integral part of our compulsory schooling system. . . . The idea of an equivalent of 'learning to read pictures' – what has come to be termed 'visual literacy' – is only just beginning to be taken seriously, although it is acknowledged that by the time we get to school we have already learnt to read images. The cultural and political ramifications of such an idea of study are enormous, but I must emphasize that I am not talking about forms of 'appreciation' or 'analysis', but rather about the use and meanings, the how and why of photographs, linked to active work on cutting and pasting, as well as picture taking.

Early teaching of reading is done through picture books which are used for storytelling or which depict things in the real world of the child that the child learns initially to name and describe. These two distinct spheres of 'fact' and 'fiction' are learnt in parallel. . . .

Fairy stories set up and position us within simple narrative structures, with socially constructed archetypal characters. They are mediated in terms of morality (good vs. bad), through visual motifs (historical costume, for example), physical characteristics (e.g. beauty/ugliness). And they offer notions of fixed character (e.g. goodness), whilst repetitiously laying down in various guises that which is ideal in terms of gender, race and class. Across the stories an agenda of 'problem setting' and 'problem solving' takes place, which is presumed to enable the child to negotiate internal conflicts. These are mediated through a double matrix of words and images.

The laying down of what amounts to a visual vocabulary reinforced across many stories, and equally embedded through repetitious rereadings of fairy stories, which the child demands to be read without deviation, is something for political consideration for those of us engaged in photography. The signs and symbols used in these stories are mobilized in all other forms of visual media throughout our lives; many of them appear to us in the guise of 'history' and 'historic events', particularly around the royal family in Britain. In particular the symbols of class (seen also as symbols of freedom and free enterprise), such as the horse, the crown, the castle, are included alongside symbols of time and travel (the clock and the golden carriage), as well as symbols of narcissism (the mirror). Symbols of labour are epitomized totally negatively through the broom or mop, whilst the labour of the servants and army is almost invisible, as is eventually the housework which is one axis of the whole story. Power relations are caught in the hierarchy of a pre-technological age, set in a 'historical' past, where the modern child is somehow sited with her family. The technological, industrial and financial base of society is totally absent, as is any account of the power of the state.

This paper is not an impassioned plea for the total banishment of the reading of fairy stories to children, for clearly this gives much pleasure to adults and children alike. What I do ask is a study of this very specific area, and in particular that the visual matrix and the narrative structure which position the child as reader be integral to any critical study of photography. It is interesting, on analysis, to comment that the Perrault-based version of *Cinderella* now underpins so many of the characteristics of what should constitute a typical working-class girl's dream world that it could almost have been programmed into a computer by an educational psychologist. . . .

Finally, if we ask the question 'what actually is being displaced, and why?' we as Marxists might come to the conclusion that we are looking at . . . a highly sophisticated form of class censorship and symbolic control as well as a making invisible of our sexual desires.

In fairy tales things often 'just happen'. In *Cinderella*, there is no explanation of how the fairy godmother managed to pop up when she does, or how it is that her magic takes the form it does. And anyway who cares? The whole point of the story is to *suspend disbelief.*

Of one thing we can be sure: that magic is introduced in order to facilitate the smooth path of 'justice' and the restoration of moral and social order for, in this case, the heroine. For the powerless child sited within the family, this could be explained in terms of the universal desire for instant harmony and gratification, militating against any violent or prolonged action on the part of either the heroine in the story or the powerless child (who nonetheless at times sees itself as all-powerful). Personally, I would prefer to describe it as a metaphor for also understanding the varying relationships between the state and groups of adults in a class society.

Just as most forms of capitalist news gathering echo the simple plot structures and culturally constructed archetypal heroes, villains and victims of children's literature, so it is easy to discern within their 'news agenda setting' that a constant theme is, similarly, the narrativization of forms of (class) conflict. Here disharmony is deflected, repressed or smashed and a state of equilibrium brought about through the benevolent agencies of the state, or the owners of industrial and financial capital. How often do we hear that a child has been 'rescued' by social workers from its family, or that the police 'restored law and order' after a riot or during a strike?

On the other hand, if we take the other major user of photography – the advertising industry – could we not perhaps discern certain similarities to the transformation work of the fairy godmother and other magical interventionists? . . . Perhaps we could stretch the metaphor further and see this early work in fairy stories as the matrix for another system of economic and symbolic domination which we enter soon enough.

Leaving the anthropomorphic and magical world of childhood where money apparently grows on trees or we merely snap our fingers in order to get our heart's desire, we enter the world of money and commodity fetishism as theorized by Marx. Here we have what Raymond Williams has called the 'magical advertising industry'. Whilst structuring and mobilizing our day-dreams, at the same time it obscures the production process from us. . . .

I have been talking about an entirely different approach to 'photography in a social context'. We must take seriously the problem of how to teach photography. If we move away from trying to show 'what is real' to the notion of theatre (as Terry and I have done in our own work) this opens up possibilities of a very different and pleasurable kind. There are some starting points:

- work on the family album – then *staging* absences and reworkings for the camera, starting with working on your own, or moving into group work very quickly (what would constitute a 'social album' as opposed to a 'family album')
- forms of staging using our own and popular press images – as a way of exposing contradictions
- photography as a form of play – using dolls or actors to stage our own events
- work on fairy tales (particularly in women's groups) so that the tales can be reworked and the invisible ideological content brought to the surface (this can be done with forms of visual cartooning)
- the making of our own 'photo stories' for girls which subvert the dominant ones
- analysing media images of the job we already do (e.g. as I did clerical work) as another way of struggling politically at work
- more work can be done on producing different types of children's books
- work on 'alternative technology' within photography to encourage children to become self-reliant in their use of equipment and materials – and as a way of discussing multiple uses of things – rather than depending on an apparently high-technology base which is never demystified for us.

I hope this has been useful. I want to emphasize that I see what I have said as one form of struggle among many.

8 · AN *OMNIBUS* DOSSIER

by Jo Spence but with introduction and afterword by Simon Watney

This was originally published in the film studies magazine *Screen*, 1983, and is significant because it outlines Jo's first experiences of working with broadcast television – a medium which excited and frustrated her, and in which she quickly became proficient. The *Omnibus* experience was also important because it gave her ideas for a project on family history: the video diary idea later developed by others.

INTRODUCTION

This dossier concerns an edition of the BBC-1 *Omnibus* series filmed in February and broadcast on 14 November 1982. *Omnibus* is a cultural 'magazine' programme, which has recently attempted to popularize itself by employing front-man Barry Norman, whose reputation was made as a television film critic and commentator. Norman's style of presentation is that of the chat-show host, and the avuncular chat-show 'look', if not its actual format, has been incorporated by the *Omnibus* series.

In its preview the *Radio Times* informed us that 'Lord Lichfield, Jane Bown (*Observer*), Beverley Goodway (*Sun*), educationalist and feminist photographer Jo Spence and surrealist Bob Carlos Clarke were challenged to photograph top model Jilly Johnson in whatever style they thought appropriate'. The programme planners thus gathered together photographers working in very different institutions: independent fashion photography, 'quality' newspaper photography and portraiture, mass-circulation pin-up nude photography, education and the women's movement, and the art market. The differences between the photography produced and reproduced by these institutions were understood solely as an issue of 'style'.

In her contribution Jo Spence attempted to challenge this issue directly, within the format of the programme itself. This dossier was put together to illustrate the problems confronting an oppositional cultural worker operating inside the dominant framework of Culture as conceived by television journalism.

Simon Watney

PART I

First approached by researcher who was looking out for photographers suitable for a programme on 'photographic style' – got hold of me by ringing the Arts Council and asking for a 'feminist' photographer. I said that although I was a feminist and a photographer, this by no means constituted anything that could be called a style. Later approached by the director, Bernard Clarke, who explained that each photographer would be offered the same model, could pick their own setting and take any kind of photograph they wished. The BBC would pay expenses for materials, props, etc., plus a fee of £150. Was told other photographers would include Lichfield or Snowdon (didn't know which at that moment), that they were approaching David Bailey, possibly Jane Bown, and a 'page three' photographer. I said I would like them to choose a model who was a mother so that I could do something on 'motherhood' or 'childcare'. (I later dropped this idea.)

Phone call from Bernard Clarke explaining that they had seen a BBC film in which I had previously appeared, made by the *Arena* team, and that they thought I would be very suitable. Contract arrived for me to sign. I received a sudden phone call that they wished me to be one of the first photographers to be done and that I should tell them what I needed. I decided to shoot in the model's own home and they gave me (for the first time) her name, address and phone number. They confirmed that Lichfield, Bown and Goodway had agreed to do the programme and that they were trying to get hold of an 'erotic' photographer. I was beginning to worry about the status of any 'statement' I might make.

I rang the model, Jilly Johnson, and asked if I could come across to meet her and to see her house so that I could choose a location within it. I was greeted by her and her husband, given a drink and made to feel very comfortable (though clearly they were not expecting someone as scruffy or forthright as me). Eventually I chose to work in the kitchen and asked if I could do test black-and-white and colour shots. Jilly agreed. Tests proved OK – i.e. exposure, sharpness, etc. – not great shots but good 'snapshots'. I rang the BBC and said I was prepared to go ahead whenever they wished and a date in a midweek morning was decided upon.

I dutifully took myself off to Holland Park and presented myself at the front door. From inside I could hear sounds of activity, and from previous experience I realized that the film crew were already set up and about to shoot as the door opened. Which they did – the camera followed me down the hall and into the living room where Jilly was doing a 'hostess' number for everybody. All potentially very glamorous and exciting. Shooting began as I was wired up with a body microphone which I was to wear at all times during shooting. This was without a trailing lead and picked up my voice without room sounds. I worried slightly about this as I wanted to use the toilet!

Jilly asked me what makeup to wear. I told her to wear her normal everyday makeup with a shade more lipstick than usual. I explained that I didn't want to deglamorize her, but that I did want to photograph her at the kitchen sink, and gave her a pinny to put on. This was considered hilariously funny all round. (At one point in the early part of the kitchen shooting session I noted a young woman of about 17 dusting the kitchen. Later, when I went upstairs into Jilly's living room to change films this young woman asked me what I was doing. I explained that I was photographing Jilly as a 'housewife'. The young woman in her turn explained that she was Jilly's daily help and that the idea of Jilly in an apron was a scream as she had never seen her do any housework!)

Meanwhile members of the crew who were not at that moment working were thumbing through books of erotic or glamour photography which lay dotted about the living room and commenting on the merits of the women in them. It was hard to concentrate on the technical side of loading my cameras, setting different ASAs [film speeds] for black and white and colour, trying to remember which camera was which, because another part of me was voyeuristically taking in the process of the production of the film. As I tried to formulate to myself exactly how to proceed to take my shots it hit me that I had walked into a baited trap. I began to feel rather ill and 'unnatural' (the director had explained that he wanted me to behave as naturally as possible, just do 'my usual routine'). He kept referring to my style as feminist and I realized that I had taken on far more than I could cope with. The terms of the conversation were always couched in talking about 'styles of photography'. I again explained (privately) that if feminism was a style, then presumably fashion photography could be called a fascist style. No response!

I had set myself a three-part task in accepting the brief to be on the programme:

1 I wanted to demonstrate that pictures are constructed, in the sense that two cameras standing side by side could take totally different pictures of the same 'moment' – merely through the use of black-and-white as opposed to colour film, and through the cropping/framing up, done through different focal lengths of lens.
2 I wanted to shoot an extra shot, after the session had finished, with the 'live' model – a still life which I hoped would comment back on the rest of the programme. (Oh to be so naive!) By this I mean that I wanted to do something which would disrupt the normal flow of ideas in a programme around style, and to do this I needed to use not the model provided at all, but something more abstract which would give an indication in a non-naturalistic way of what I felt about the whole idea of the photography of women and their faces/bodies. I wanted to do this in a way which would not *use* the model herself in a way which would upset her, but rather move to a notion of setting something up specially ('radical advertising', as I called it at the time – a comment predictably excluded from the final footage).
3 Finally, when all the prints of the five photographers were on display and we were called back to comment on our work, I would try to talk about how the context in which a photograph appears leads to only *certain* meanings being possible (all basic semiology). Additionally, because I wanted to introduce an economic comment on the whole thing, as well as indicating that women's bodies are treated as commodities, I would go to this session armed with information from *Campaign* which would clearly indicate how papers such as the *Sun* and the *Star* advertised *themselves* to industry as a site for advertising, through the use of nude women.

I realize in retrospect that this was all wildly ambitious, but even so it was totally inadequate. It's impossible to take on something as difficult as this by my/oneself.

The shooting proceeded in the kitchen with me offering 'real' instructions to Jilly about what to do. I felt she was decidedly uneasy about the whole thing but had to make the best of it, which she did by laughing and joking the whole time, lapsing into a working-class accent because she had on an apron and was asked to light up a cigarette. Jokes were made about 'kitchen sink schools of photography'. All very predictable and bearable. However, I could feel my own 'image' of Jilly sliding into something untenable – as I got hotter and hotter, trying slowly to explain what I was doing, so any idea of *cinéma vérité* (anyway a suspect technique) collapsed. At various points in the session the director, hidden behind the lights, would ask pointed questions. This form of shooting is quite clearly an attempt to bring out surprise elements in the scenario, but is quite difficult to negotiate when you know what the technique consists of already. As I was talking I tried to think ahead to what I 'ought' to say (the problems of propagandizing), and how I could explain that this was not 'my' work, but came out of a body of developing ideas. But of course I had overlooked the fact that the programme was in the 'popular arts' slot and that the overall structure of it would finally emerge as a validation of particular notions of an art practice (genius, frantic sessions of work, creativity, expensive artefacts).

I took thirty-six colour shots. When these were finally presented to camera I realized that I had shot thematically (that is, I had followed through certain trains of thought) and I set out these 'thoughts' as far as I could reconstruct them: laying out my proof prints in lines which indicated that some pictures were useless for the purposes taken (the model had her eyes shut, had turned her head, etc.); that some were marginal (there were slight differences of expression to choose from); and that some were certainties – either because everything had 'clocked together' in the making of the picture, or (in the case of the dishwashing liquid shot) it was the only one I had done and had somehow 'worked'.

I was aware as shooting proceeded that even if I said 'what I liked', or did 'what I liked', anything could be edited out later, have a voice put over the top, be preceded by a question which wasn't asked at the time but which would throw my answer into a different light. I was also aware as time went on that it would be impossible for much of what was being shot to be used. However, I had at the back of my mind the fact that it was to be a fifty-minute programme, that they were treating the matter 'seriously' and that therefore nothing should be hurried. Little did I know that it would be reduced to thirty minutes to fill a vacant slot in the *Omnibus* schedules and that carefully argued points would be hacked to pieces and butted together again in a kind of frantic collage of ideas in order to make the material fit the time allocated.

When the filming and photography of the first part of the session had finished, purely as an act of bravado (desperation) I asked if I could take some panoramic shots of the production process (which of course would not include myself). This was thought to be very funny and the crew turned off the equipment and allowed me to do it as a kind of indulgence. I then explained to the director that in order to take the second session I would need to buy some fresh food from the local supermarket and that I would not need Jilly for this. I explained the idea to him and he appeared to be delighted, clapping his hands and saying 'I'd hoped you would come up with something like that'. He explained that going to the supermarket, walking down the street, etc. would make good bridging shots for the film. I asked did he mean that it would help to narrativize it? (Meanwhile Jilly was asked what she thought of the session: 'Not much'.)

I was then filmed setting up my props and producing my extra shot. As I finished shooting the director said to me, 'I believe that what you are doing is political photography.' I replied yes, 'but with a little p'. I also explained that I was a feminist but also an educationalist, which meant that I used photography to explain to people how photographs 'work', and that such work came from other work which was going on in various parts of the world. This was cut from the programme. (Total time of session: two hours.)

PART II

I was invited to bring the results (developed and printed at Sky colour labs) to a further shooting session at the BBC where all the work would be pinned up and each photographer asked to comment on their results. We were not to meet each other (thank God). Auntie laid on good hospitality for this occasion – lots of little things on toast and oodles of booze. Publicity stills were taken and each of us was given the 'big star' treatment. All as a preamble to our being allowed to say what we liked in order for it later to be hacked to pieces in the cutting room.

PART III

Rather ashamedly, I told about four people that the programme had been made and that there was no scheduled date for viewing yet. I was already beginning to worry about what I had become involved in. I wrote to the BBC and asked specifically that I be labelled not a 'feminist photographer' but an 'educational photographer' – as a way of avoiding the clichés and stereotypes which I was beginning to realize would emerge from such a programme.

This was all done in February 1982.

PART IV

Late October of the same year: I received a letter from the BBC announcing the transmission date eight days later but my request for a preview was turned down. Clearly by this time it was already in print in the *Radio Times* and the publicity machine was in gear. I realized I had been far too lax in asking for control over what happened – but this had not appeared to be necessary until it was too late.

I find myself now in an ironic position. The programme when I viewed it was (as the previews in *City Limits* and *Time Out* had said) voyeuristic, titillating, etc., etc. Any efforts to explain a particular position within photographic practice were indeed trivialized or marginalized (I hadn't expected them to be the centre of the programme, incidentally) and the structure of the final film, constructed through editing, totally validated the dominant art practice of white male genius – as against ranting/plain/well-meaning woman. The model, whose participation allowed another structuring presence within the film, appeared to be free to say what she wished – but of course Jilly could only put her position within that which had already been set up by the BBC. As part of the advance publicity a spread appeared in the *Daily Mirror*.

One week later: Jilly Johnson appeared on *The C(h)at Show* (London Weekend Television), an all-woman show which although not feminist is clearly a result of the women's movement. This week the discussion topic was fashion and Jilly gave an account of how happy she is not wearing clothes. Fortunately, photo-journalist Angela Phillips was able to speak from a feminist perspective without constant interruption.

I received a letter from Cussons requesting prints showing their product, Morning Fresh washing up liquid, which I'd used as a prop on the programme. So much for art!

AFTERWORD

It is significant that the ways in which photography is presented on TV are still so completely taken up with the notion of the individual photographer/artist, regardless of the site or contractual situation of his or her work. One related aspect is the idea of photographic 'truth' – even when, as in this case, the programme clearly indicated the constructed nature of *all* photographs. The editorial work in the making of the *Omnibus* programme was fairly typical insofar as it suppressed the fact of its own existence, while managing (doubtless unconsciously) to isolate the photographers from the institutions in which they work – fashion, journalism, advertising, education and art – and the discourses which those institutions generate and control. Still less could the programme represent those institutions' interdependence on one another, and the systematic way in which they operate together to validate and organize dominant ideas concerning gender, sexuality and work.

Simon Watney

9 · REMODELLING PHOTO-HISTORY

An afterword on a recent exhibition (with Terry Dennett)

First published in *Screen*, vol. 23, no. 1, 1983, this article is a reworking and a commentary on a series of photographs created for an exhibition at the Massachusetts Institute of Technology, curated by Linda Benedict-Jones. *Putting Myself in the Picture*, Jo's autobiography, included this article, which she saw as essential to this anthology as a pivotal point of working practice. It marked the final break with classic documentary photography and the first public showing of the development of the method of photo theatre, from which Jo moved – with Rosy Martin – to phototherapy.

HOW THE WORK CAME ABOUT

This collaboration between two photographers (using themselves both as photographer and as photographic object) stems from our joint interests in photography and in politics. We've attempted to engage with some of the current theories of visual representation, while at the same time offering a critique of standard histories of photography which still mostly exclude details of institutional, state, class or economic determinants, being grounded instead in 'great inventions', 'great names','great companies'.

We also hoped that the tension between us as two individuals, with overlapping philosophies of historical materialism – grounded here in Terry's study of specific apparatuses and the economic point of production as central to any understanding of history, and Jo's interest in women in a class society in relation to *re*production and domestic labour – could productively raise a series of presently unvoiced questions. The work also comes out of our (separate) experience – as a scientific photographer and photo-historian (Terry), and as a commercial and portrait photographer, now analysing a visual/socio-economic history of the family (Jo).

We produced *The History Lesson* [also called *Remodelling Photo History*] in response to an invitation to an exhibition organized in the United States at the Massachusetts Institute of Technology. Called 'Ten Contemporary British Photographers', it opened at MIT in February 1982, before beginning a tour. The organizer reported that our work provoked considerable discussion, with the comments 'Too obvious' at one end of the spectrum, and 'Can't understand what they're doing' at the other. We both felt that it could have another life as a short, polemical, 'tongue-in-cheek' teaching work for photographic and art courses and workshops in this country. To this end a second set of laminated prints is now available for loan or hire. So far these have been used on several very different occasions and have always provoked lively and productive discussions between students and teachers.

We were especially keen to provide a starting point for discussion between men and women in the controversial area of the representation of the female body (where it is argued at one extreme that to even show the female body is problematic, while at the other some still seek to tinker with the dominant 'stereotypes' of women without engaging with wider questions of cultural production). During discussions in mixed groups it has become apparent that people continually collapse 'the real' into notions of 'visual representation' – talking about the photographic images in the classroom as if they were a reflection of the bodies of the women who stood before the camera in the first place, which in themselves produced specific 'effects' on men. This makes it difficult to get beyond personal confrontation between those present, often silencing and shaming individual men, closing down discussions, and never moving to a point where the institutions and signifying practices of photography could be analysed.

Another observation from this work, noted in discussions applying psychoanalytic theory to photography, has been a problematic separation of questions relating to sexuality and the family from any consideration of apparatuses and institutions involved in the regulation and repression of people's labour, and of their sexual and reproductive lives. While acknowledging that this other work exists it is seldom dealt with on photographic courses.

Photographic theory (scant as it is) has now run so far ahead of most people engaged in the everyday world of photography that very often students turn away in despair from *any* notion of theory. Both of us are concerned that useful critical work should be given forms which make it more accessible. We are beginning (hopefully) to produce images and texts which could be used in the photographic press itself as a tiny wedge against the sexist, racist and class assumptions underpinning most of these publications, rather than continuing with the marginalization of such work to 'art', 'serious' or 'political' magazines.

WORKING METHOD

From the start we made a joint decision not to rely on what we could find to photograph (in the classic documentary sense), or solely on forms of montaging of visual elements at the post-shooting stage of production, or on 'subversive' texts. Instead we moved to a form of 'photo theatre'. This is a totally non-naturalistic mode of *re*-presentation which aims to create 'a spectacle' while drawing upon, and yet slightly disrupting, well-known genres of photography. (A good example of this can be seen in *Colonization*, where Jo as social actor is dressed and placed in an environment which is then photographed in anthropological style. The fragmented foot is then photographically treated as if it were within a medical discourse – but note too how the foot has been colonized here by nail polish.) In this way we have a twin performance: the staging and acting out of a tableau for the camera, and then a two-dimensional signifying performance on paper.

Within this framework we were able to have extended discussions after our normal hours of (paid) work, to pre-visualize and script everything (but still leave room for an element of spontaneity at the shooting stage). It also meant that we could reshoot anything we were not entirely satisfied with. We did this work sporadically across several months, using weekends to drive around looking for props and locations, and to do the actual shooting. (We could write a book about the experience of trying to photograph the naked female body out of doors on 'public property': in legal terms it constitutes a form of indecency.) Drawing upon our long since forgotten professional experience we were able to choose how to depict a range of styles and genres (both contemporary and historical) to indicate some of the ways in which women's labour and sexuality have been represented, within and across various institutions of photography and state apparatuses.

2 Jo Spence/Terry Dennett, 1982
The History Lesson [also called *Remodelling Photo History*] (7 photos):
(a) *Colonization*, p. 79 (b) *Revisualization*, p. 80
(c) *Victimization* p. 81 (d) *Madonna and Child*, p. 82,
(e) *Questions from a Worker Who Thinks*, p. 83
(f) *Industrialization*, (1 of 2), p. 94 (g) *Industrialization* (2 of 2), p. 95.

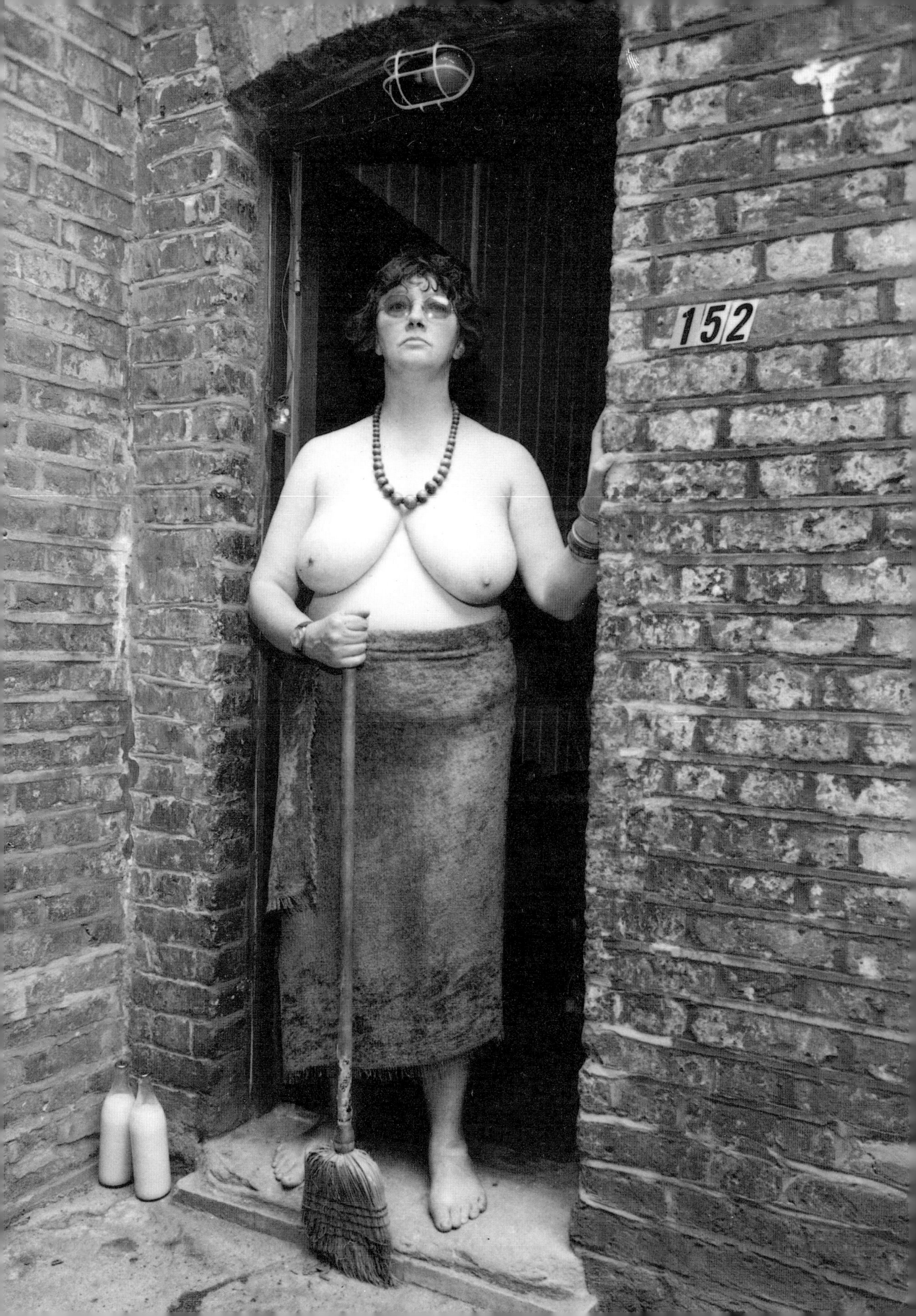
152

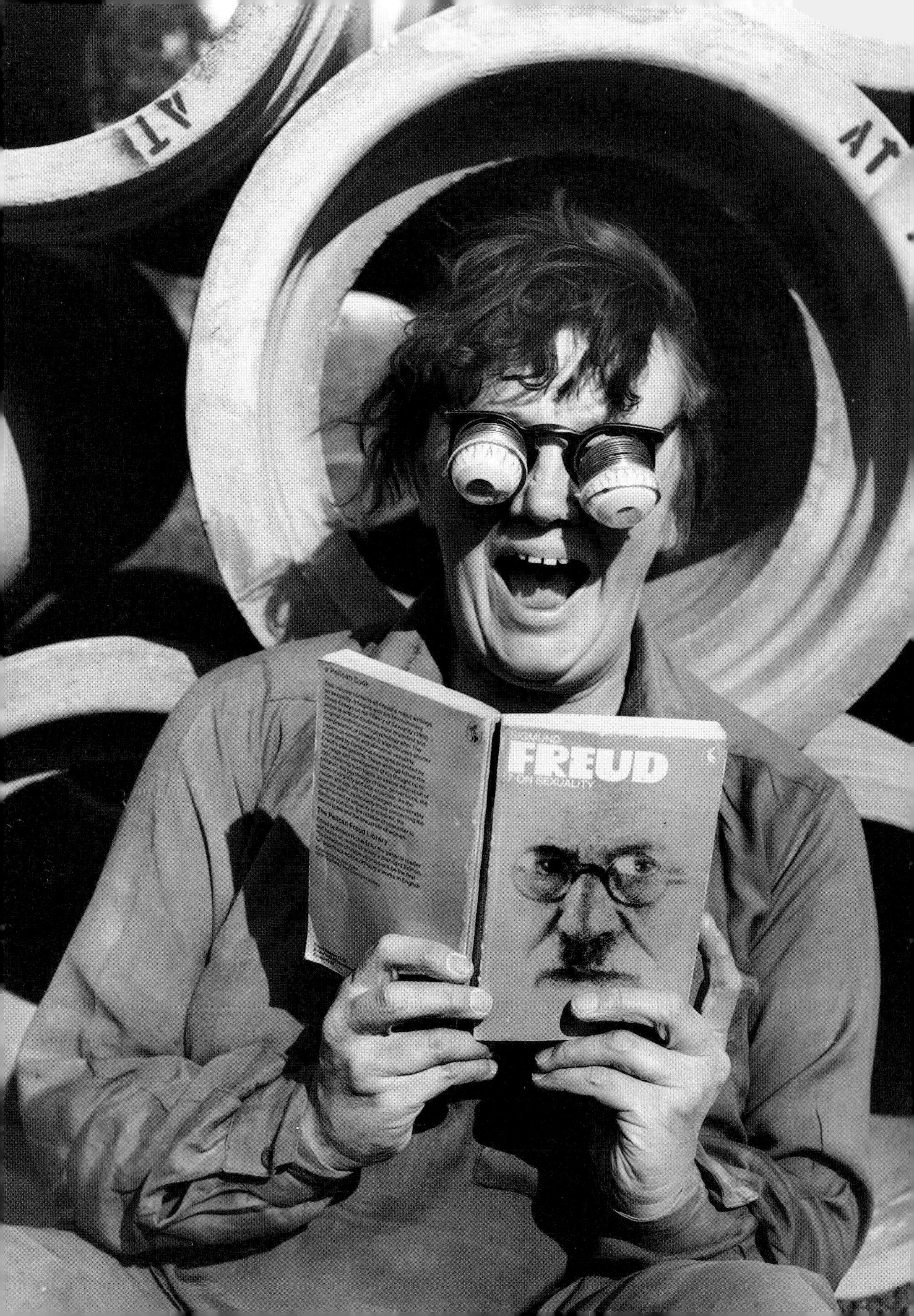
SIGMUND
FREUD
7 ON SEXUALITY
a Pelican Book
The Pelican Freud Library

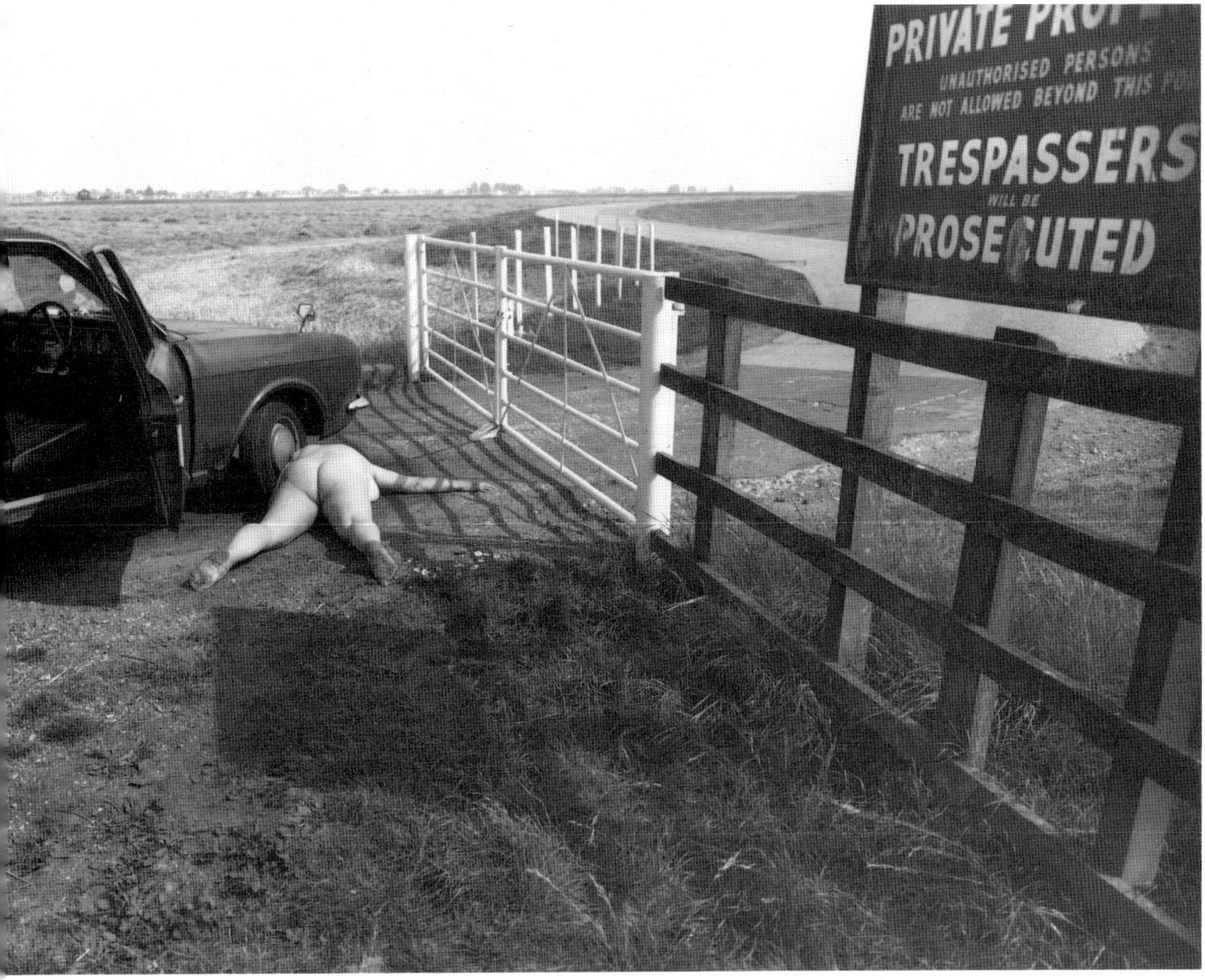
PRIVATE PRO
UNAUTHORISED PERSONS
ARE NOT ALLOWED BEYOND THIS
TRESPASSERS
WILL BE
PROSECUTED

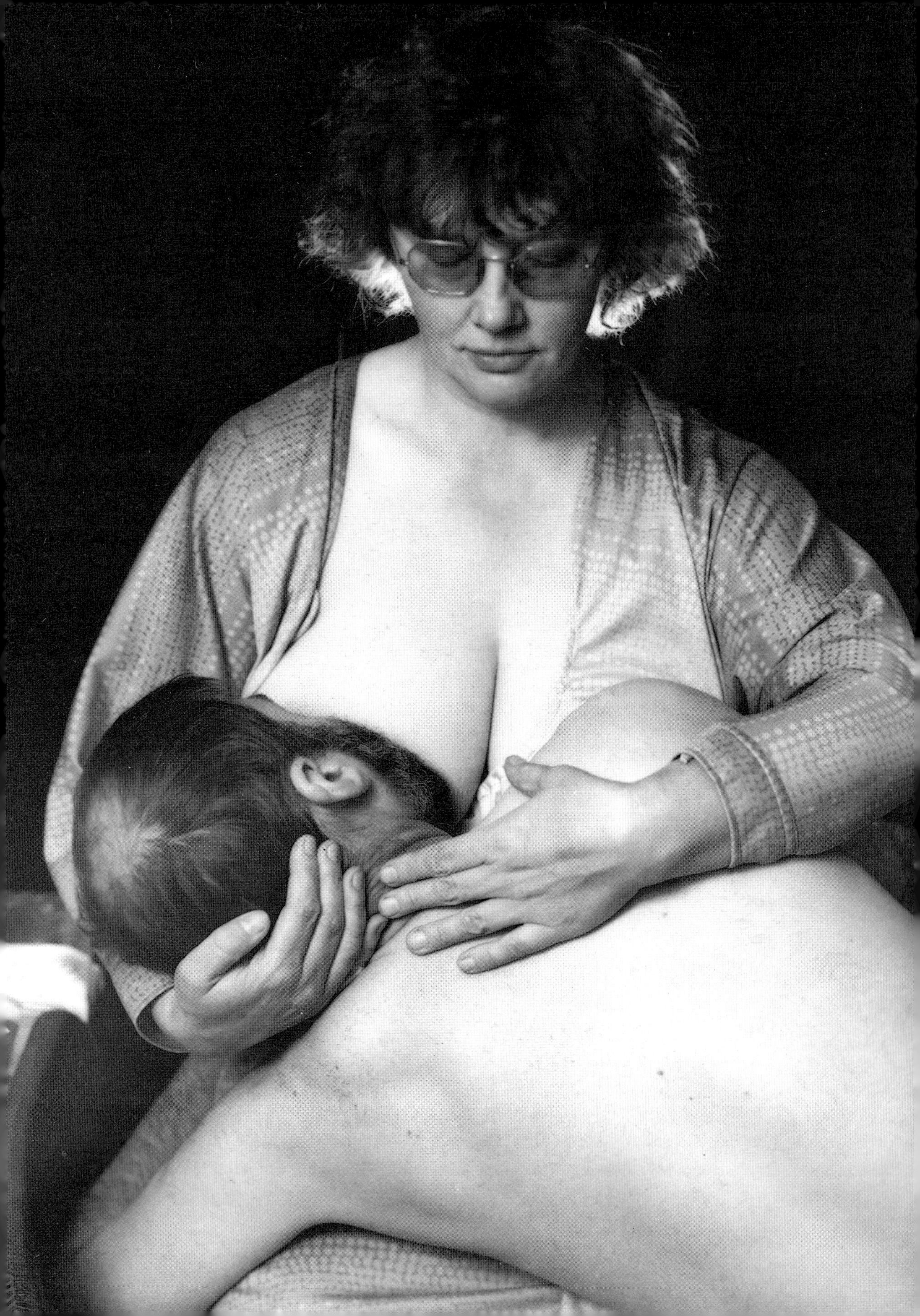

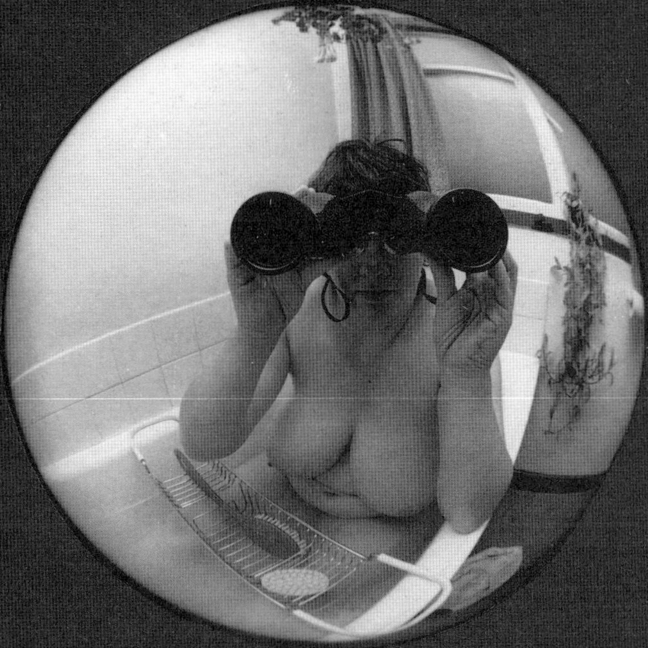

Who built Thebes of the seven gates?
In the books you will find the names of kings.
Did the kings haul up the lumps of rock?
And Babylon, many times demolished
Who raised it up so many times? In what houses
Of gold-glittering Lima did the builders live?
Where, the evening that the Wall of China was finished
Did the masons go? Great Rome
Is full of triumphal arches. Who erected them? Over whom
Did the Caesars triumph? Had Byzantium, much praised in song
Only palaces for its inhabitants? Even in fabled Atlantis
The night the ocean engulfed it
The drowning still bawled for their slaves . . .

Every page a victory.
Who cooked the feast for the victors?
Every ten years a great man.
Who paid the bill?

So many reports.
So many questions.

BRECHT

Of course this work does not attempt to be a definitive statement, but merely a way of beginning a visual mapping process. In parallel with this we wanted to begin a study of visual sexual difference, moving to the male body – whatever we felt would constitute an equivalent set of images – but the asymmetry of male/female representation made this difficult to conceptualize.

As well as providing materials for a 'history lesson' we wanted also to re-examine the model/photographer relationship which is generally one-sided (though not universally so: police photography has a fairly rigid set of routines and a fixed power relationship, artist and model relate in an entirely different – but nonetheless rigid – way, while snapshotting is a variable power relationship). At the same time as we drew upon our own knowledge of dominant signifying and technical practices of portraiture, record, still life, documentary realism, 'nude photography' and the snapshot, we also traversed signifying practices from within anthropology, fine art, news, advertising, science, law, medicine, welfare and charity institutions. For this work we have not attempted the futile task of trying to invent another photographic language, but rather have tried to indicate how photographs which are usually given currency and circulated within different (and contradictory) spheres, can when brought together enable the viewer to begin to make new, and perhaps political, connections. We thus worked within the rough parameters of the given practice. With one exception (where we used a 35mm camera with a fish-eye wide-angle lens) we used throughout a 5" × 4" Linhof stand camera, with 150mm or 65mm lenses, working always on a tripod. We shot on Ilford FP4 black-and-white cut film, using daylight or on-camera flash. Additionally, we decided that a very sparse use of text – what amounted to a *recategorization process* – was all that was needed. Further work for students in deciding upon and trying out new forms of categorization to see how meanings can shift about could perhaps be productive here.

We structured the final work so that it would 'hang' off the upright central panel (*Victimization*). The upper image uses an obviously narrative style which has proliferated in fashion and erotic photography in the past ten to fifteen years, notably in the work of Helmut Newton. Here a crime often appears to have been committed and the female body is used as a sado-masochistic motif, erotically displayed for the camera. However, we tried to strip the image of its eroticism and shift towards a type of reportage. By siting our 'victim' on the boundaries of that which is geographically signalled as 'private property', we hoped to create an ambiguity as to whether the victim had been trying to escape from or into this fenced-in world.

The History Lesson attempts to explore the relationship between the apparatuses which *use* photography, the institutions which *validate* or teach photographic practices, and the role of women in the family. We also wanted to indicate throughout a certain consistency and overlap in the ways in which women and other subordinated groups are represented. Thus the project offers a starting point from *within photography*, but one which should allow us to move beyond the eternal textual analysis of single images. Only then can we ask what is *not* being said, what cannot be said (what is visually unsayable), what is being displaced or rendered structurally absent.

In asking what is absent we enter the realms of the analytical, be it through psychoanalysis or historical materialism. The former engages with the construction of gendered subjectivity and 'unconscious desire', positioning us within texts in specific discourses, the latter with the possibility of conscious scientific and historical knowledge, and the possibility of political change. Both address memory – that which is considered unthinkable/unspeakable, censored from consciousness, and that which in terms of class/power struggles is *rendered invisible*, not spoken about or shown, and often is indeed actively suppressed.

MOVING ON?

From this initial mapping process we moved into another phase of the project where notions of specific reworkings of dominant icons (e.g. the mother and infant relationship as epitomized in the 'madonna and (male) child') now enabled us to formulate new questions. The idea of staging woman as universal 'love object' and 'eternal nurturer' was fraught with personal and political problems, for at this point we began to include more explicitly the male figure inside our scenarios. Easily done using actors, or when drawing or painting – not so easily attempted when it begins to foreground the private and public relationship between two specific photographers with a 'personal' history, working within a public 'history of photography'. In pre-visualizing each element in the project, we were often concerned about offering potential readings which might be construed as 'pornographic' – most especially in the madonna image – but we wanted there to be a tension about the status of any reading. This, however, is totally separate from any 'effect' the staging of such scenarios might have on us! Would our families ever see it? What about the neighbours? Would our colleagues think we'd gone mad? In other words, would people start to wonder if we were 'really like that'...? Thus at this point 'representation' and 'the real' began to coincide, pointing to another area of work which we are now developing.

PLEASURE

Apart from hoping to give *critical* visual pleasure to our audience, part of our project has been to find a pleasurable new way of working together. Previous collaboration had always revolved around notions of photography for 'social and political action' and we wanted to do something which would allow us to explore our personal, as well as our photographic and political, relationship.

Towards the end of the project, where a more specifically feminist voice is allowed to speak out – often ironically – Jo enjoyed moving from considerations of the dominant practices to a different kind of portraiture. She also realized that throughout (almost unthinkingly) she had been making statements about her right to 'exhibit' herself as a 47-year-old social actor, in daring to offer some very different renderings of the female body from those, say, in women's magazines. In that particular homogenized and declassed world, where everything is idealized (or potentially able to be so through the offer of endless 'improvements' to self, home and family), women are enjoined to identify with the universalizing effects of photographic styles in fashion and advertising which minimize skin texture and colour, disguise sagging flesh and flabby, tired or diseased bodies, and efface the ageing process.

In the course of this project we also discovered the difficulty of making a non-linear piece of work without a narrative resolution. Instead, we decided to have the 'object of the look' metaphorically cleanse herself and look back, reflecting the voyeuristic activity of both photographer and viewer in looking at her. Thus our inclusion of the vignetting 'tunnel effect' of the lens used to take the picture.

Finally, we wished to pose some questions beyond the scope of these images. Since we'd been working within a Brechtian tradition of distanciation, trying to transform feeling into thinking through a form of 'educational entertainment', we turned to Brecht's own writing. His questioning poem, coming from outside photography, seemed relevant to the overall problems of history – both of the individual gendered subject and of our positioning within a hierarchical class society. (Incidentally, what we can't or don't ask of most photographs is questions of *their* history.)

10 · TEN YEARS OF PHOTOGRAPHY WORKSHOP (with Terry Dennett)

Written as a contribution to the critical compilation *Photographic Practices: Towards a Different Image*,[1] it introduced the work and ideas of Photography Workshop to an international audience and resulted in the setting up of similar small projects in Africa, India and Brazil. Subsequently, many students told Jo that it was this article that first made them realize that they could be photographers without official sanction or 'qualifications' – and without grants.

As a group which has been involved in many debates within photography and the politics of representation as they have emerged recently in this country, we feel slightly strange in writing about ourselves. Ever since Photography Workshop was formed in 1974, from the shared photographic and political interests of its founder members, it has either been ignored *as a group* (most of its work is attributed to single members) or else rejected outright (as in the case of our working hard to found, run and then write for *Camerawork* magazine). And one of the ironies of the Left and women's movement must surely be this: that groups which are set up and do innovative work usually split into differing political segments; these segments then go on to found new dynasties, or just quietly fade away. In time, the original differences, cracks, fissures and explosions come to be neatly laundered over, erased from the memory of those involved because they are too painful, not fully known to those who came later because 'nobody told us about it' and, finally, mythologized through the accounts of others writing about them from outside. It is surely contradictory, then, that very little is actually known about most groups who are involved in the politics of representation; that, although they themselves raise fundamental questions about representation, the question of how they represent *themselves* is almost always ignored. This prevents the emergence of any serious mapping process becoming discernible from 'outside'. It also prevents the development of dialectical or polemical discussion in any real sense and means, too, that we go on 'inventing the wheel' over and over again.

In this sense, then, Photography Workshop is an unusual group. It started with two core members and ten years later it still has the same two core members. And this is *our* account. The drive for the work of the group has always come out of the obsessions, bitterness and passions of these two members, sometimes collaborating with others, or working together, or working alone. We believe it is this passion and determination to survive in the face of all criticism that has helped us to be here today. However, in the course of this survival the group has changed drastically. We started with the ultimate in 'independence' – poverty – moved on to the use of voluntary labour, donations, ploughing back the earnings of members; we always housed ourselves in our own home and very latterly decided to apply for a grant. We have ended up with a combination of all these things. We now have a small grant from the Greater London Council for very specific purposes, still work voluntarily, and are very poor. But nobody tells us what to do – we can make a lot of noise or be silent if we need to. But we don't have to behave like performing seals for the grant-funding bodies. Throughout we have always attacked particular types of opportunistic radical-professionalism and have tried to open up the very big question of how to rework and redefine the term 'amateur'.

The question of labels hangs around all groups; we have found it strategically useful, for instance, that one of our core members has been blandly labelled as a 'feminist photographer' (a very generalized term), whilst on the other hand we are often called vulgar Marxists (when we know we are not). In fact, much of our work has been about history, both of the individual subject – 'Who am I?', 'How do I know that?', 'How did I get to be that way?', 'How will new knowledge of the past affect my future activity?' – as well as the broader political perspectives of belonging to a class (however fragmented or ill-defined), and in understanding how our race, age and gender shape our conscious and unconscious desires. We have been interested, too, in the relationship between these questions and the institutionalized bases of photographic practices.

What follows is a progressive chronology of our work for the past ten years. We have tried not to ascribe motives, beyond our initial aims, and to be as descriptive as possible about our attempts to help in the broader cultural and political struggles to change society. We do not see this as a trumpet-blowing exercise: our history as a group has been fraught with mistakes, but each of them has taught us to grow and to know better how to survive and to share. Underneath everything has been a desire to pass on information and to make it possible for others to realize their political and personal potential in the widest sense. Above all else we think it is important to say that the ten years' work brought us a total of £8,000 from funding bodies – which works out at an incredibly low annual average. The rest we raised ourselves. We think that working on this scale should be seen as a useful political activity because we always hope that a point will emerge when there are enough small groups within photographic practice to become federated, so that we can all increase our power base through the making of alliances.

Photography Workshop Limited is an independent educational, research, publishing and resource project. Founded in 1974, it carried out an extensive programme until 1979 of workshops on photography – lecturing, research, exhibition production and publishing. In 1980 it became a registered charity and non-profit-making limited company (registration no. 280873). Its programme from 1980 until the present time has been based around an extensive research and retrieval programme. It has helped many groups in the community, the labour and women's movements, and adult education, towards a better understanding of the progressive potential for making and using photography.

The Workshop's research programme has, until recently, been carried out on a self-funded basis, without grant aid, through donations, sales of literature, lecturing, teaching fees and exhibitions. It currently includes work on visual representations of labour, race, gender and sexuality in the popular mass media. There is extensive research/retrieval into the technological and social history of photography, as well as into the cultural history of the labour movement. Our overall perspective is towards the use of such material in community and educational/arts projects/workshops in London and elsewhere.

We have been instrumental in helping with a number of other projects: these include the setting up of the Half Moon Photography Workshop and, jointly with the Half Moon Gallery Ltd (later to be called Camerawork), the magazine *Camerawork*; initiating and working with the Hackney Flashers Women's Photography Collective; publishing the first serious collection of essays on photography, history and politics in this country (*Photography/Politics: One*); publishing the broadsheet *The Worker Photographer*, as well as various teaching kits and posters.

At the same time, members involved in research have systematically written up their work in a variety of educational magazines, as well as setting up or collaborating in teaching workshops, lecturing throughout London and the home counties and trying, with the aid of slide shows, to make accessible a variety of differing approaches to photography. Such approaches also entailed the making of small teaching exhibitions, as well as writing in cultural and art journals.

The Workshop has also produced a variety of permanent and temporary touring exhibitions, and has much partly finished work now in the pipeline. These exhibitions (many of which can be interchanged or juxtaposed with each other to suit particular needs) have been used in arts centres, community and youth projects, as well as within a whole range of formal and informal teaching situations, weekend and day schools and at conferences. We have established a wide network of users throughout the country as well as in London.

At the moment, because our voluntary staffing situation is so overloaded, we have placed several of our touring shows with the Cockpit Gallery, Holborn, where they are used extensively by educational, community and youth projects.

A brief chronology of projects from 1974 to 1983 follows.

1974–1976

Photography Workshop was set up in 1974 and immediately began a programme of workshops to teach photography to children, outside of formal schooling. This culminated in 'The Home Made Show: alternative and low-cost technology in photography', and the touring show 'Children Photographed'. In those early days most of this work was done at weekends within the adventure playground movement, in free schools and in independent children's projects. At the same time we began to research the 'hidden history' of the cultural activities of the labour movement and the trade unions, particularly centring upon the period of the General Strike in 1926. Out of this came a travelling exhibition.

In 1975 Photography Workshop temporarily merged with the Half Moon Gallery Ltd. Out of this merger came the Half Moon Photography Workshop and the production of *Camerawork* magazine. Various other shows were researched and produced by us at this time. At HMPW an Education and Photography group was set up, which convened and ran four weekend workshops on Photography and Youth. These brought together such apparently disparate elements as critical input from commercial educational television, the BFI Education Department's work on the semiology of the image, work on literacy and with welfare agencies, and work with handicapped children, and drew upon the advanced ideas from existing youth projects in the field, such as Blackfriars Settlement. 'The Thirties and Today' was produced by the Labour History Research Group of Photography Workshop under the umbrella of HMPW.

1977–1979

Photography Workshop was involved in the calling together and early coordination of the Hackney Flashers Collective, an agitprop group which produced exhibitions and posters around issues of women, work and domesticity – moving away from simple 'window on the world' techniques to ask questions about mediation and ideology. They also produced a teaching slide pack and a much-used bank of images on class and gender....

PHOTOGRAPHY WORKSHOP'S ORIGINAL STATEMENT OF AIMS

To provide an ongoing research, information and advice resource, and to publish and distribute in whatever form most useful, such research, basic bibliographies, etc.

To continue to establish a permanent, readily available, non-commercial photographic archive which will also encourage the depositing of negative and slide collections and thus ensure their continued use after the owner's death.

To continue to establish a register of slides and prints available for loan at minimal cost for campaigns, lectures, educational projects and community arts use.

To positively encourage self-reliance in photographic users and makers, with the aim of working towards group activity, collective practice and the pooling of resources and information as a general principle in contemporary photography.

To systematize the investigation of alternate chemical and photo technology so as to develop a basic independence from monopolistic companies. (This is an essential first step towards demystifying technology.)

To initiate projects and promote interest in the critical use of photography and various media as educational and communicational tools.

To self-publish concise educational worksheets on various aspects of photography, which can also eventually be put together as a teaching aid. Also to make available technical and useful information in poster and broadsheet form.

To promote the collection of existing local and photo history from all sources, including public and private institutional archives, old personal and family photographs, long-established local commercial photographers, local history and conservation groups, local newspaper files, and with special emphasis on the family album as a valuable social document.

To encourage the photographic recording of personal, group and local history by people themselves, with or without the assistance of professional photographers.

To encourage the preservation of existing industrial and commercial photographs and work records, and to guarantee their safekeeping as documents of historical and political use which are readily accessible.

To continue to help to participate in the setting up of short-term groups to carry out specific documentary/mediation projects, as requested by educational, community and subcultural groups. Additionally, to act as intermediaries in the exchange of details between those wishing to teach or learn photographic skills.

(*Note:* Some of these aims have been realized – others not.)

Critical autobiographical work on a 'history of self' in relation to a 'history of photography' questioned the function of family photographs in the production of knowledge about our lives. A laminated exhibition was produced for the 'Three Perspectives in Photography' exhibition at the Hayward Gallery and was later made into a TV arts programme by BBC 2/*Arena*.

The re-emergence of Photography Workshop after the split with the Half Moon was very productive. As well as working on the two new publications [*The Worker Photographer* and *Photography/Politics: One*], we set up a series of evening classes on Feminism and Photography in collaboration with the Cockpit Cultural Studies Department.

Photography/Politics: One, which was self-published, was distributed for us by Southern Distribution. We printed two editions and had a wide readership in all English-speaking countries, as well as throughout Europe. The book was produced by four editors who worked over a period of eighteen months on a voluntary basis, finally calling in a designer. As we produced the first English-language socialist 'annual' of photography, we are obviously glad to have done this work. In retrospect, though, we would never want to get involved in this type or scale of production and finance again. The cost of printing was paid for out of Jo's severance pay from HMPW, and the rest came from donations and forward subscriptions.

'*Photography/Politics* breaks important new ground, not least in its quiet demonstration of the total inadequacy of traditional approaches to photographic media and their effects upon our lives . . .' (*Time Out* review).

The Worker Photographer was produced by a small voluntary group working within the labour movement, under the Photography Workshop umbrella. It attempted to open up once again discussions started within the socialist movement of the 1920s and 1930s about the class nature of photography and its specific forms and importance as a weapon of cultural struggle.

It had some success in showing the 'hidden story' of labour photography and journalism, exemplified by the concepts of the amateur 'worker photographer' and 'worker correspondent', and was responsible for the reintroduction of these concepts back into the language of the radical movement in Britain. On a practical level, however, it was a premature experiment from which no further journals or stable groupings developed, to our knowledge.

1980–1982

An extensive period of research, workshops, lecturing, teaching, preparation of teaching materials. As an example, we produced *Remodelling Photo History*: a collaboration between two photographers [here referred to as *The History Lesson*]. This was done, initially, for inclusion in a show on British photography prepared for the Massachusetts Institute of Technology, later touring America. We also made a small, laminated version for use for teaching in this country. This work attempted to look at the broader institutional base of photography. In looking at various photographic discourses, we endeavoured to foreground their interconnectedness through our reworking of photographic styles and genres. This was a conscious move away from the (autobiographical) idea of *images of self* into the more psychoanalytic and post-structuralist-based disciplines which have examined *self as image*.

1974–1984: SETTING UP AN ARCHIVE

The Workshop has now accumulated a very large body of work which forms a more than rudimentary archive. This consists of 35mm colour transparencies, 35mm black-and-white and colour negatives, black-and-white and colour prints, a collection of xerox reprints, pamphlets, books and audio-visual aids. The work has concentrated on several different areas:

1 a collection of 'popular' and ephemeral images from a wide variety of publications
2 research project materials which document the social and cultural history within the labour and trade union movements

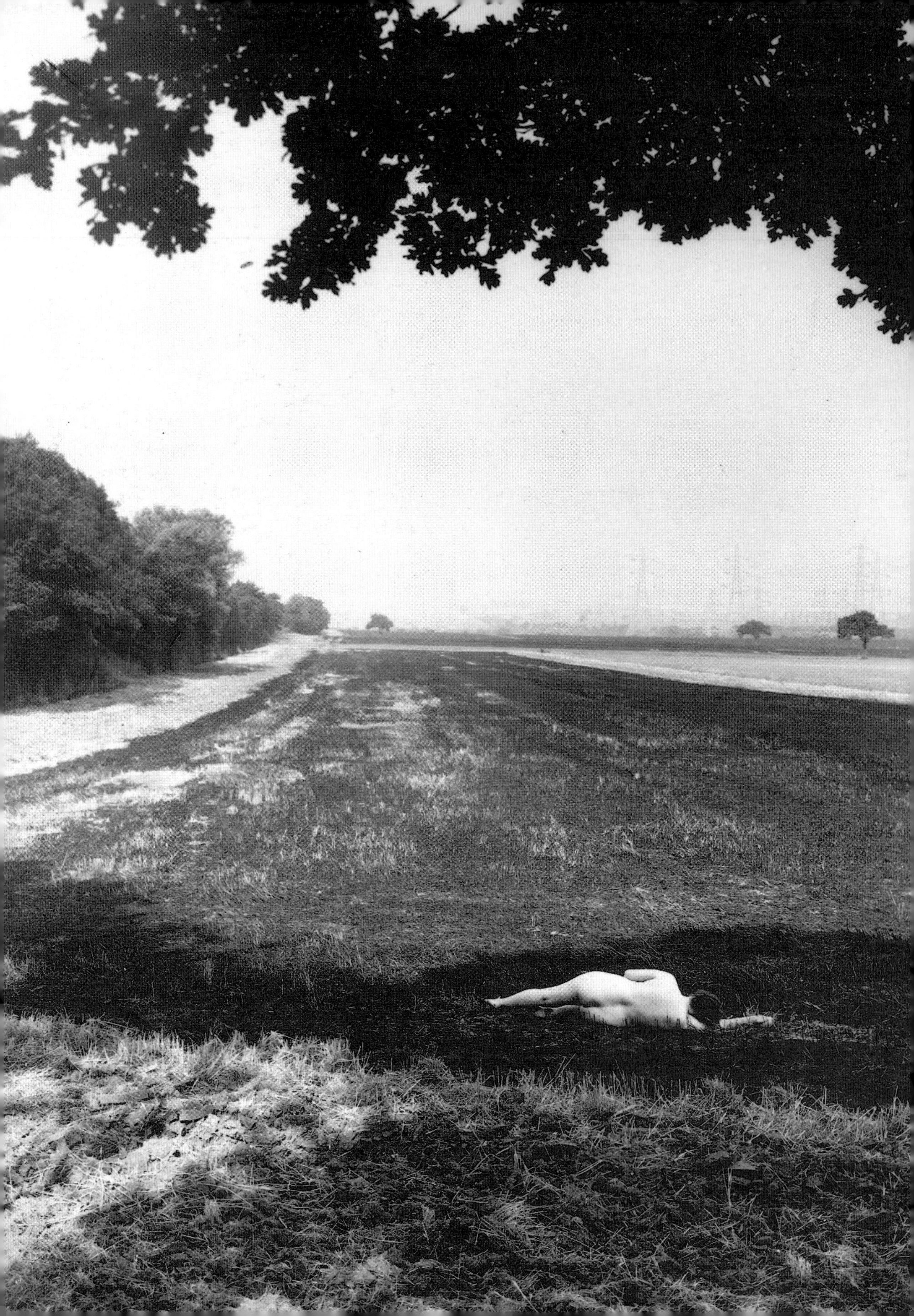

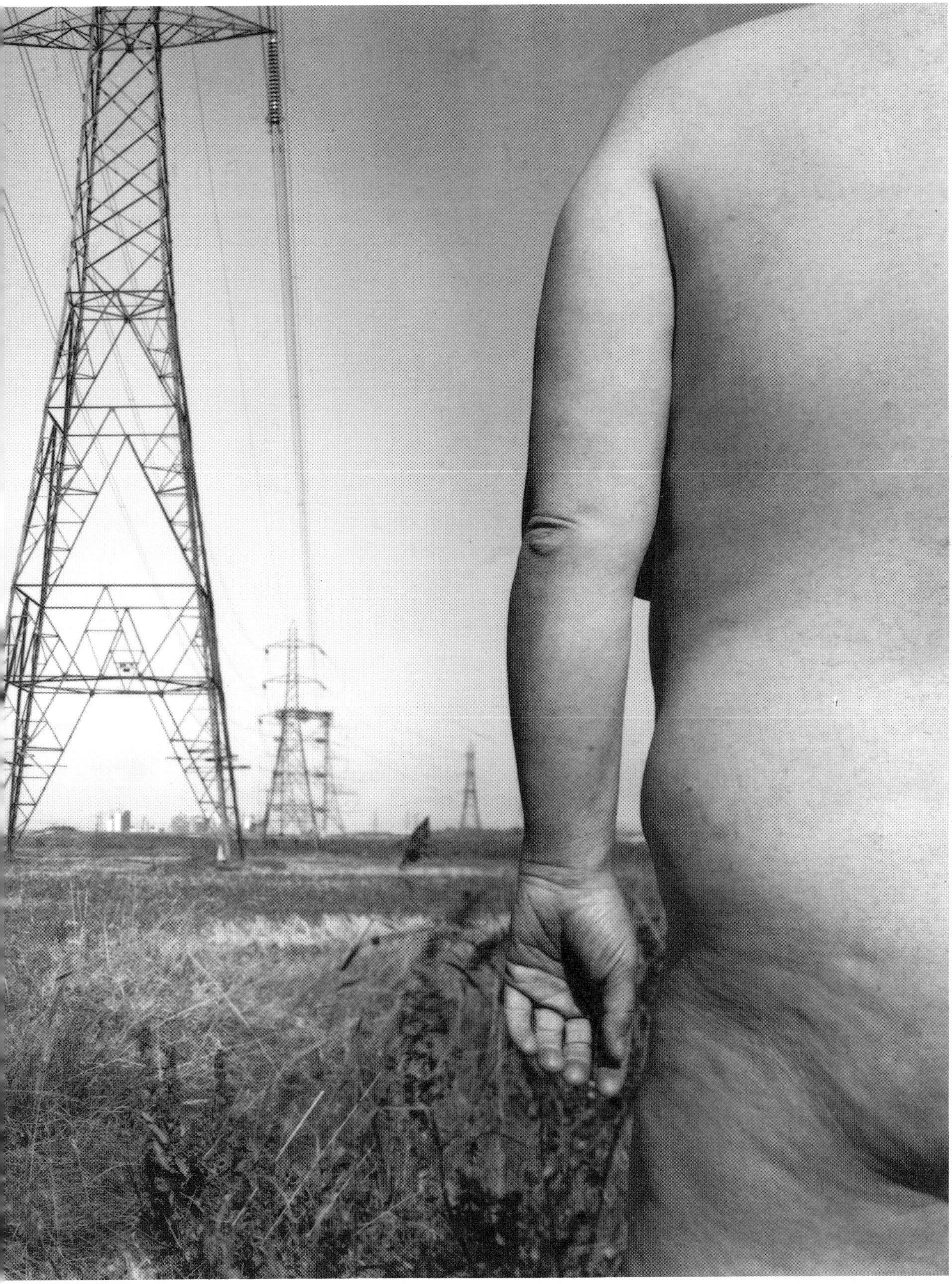

3 a resource which concentrates on the social and technical history of photography from the 1870s onwards
4 a book/pamphlet collection
5 copy negative archive of the *Workers' Film and Photo League*
6 a 35mm slide collection of ephemera and advertisements about sexism, racism and class bias
7 cartoon collection – historical and contemporary
8 postcard collection.

We would emphasize that this material does *not* form the basis of a commercial archive, but that we only charge a small search fee for the cost of making prints. In many instances no copyright is involved, so there is no question of material being used commercially. The archive exists, rather, as a resource for researchers, educationalists, cultural workers and people engaged in a variety of artistic and educational pursuits. Much of the material takes as its focus the need for groups to be aware that *they can represent themselves* through photography, images (both moving and still) and language. In the past we have found that the non-commercial nature of the archive has meant that it is especially welcome to those seeking materials who have little or no funding (e.g. projects by the unemployed, nursery campaigns, etc.).

'The starting-point of critical elaboration is the consciousness of what one really is, and is "knowing thyself" as a product of the historical process to date, which has deposited in you an infinity of traces, without leaving an inventory.'

(From *The Prison Notebooks* by Gramsci)

'In 1928 they said a depression could not happen, can you believe those same voices in 1983? This is what happens in the downwave. Whole countries go bankrupt. Banks large and small go bust. Companies crash, whole industries disappear and millions lose their jobs. House prices tumble. Building societies shake, office blocks become unsaleable, land values slide, and share prices slump. People live differently, think differently, wear different clothes, watch different films, hum different songs, and see sex differently . . .'

(From *Downwave (Surviving the Second Great Depression)* by Robert Beckman)

11 · QUESTIONING DOCUMENTARY PRACTICE?

The sign as a site of struggle

This was a keynote paper given at the first National Conference of Photography, organized by the Arts Council of Great Britain, in Salford, on 3 April 1987. Though she had been flattered to be asked to give a keynote paper, and to have the chance to put class on such a major agenda, the hostile reception her paper encountered was one of Jo's most scarring adult experiences. Several years afterwards one of her detractors apologized and said that the motive for criticizing her as racist was actually part of the lobbying around getting black photographers' needs recognized in arts policy: one of the keynote speakers had to be attacked – that it was Jo was coincidental. However, many others saw it as scapegoating – and believed it inappropriate as Jo had worked on race issues.

As discussions and questions about documentary practice are such a minefield it is unlikely I'll avoid stepping on many before I've mapped out my thoughts, but I'll try. I'm glad that the organizers have asked a woman to speak, who is middle-aged, comes from an economically poor background, is 'working-class identified' but now ostensibly middle class, and has herself experienced dis-ablement through illness. However, I can only represent my own views here and cannot begin to pretend to speak for others outside the identity categories I inhabit. Nor will I hide the fact that part of my identity has been formed from within a specific set of cultural debates and clashes in relation to visual representation, which embrace feminism, Marxism and psychoanalysis. However, I do not occupy a 'correct position', nor do I wish to be dogmatic, but

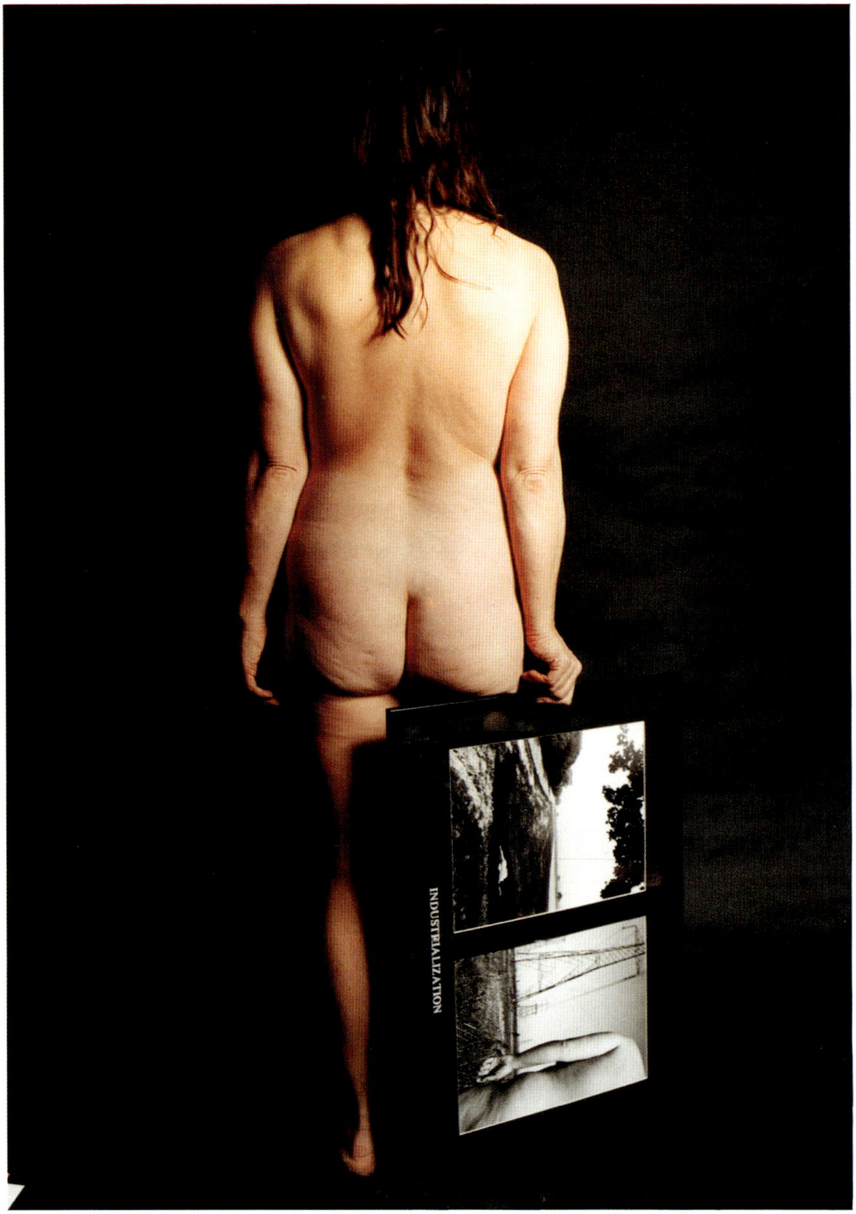

3 Jo Spence/David Roberts, 1988
Untitled
Rising like a phoenix I create a further image which represents my decision after being hounded from the first National Conference of Photography for giving an 'inadequate!' keynote paper about class and power relationships. I retreat into my illness and turn my back on the photographic world. There seems to be no safe position from which to speak.

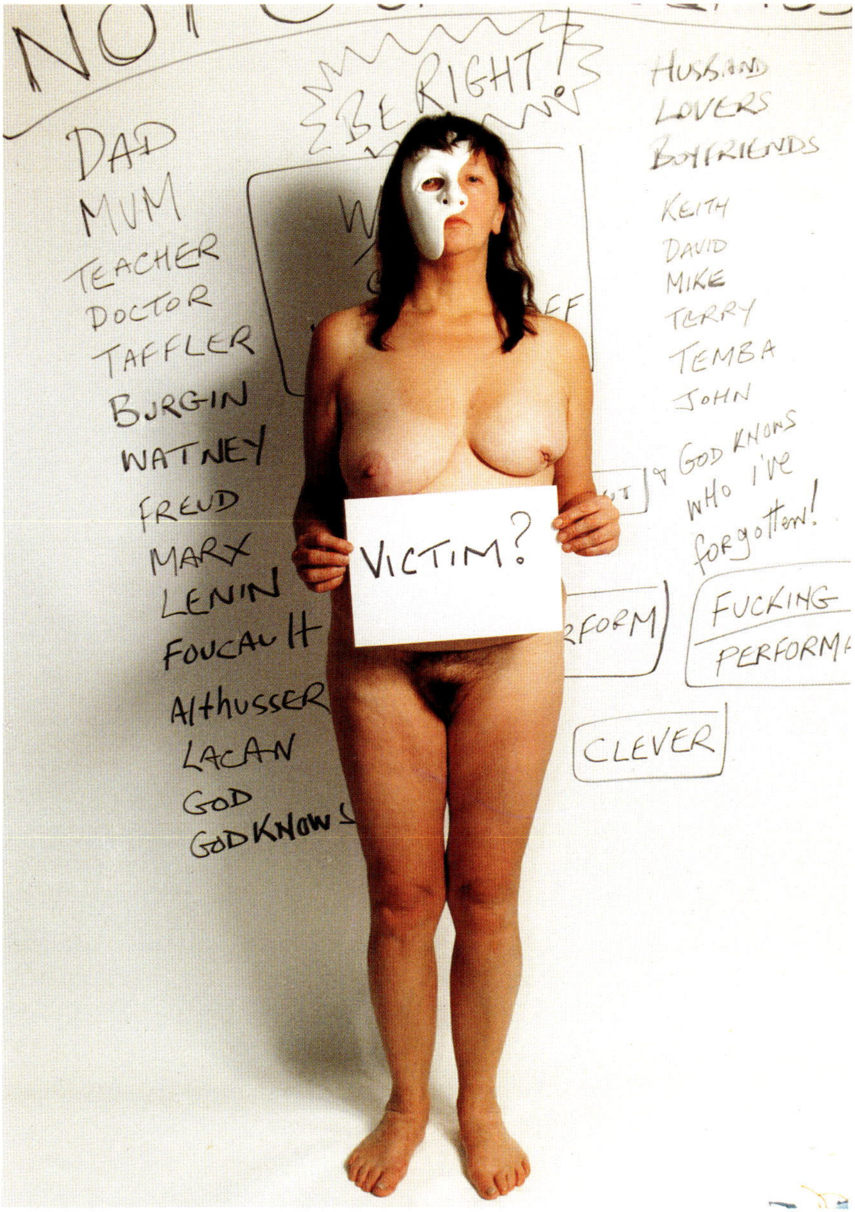

4 Jo Spence/David Roberts, 1989
Not Our Class? (from a session on class)

am interested that it should be possible to have a dialogue in which we all learn from each other. I have not come here to be preached to, nor do I intend to preach.

In common with many people here I am interested in photography and its relationship to power and powerlessness. In that respect I speak with forked tongue as, like many others, I consider myself to have a foot in both camps. As a practising photographer and writer in the field of education, of course, I have some power even though I am often taking a critical stance and feel very vulnerable, ignored and powerless for doing so. But I also speak as somebody who for many years has earned very little and who is ill, and in these other aspects of my life I have less power. Although it is seldom acknowledged, many of us present here occupy and negotiate a terrain which is constantly shifting in relation to our identities, and none more so than within photography where we often use different photographic strategies to meet different needs and wear different hats on different occasions. Additionally (let us whisper), hardly any of us support ourselves entirely from our labour as photographers, or many of us are on short-term grants and put up with disgusting terms of employment.

It is the *complexity* of this fragmented notion of identity which I feel could most usefully be addressed throughout this entire conference, most especially in relation to documentary photography. Documentary photography in its most critical form is usually a method of petitioning those in power, or is used in order to change 'public opinion', that notice be taken of something which needs to be attended to, which is being ignored. It assumes, in the way in which it addresses an audience, that there are universal people 'out there' who have uncomplicated, rational minds, who can perhaps be persuaded or shamed into action by the petitioning claims of such photography. Leaving aside political and economic factors, such appeals to the intellect take little account of the matter of how our minds work out of consciousness, which may not be in any way congruent with the so-called rational mind.

Because of these complexities of social and cultural identity, and because of the vast agenda of social and political problems with which photographers have chosen to concern themselves (which is always linked to questions of audience),

5 Jo Spence/David Roberts, 1988
Write or Be Written Off
In 1983, after being diagnosed as having breast cancer, I silently faded away from the social and economic life of cultural production. At gallery openings instead of being asked 'How are you?' I was often asked 'What have you been doing?' Finally, it feels safe enough to speak to (or to endure the gaze of) only my husband, as I go into deep depression.

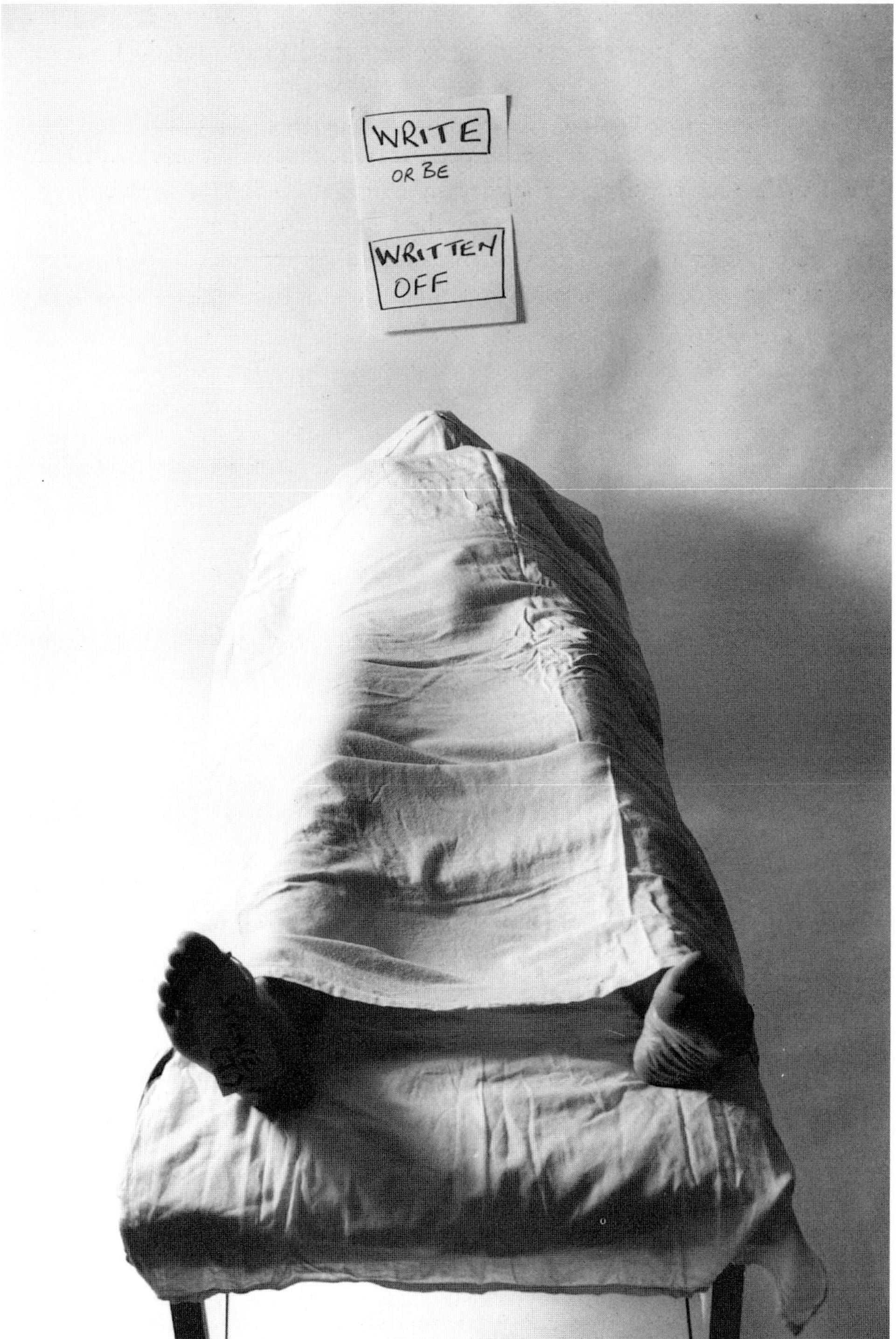
WRITE
OR BE
WRITTEN
OFF

we need a complexity and spectrum of practices to be discussed and validated here. This validation, which should take good account of the simplest attempts to engage with photographic practices, is preferable to a hierarchy dominated by intellectuals who talk in jargon and who are accountable to no one. The political agendas of the academic avant-garde are often totally different from, and longer term than, the short-term demands of campaigners to have immediate material needs met. Photographers will all be concerned with their own individual hierarchy of needs, or the needs of the group they represent, and we should respect this. I don't suppose I'll be thanked for saying this either, but I would also hope there will not be the continual and unhelpful bandying about of blanket terms like race, disablement, gender, sexuality or class that I have experienced at so many other cultural events, where people have been shouted down and prevented from speaking by guilt-tripping insults about hierarchies of oppression. We must not beg the question of cultural and economic oppression but consider that everybody here has something to contribute to debates. Everybody should be encouraged to speak: if people do not speak then we should find out why this is so. (As an example of cross-cultural perspectives there will be, for instance, in the workshop Rosy Martin and I will be doing on phototherapy, a mapping out and discussion about the historically specific construction of white heterosexuality for us as working-class girls growing up in Britain in the 1940s, 1950s and 1960s, and how we have begun to unravel the knots of this in order to understand that identity and sexuality are cultural constructs.)

For more years than I care to remember I have been involved in photography and have witnessed major changes in its thinking and practices. What I feel we have now in the 1980s is a fantastically broad and exciting map of reflexive theories and histories of photography which are still being unravelled. This offers us many starting points and ways forward but is quite bewildering to newcomers. We need to find common aesthetic and political ground so that we can federate ourselves for education and solidarity. We should treat such a notion of federation not as the major centre of our lives but as a resource from which we can go, intellectually refreshed, back into the various streams of commerce, education and politics. But maybe that is too much to expect at the moment!

Much of the theory of photography now on offer appears to be impenetrable and offers no reason why it is there or why it is validated continually in the journals of higher education without much reference to grassroots photographic work. Theory just seems to exist and the idea that theory is good for you has become a truism. However, we cannot live without theory, and it is important for all of us to continue to try to engage with the analysis and theorization of photography, and to ask for answers to the question of why and how radical or progressive theory can be liberating, both for us as individuals and in terms of group identities.

Moving on: commercial photography (which also has a highly theoretical base which never makes itself visible) is still dominated by incredibly narrow definitions of photography which are straddled by news and advertising and a multitude of state uses of photography, many of which employ the window-on-the-world documentary mode of representation. Often these are a thinly disguised form of surveillance, a way of offering phoney evidence of surface phenomena, or of defining individual or group cultural identities which appear to be grounded in the 'real world' but are in fact total fictions offered up for consumption. We must never forget that all this is the background to any kind of radical professionalism in which we are engaged. Such images as we produce which we feel challenge the dominant ideology, even if they initially attempt to show something which has never been seen before, will soon be sucked up by the industrial machine of the mass media. We must expect this and have strategies for dealing with ways in which work is appropriated.

Equally fictitious are the fantasies (apparently more pleasurable, often engaging with our unconscious desires and traumas) offered to us by advertising. Some of us are also offered images of the fragmented female body, which are often called pornography. These images appear to present men with a kind of pseudo control over women in which they can day-dream of being dominant whilst in fact they continue to occupy a kind of childlike notion of omnipotence. This is often in contradiction to the economic and political impotence of many men. These interconnected spheres of image-making create regimes of desire in which we are always flattered into assuming positions which are difficult to escape in imagination – even if our daily lives totally differ.

As well as setting out tasty visual dishes of victimization and heroics, from surviving plane crashes and runaway horses, to winning the pools or being voted slimmer of the year, the dominant media continue to underpin the self-exaltation of the power and owning capacity of dominant groups which create glamorous and idealized images of themselves. There are no countervailing institutions or agencies of photography with the power to challenge any of this: our work is fragmented across a range of sites. The very real professional power of the middle classes, as managers and mediators, how it is attained and kept, continues to remain totally invisible. For those of us who are middle class, this, I feel, should be a priority as an area of work. Instead of going off into the interior, as cultural social workers, perhaps turning the photographic gaze upon one's own individual and group identity may be useful.

Overlaid with these image repertoires are the types of pictures which we choose to make and select of our own lives, which we keep in family albums or personal photo collections. This is termed 'amateur photography' by those who define photographic markets. The agenda of images given a currency here is even more limited, and yet most of us continue to collude in the fantasy that – pleasurable as they may be to each of us – the complexity of our lives can easily be encapsulated in these tiny prints. Where then, within the private sphere, do we keep a counter-history, which will remind us that what is being said 'out there' is *not all there is to be said*? When do we begin to reinvent a documentary practice within the family where the most insidious of power struggles go on, between men and women and between adults and children?

It is only by having a theory of what it is possible to speak about or to represent visually that we can begin to understand what is absent from all these agendas. It is my contention that as photographers, long before we try to look for techniques to represent others (via documentary photography or whatever), we need to begin to think seriously about the question of how to represent ourselves, to ourselves, even if we do it as a technical or theoretical exercise. It is only if this is taken seriously as a political question that we can begin to home in upon the real problems of representation or documentation – which are primarily those of institutional, family and self-censorship. We are so full of shame and desire and fear and trauma, underneath it all, that we can hardly say anything about ourselves. Yet as photographers we seem to have plenty to say about others. If we can begin to understand the roots of self-censorship (learnt within the domination of the child by the family, schooling, peer groups, doctors, the various forms of media and the state), we will be able to trace all the ways in which we watch ourselves and continually block off what we 'really want to say'. All the things we cannot bear to face about ourselves, what is called in psychotherapy the 'shadow side', are then parcelled up and projected back out onto other individuals and groups, which become the embodiment of all that we fear and hate in ourselves. I say this as someone who has undergone various forms of psychotherapy, as the result of a near nervous breakdown. If social and cultural identities are constructed and not biological or God-given, if they are not fixed but changeable, then we are not dealing with notions of bias, in which these representations are distortions of the real, but rather we need to find new and more reflexive ways of conceptualizing and mapping out not only the product, but also the process of who *we* are and how we got that way – as individuals or group members. In the unblocking processes of psychotherapy I experienced a need to represent myself to myself in a range of ways from the symbolic, to the fantastic, to the mimetic, from the validatory, to the critical, to the contradictory. All of these ways became ways of telling myself different, and more honest, stories so that I could understand better how I came to be formed psychically, how my subjectivity came into being, and how I had negotiated in the world to survive. Photography – in particular phototherapy – helped me here and I now have an amazing visual map of my psychic and social history. These images are all fictions or fantasies but are the visual embodiment of the structures and relationships which held my life together.

The problems of the dominant practices of documentary photography still remain: though such practices may be useful for showing what appears to be happening in the world, they are still incapable of showing how institutional structures work. Nor can they indicate how we feel or negotiate within them. Documentary photography is also fairly useless when it comes to questions of social self-documentation as individuals, when most of what we might wish to document (such as sexual harassment, racial discrimination, power struggles within the family) is a cause for shame or embarrassment, when we fear that we might be judged by revealing the very concerns we are engaged in understanding and perhaps challenging. Never is this more apparent than when trying to deal with questions of sexual identity where the camera is tabooed or forbidden. Documentary photography in any straightforward sense would be ridiculous here and so we need to restage scenarios for the camera as a way out of the impotence that comes from this impasse. This image production work should be seen as a private activity.

I feel it is totally relevant to bring up these problems here, for it is important to understand that whenever there is a photographer and a photographed, wherever there is a story to be told, unless the photography, or an exchange of knowledge, is reciprocal then there will always be an imbalance of power. What I mean by this is that if a documentary practice involves only the exposure or revelation of one party, then it is an unfair transaction. I am not suggesting that all photography be done on a reciprocal basis, but that we mark out this territory as problematic. Augusto Boal states in his book *Theatre of the Oppressed* that within a poetics of the oppressed 'one must keep in mind the main objective to change people from "spectators", passive beings in the theatrical tradition – into subjects, actors, transformers of the dramatic action.'[1]

Equally, a photographer 'takes' pictures of someone which are then used for a purpose outside the control of the subject (matter) photographed (who is not consulted on their use, or asked to put a personal story or text with them). This means that questions of cultural identity will always be imposed from outside, and we will be forced to collude in such a tying down process because of the poverty of ideas of how to invent and define ourselves. In all documentary photography, where people are represented, the question of identity is paramount. To be specific, and to give an example of what I mean, when I was ill in hospital and taking photographs of the ward rounds of the consultant, it was possible to show the interaction between different classes, races and genders of

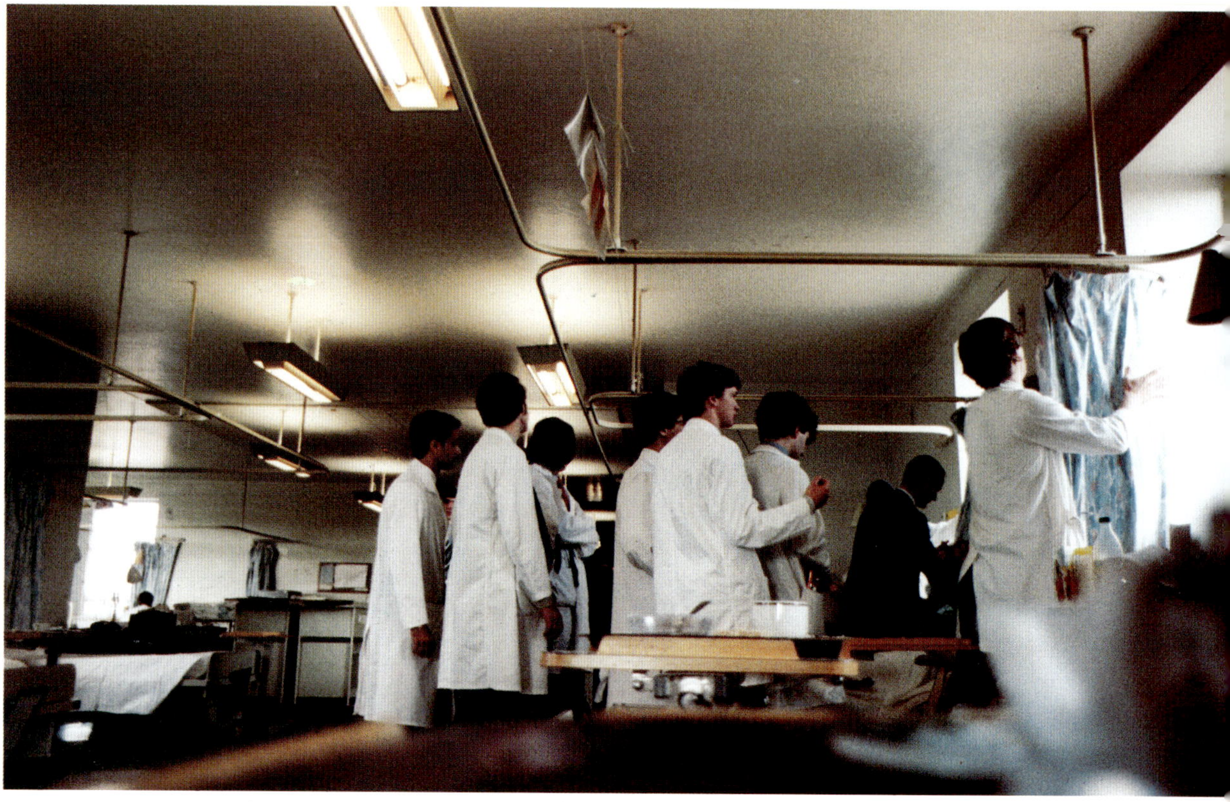

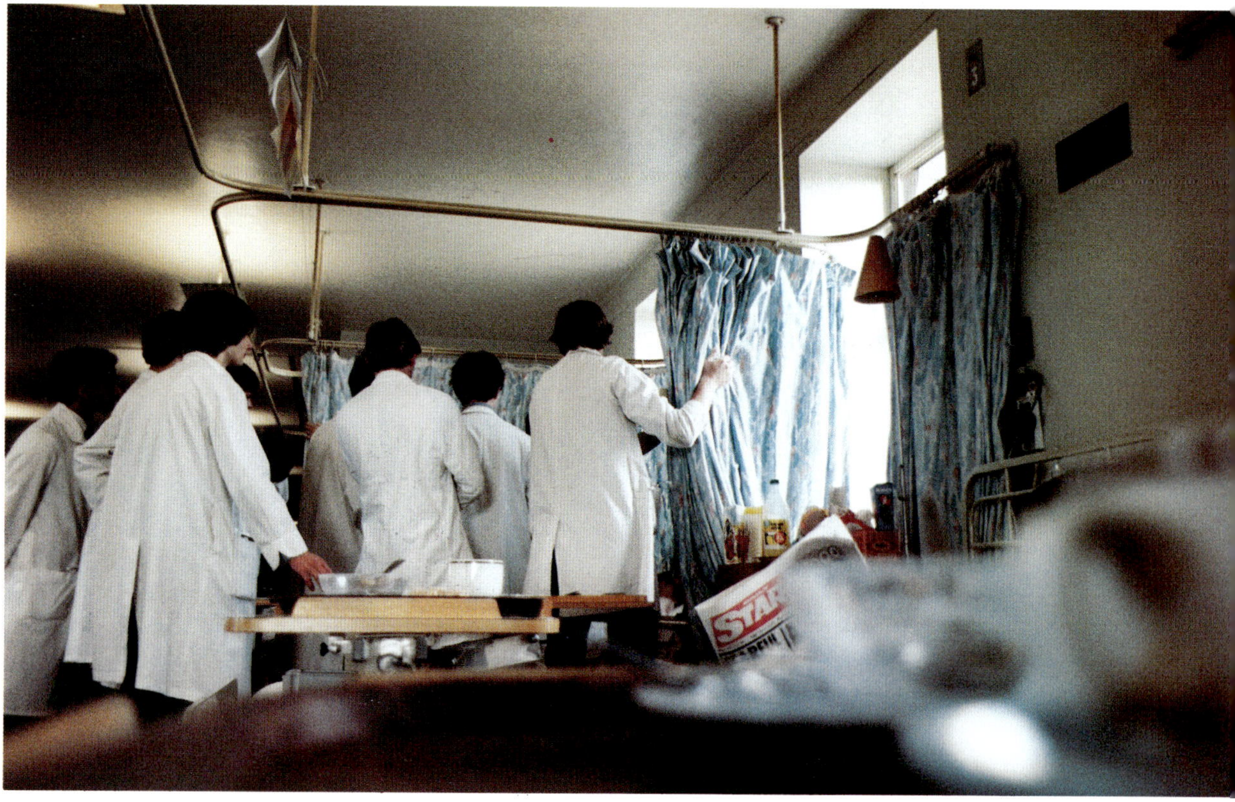

people at their workplace, and between doctor and patient, but it was impossible to show how I was situated within that as a powerless patient, how I knew so little about my body that I had internalized my subjugation to the medical profession, or how the medical profession came to have the power of life and death which is rarely questioned. And please feel free to read this as a metaphor for all other types of powerlessness which we experience at the hands of people onto whom we project benevolence. When I came out of hospital I needed to do research and to turn to theory to understand the essence of the political power of the medical profession. I then needed to seek for other ways of representing that reality which, eventually, involved the staging of personal tableaux for the camera. In this way I was able to produce photographs which helped me to ask questions, rather than to appear to give answers.

Speaking less specifically now, not only do we need to use photography to try to make visible what is not being talked about by those in power (dealt with so skilfully by Heartfield and Peter Kennard, for example)[2] but the other side of the coin is that only by using photography to ask new questions can we then begin to understand the systematic denial of the reality and fantasies of groups and individuals who have plenty to say, who have been silenced, or who are still fighting to speak....

When individuals or groups decide to document, reclaim or reinvent their own histories and identities they are termed self-indulgent or narcissistic. But let us not forget that Narcissus had a great deal of awareness that the self he saw in the mirror was tantamount to an 'unreal self', and was merely a self-image fabricated out of the views, needs and attributions of others. Through self- and political knowledge it is possible to move beyond the idea of the 'perfect image'

6a–b Jo Spence, 1982
The Designer Can See What is Best
(from 'The Cancer Project', Nottingham)
The consultant's ward round. He enters the ward dressed in an expensive suit and is surrounded by a flock of white-coated students. When he gets to my bedside I immediately stop taking photographs.

'The analogy between the war on cancer and the war in Vietnam is more than metaphorical. Since the rise of the cellular hypothesis – that cancer is a mysterious, tumorous condition of localized origin – the medical establishment has sanctioned only three methods of treatment: surgery, radiation and chemotherapy. On a larger scale these are precisely the three major weapons (search-and-destroy, bombardment and chemical warfare) utilized militarily against social problems (i.e., political and economic insurrections) in Vietnam and other parts of the Third World.' – Alex Jack, *Cancer Control Journal*, vol. 5, no. 3/4.

or 'the perfect lifestyle'. Ideological liberation lies in the examination, analysis, transformation, destruction and, finally, separation of the ever-evolving core of self, from that Other self, which has previously been condensed into one set of images.

In a recent interview on television, Dennis Potter, who is one of our most exciting and political 'image makers' as a playwright, said that as a cultural worker

> you should attend to that which you can attend to ... work where you find yourself. Make it a detective story about how you find out about yourself – you have a superfluity of clues and very few solutions. Maybe the very act of gathering the clues and the account of remembering not merely events but how those events have lodged in you, and how those events have affected the way you see things which begins to assemble a system of values, will become valuable. Only when it has all been assembled can you (metaphorically speaking) get up out of your bed ... use different conventions and make them co-exist so that the past and the present are not in strict sequence (even though they were, in a calendar sense, they are not in your head in that sequence, and neither are they in the terms of the ways in which we discover things about ourselves). In thought an event from the past can follow yesterday instead of precede it ... out of the morass of evidence and clues and searchings and strivings which is a metaphor for the way we live, we can start to put up the structure called self and we can then walk out of that structure saying 'at least I know and you know better than before what it is we are'.... In *The Singing Detective* the illness is the catalyst which was the starting point of extreme crisis, no belief, and a cry, and a hate ... out of which were assembled the fantasies out of which eventually came facts, out of which came knowledge ...

This brings me finally to the question of The Female Gaze. What is the role of women within photography? This is something which Rosy Martin and I will be talking about in our workshop, in order to begin to attempt to deal with this major political question.

NOTES TO PART ONE

2 THE UNPOLITICAL PHOTOGRAPH?

1 See Roger Mayne, *Camerawork*, no. 6, 1977.
2 See H.M. Enzensberger, 'Constituents of a theory of the media', in *Raids and Reconstructions: Essays in Politics, Crime and Culture*, London, Pluto Press, n.d.
3 A reading list on this and related topics is available from Photography Workshop, 152 Upper Street, London N1 1RA (send SAE).

See also:

IMMRC (ed.) *Marxism and Mass Media: Towards a Basic Bibliography 4–5*, New York, International General, 1976.

Greenhill, R., Murray, M. and Spence, J., *Photography*, London, Macdonald Guidelines, 1978. This gives a good general introduction to the question 'Who is photography for?' It also discusses professional practice, and how pictures are used.

3 WHAT DID YOU DO IN THE WAR, MUMMY? CLASS AND GENDER IN THE IMAGES OF WOMEN

1 I am using the term 'sign' in its semiotic sense. The sign consists of two interlocking elements: the signifier (what means) and the signified (what is meant). Cf. Jonathan Culler, *Saussure*, Glasgow, Fontana, 1976, especially pp. 18–23.
2 On such determinants of productions, see John Tagg, 'The currency of the photograph', *Screen Education*, no. 28, Autumn 1978. On determinants of reception, see Stuart Hall, *Encoding and Decoding in the TV Discourse*, Birmingham Centre for Contemporary Cultural Studies Stencilled Paper no. 7, n.d.
3 Stuart Hall, 'The social eye of *Picture Post*', in *Working Papers*, no. 2, Birmingham CCCS, n.d.

See also:

CCCS Women's Studies Group (eds) *Women Take Issue: Aspects of Women's Subordination*, London, Hutchinson, 1978.

Williamson, Judith, *Decoding Advertisements: Ideology and Meaning in Advertising*, London and Boston, Marion Boyars, 1978.

Winship, Janet, *Women at Work Bibliography*, Birmingham CCCS Stencilled Paper no. 54, 1979.

5 THE SIGN AS A SITE OF CLASS STRUGGLE: REFLECTIONS ON THE WORK OF JOHN HEARTFIELD

1 See U. Eco, *A Theory of Semiotics*, Bloomington, Indiana University Press, 1976. He examines in considerable detail various types of pictorial signs and the problematical nature of their relationship to the reality which encompasses them.
2 There is no room to deal here with the child's phantasy of the 'family romance', a term coined by Freud, wherein (as a partial description of the term) a child deludes herself that she was not born of her real parents, but is, rather, of noble origin. Such delusions of grandeur can be continued right through into adult life via certain structures of romantic fiction. Eventually the heroine will be cast adrift in a sea of glorious signifiers, replete and satisfied to have transcended her humble origins now that she is at last fairy-tale bride.
3 John Berger, 'The political uses of photo-montage', in *Selected Essays and Articles*, London, Penguin, 1972.

4 Tim Mason, Letter to *New Society*, 30 October 1992.
5 Stephen Heath, 'Film performance', *Cinetracts*, 2, 1977.

Recommended reading includes:

Althusser, L., *Lenin and Philosophy*, London, New Left Books, 1971.
Curran, J. and Cuervitch, M., 'Retrospective', in *The Audience*, Block 3, Units 7 and 8 of *Mass Communication* course material, Milton Keynes, Open University Press, 1977, p. 55.
Dennett, Terry, 'The evolution of an illustrated workers' literature', in *Photography/Politics: One*, London, Photography Workshop, 1978.
Goodwin, J., 'Ideology and intellectual cinema,' *Quarterly Film Review*, Spring 1978.
Hood, S., 'Brecht's theory of alienation', *Block*, 20, 1980, pp. 11–12.
Korner, W. and Stuber, J., 'Germany: Arbeiter Fotographie', in *Photography/Politics: One*, London, Photography Workshop, 1978.
Mason, Tim, 'Women in Nazi Germany, part 1', *History Workshop Journal*, 1, Spring 1976.
Morton, C., 'The *Arbeiter-Illustrierte-Zeitung*', Polytechnic of Central London thesis, 1979.
Munzenberg, W., 'Tasks and objectives, 1931', translated from *Der Arbeiter-Fotograf in Germany: the New Photography 1927–33*, ed D. Mellor, London, Arts Council, 1978, pp. 51–3.
Seiman, E., 'Heartfield's millions montage: (attempt at) a structural analysis', in *Photography/Politics: One*, London, Photography Workshop, 1978.
Sontag, Susan, 'Fascinating fascism', in *Movies and Methods*, ed B. Nichols, Berkeley, University of California Press, 1976.
Voloshinov, V., *Marxism and the Philosophy of Language*, New York, Seminar Press, 1929.
Willett, John, *The New Sobriety: Art and Politics in the Weimar Period 1917–33*, London, Thames & Hudson, 1978.

Plus:
John Heartfield, London, ICA/Arts Council catalogue, 1969.
John Heartfield: Photomontages of the Nazi Period, London, Gordon Fraser/Universe Books, 1977.
John Heartfield 1891–1968: Graphics . . ., London, Camden Arts Centre, 1980.

7 FAIRY TALES AND PHOTOGRAPHY

1 Editor's note: Jo left no bibliography for this essay, just a note telling herself to find one. No one can, now. However, the following works by Jack Zipes would have been important to her.

Zipes, J., *Breaking the Magic Spell: Radical Theories of Folk and Fairy Tales*, London, Heinemann, 1979.
——— *Don't Bet on the Prince: Contemporary Feminist Fairy Tales in the USA and England*, Aldershot, Gower, 1986.
——— *Fairy Tales and the Art of Subversion: the Classical Genre for Children and the Process of Civilisation*, London, Heinemann, 1983.
——— *The Trials and Tribulations of Little Red Riding Hood: Versions of the Tale in a Socio-cultural Context*, London, Heinemann, 1983.

10 TEN YEARS OF PHOTOGRAPHY WORKSHOP

1 S. Bezencet, and P. Corrigan (eds) *Photographic Practices: Towards a Different Image*, London, Comedia, 1986.

11 QUESTIONING DOCUMENTARY PRACTICE? THE SIGN AS A SITE OF STRUGGLE

1 Augusto Boal, *Theatre of the Oppressed*, London, Pluto, 1974.
2 See, for example, on John Heartfield, *AIZ: John Heartfield 1930–1938*, ed David Evans, New York, Kent Fine Art, 1992, and on Peter Kennard, *Target London* (set of photomontages, posters and text in box), London, GLC, 1985.

PART TWO

A CRISIS OF REPRESENTATION
Health and Bodies

12 · THE PICTURE OF HEALTH?
Part 3

In February 1986, the feminist magazine *Spare Rib* began a three-part series about cancer. Kit Mouat in Part 2 (*SR*, 164) wrote about cancer control by the medical establishment and the drug industry. Jo wrote Part 1 (*SR*, 163) and this article, Part 3 (*SR*, 165, April 1986), about dealing with the breast cancer she discovered in 1982. It is included in this anthology not only because it illustrates her awareness of power politics in illness, and her struggle to represent them. It also demonstrates her continued concern to pass on practical solutions that she had learned as she realized how much the body was 'not just a bloody sign' but something vulnerable that needed attention. She even added at the end of this article 'A full resource list of organizations, reading material and addresses relating to cancer treatments can be obtained by sending a large SAE to Jo Spence' and gave her home address, signalling her willingness to be directly useful whatever it cost her personally – almost.

I offer here some questions and ideas for consideration. Some of these came up during the course of orthodox treatment, some afterwards during my investigation and moving into, then enjoying, my new health regime. I would emphasize that I have found no evidence to contradict the notion that cancer is

7–8 *overleaf* Jo Spence/Rosy Martin, 1984
Infantilization (from 'The Picture of Health?')
Making visible the feelings of powerlessness and infantilization at the hands of the medical profession.

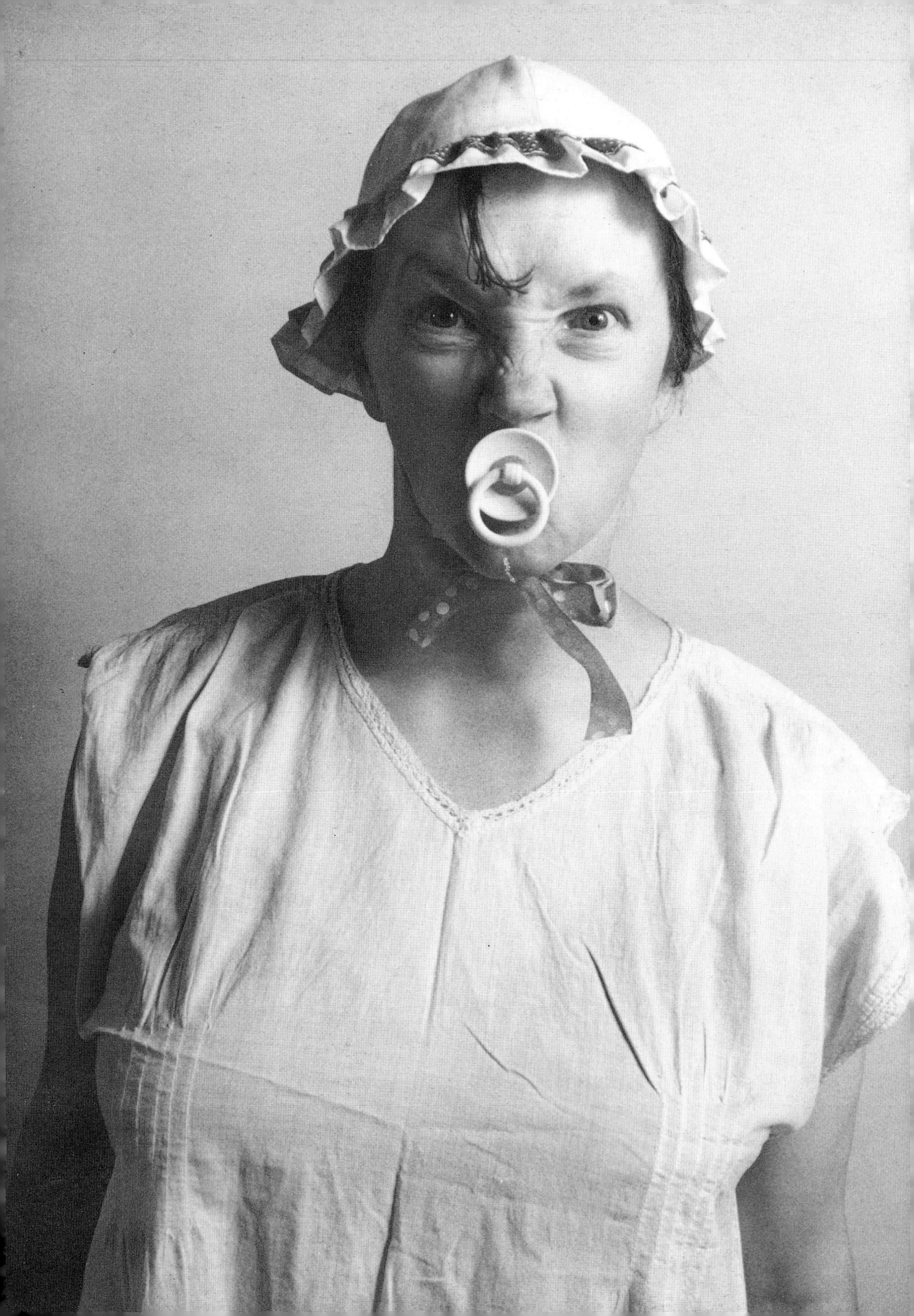

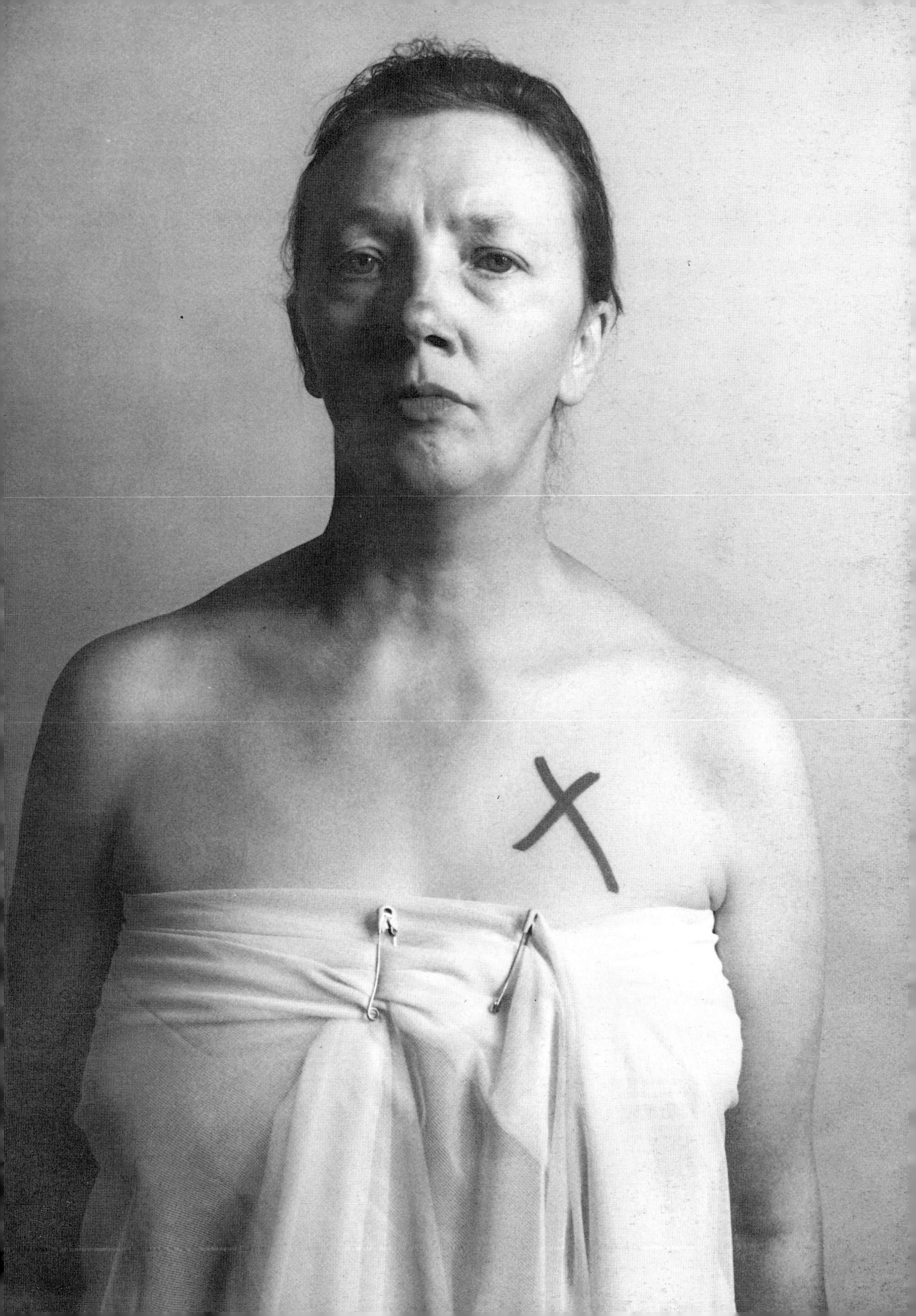

a complicated process to reverse or rid ourselves of, and whatever is offered here is merely information, not a way for anybody else to proceed. If women decide to combine orthodox and supplementary treatment they will of course be supervised by a doctor. But if, as in my case, there is a rejection of orthodox medicine, it is still nonetheless vital to be supervised at all times by a qualified medical practitioner. Because the treatment I chose, traditional Chinese medicine, is still in its pioneering days in this country (though it is regularly used in China), it is not easy to have access to a network of practitioners. I was lucky in that I found a practice where they were willing to take me on as a patient, in spite of the fact that it is illegal for anybody who does not have an orthodox medical qualification to treat cancer.

However, as they are not treating the cancer, but my entire condition, this seems to be a way round the double bind that those of us who wish to choose to proceed outside the NHS are in. Of course there are private health insurance schemes which one can negotiate with to have a range of treatments for cancer, but as I am opposed to this in principle, I have had, of necessity, to find a way to move forward outside the NHS, whilst operating on a very low income. Because I am a socialist I support the idea of a national health service within a welfare state, but because I am also a feminist I will fight with others against patriarchal medicine as it is currently practised in this country. Also, concentrating on the whole woman is in no way in opposition to group struggles over the social and political causes of illness.

In using the term 'orthodox' throughout I mean the dominant system of medicine as practised within the NHS. In using the term 'supplementary' I mean the other therapies which exist in the private sector which need to be paid for, but can be used in combination with orthodox medicine. In using the term 'alternative' I mean all therapies which are practised outside orthodox medicine, most of which have to be paid for.

PATIENTS' RIGHTS

Before you go to a doctor or to hospital it is important to know that you have the right at all times to refuse treatment (unless you are considered to be insane, suffering from an infectious disease, or considered incapable of looking after yourself). A patients' rights leaflet is obtainable from the National Consumer Council, from Citizens' Advice Bureaux, or from your local Community Health Council.

You have the right to ask that a friend or partner of either sex be present during examination or consultations. You have the right to refuse to sign a 'patient consent' form if you are not happy about the surgery offered to you.

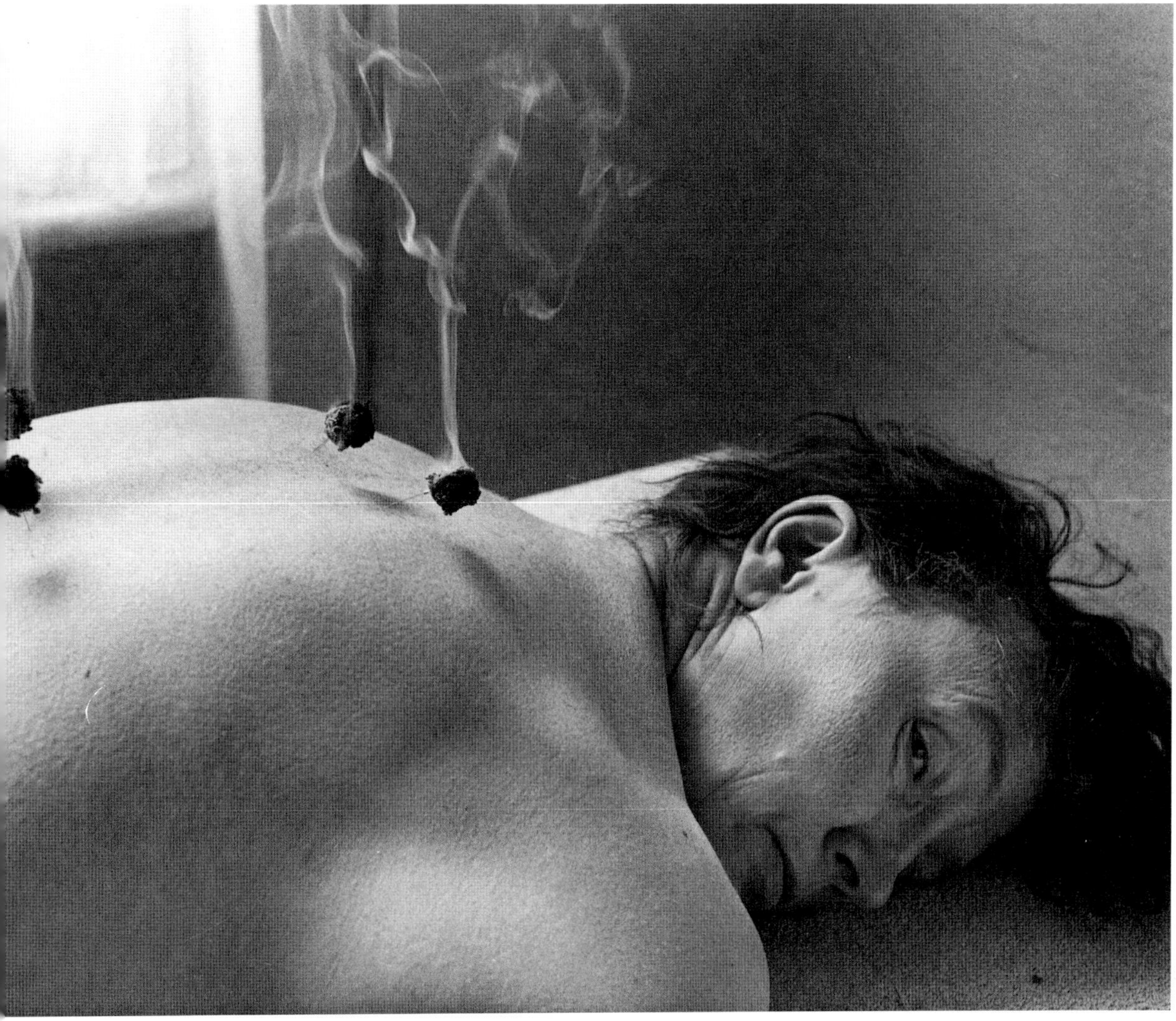

9 Maggie Murray, 1984
Alternative Health Treatment Using Traditional Chinese Medicine
(from 'The Picture of Health?')

We should have the right to know not only 'side effects' and survival rates for treatment but also what non-orthodox therapies or complementary treatment are available on the NHS. (Important to note that the Homoeopathic Hospital in London offers orthodox treatment for most cancers, although iscador (mistletoe) injections are considered suitable for some types of breast cancer.)

If opting for mixed treatment (i.e. orthodox and complementary therapies in combination), it is important to establish with your doctor that this is *your* decision and you don't expect it to be undermined in subtle (or unsubtle) ways.

You do have the right to know if you are part of a 'trial' in which pairs of patients are double-blind computer matched via their similar symptoms and then each given different treatment, which is monitored. There are at least six major trials going on in this country in different regions. What does being part of a 'trial' mean in relation to your right to make decisions about your own body? I was (unbeknown to me) part of a trial in the Nottingham area and was never told until I attended another hospital who 'didn't believe in such trials'.

We should have the right to know that different consultants actively oppose each other's treatment for the same set of conditions (in some hospitals mastectomy is still fairly automatic, in others not so). Sometimes consultants in the same hospital have different methods of treatment.

You should make it clear if you wish to refuse to have your disease progressively documented by a medical photographer for use as teaching materials, lecturing, the writing of papers or the illustration of books (most consultants ask to have two sets of slides done of 'interesting cases' – one for the patient's records and one for their own private collection). Why don't we document our own health, keeping an inventory of all chemical intake throughout our lives? This is often requested of you if you decide on a naturopathic detoxification programme.

Try to keep copies of all letters you handle which are about you (open them – nobody can do much about it). Ask for the right to read your notes and ask as many questions as you feel you need to. There are 'management techniques' for handling awkward patients – try to watch how you are being 'handled' if you are not too frightened. Some people have even managed to make tape recordings of their consultations which are very useful later for a variety of reasons.

Try to get advice from the welfare rights people on the difficult decision of whether to sign off from work (or unemployment) as 'sick' or not, which often mucks up payments to you for weeks on end. Also whether or not to have the disease named on certificates. (Do you want personnel to have you marked out as a potential health risk?) [This is] part of the whole syndrome of the 'victim hiding the problem', also linked to the compulsion for you to conform and wear a prosthesis after removal of a breast. To get rid of the evidence of what has been done to you.

You should have the right to know just what your NHS doctor is 'allowed' to prescribe for you if you opt for supplementary or alternative therapies which include massive doses of vitamins or minerals. The MIMS guide to prescribable medicines is held by all pharmacies and you can ask them to look things up for you. In my experience, the nearer a patient is perceived to be to death the more likely the GP is to cooperate with complementary prescriptions.

If you are interested to know your rights in relation to making decisions about your death then contact the Euthanasia Society. Far too much fear around breast cancer resides in our inability to face the fact that either the disease or the treatment might kill us....

ALTERNATIVE APPROACHES TO SURVIVAL

If you have been told you have cancer I feel it is important to read all the *positive* stuff on how to survive you can get your hands on. Reading death statistics will cripple you emotionally unless you somehow manage to turn it on its head and say to yourself, 'I intend to be a survivor'. Alternative bookshops are good stockists of books and pamphlets on alternative health and critiques of orthodox medicine. If you can't afford to buy the stuff, once you have located it then you can order it from a library. If you are reading for 'prevention' of cancer then the order in which material is read seems to me to be very different and might even include quite a lot about orthodox practice itself.

You need to coldbloodedly sit down (on your own or with an ally) to work out what resources you need, what you can afford, what you will have to ask to be given, and what dearly held previous beliefs about yourself and your invulnerability as superwoman will have to be examined pretty quickly. Also find a strategy for letting others know you have needs so perhaps theirs will need to be deferred for a while!

In the hospital where I was, all the women were going straight back to their jobs and/or looking after their families as if nothing had happened. The turnaround time for mastectomy then was three to four days if all went well.

Your needs might include the following:

1 a network of support (even if such a network doesn't perceive itself as such)
2 some kind of counselling (some regions have voluntary counselling schemes through the hospitals, or else these can be located through CancerLink)
3 money! You need to maximize your resources and assets.

If you feel you want to investigate alternative approaches to breast cancer,

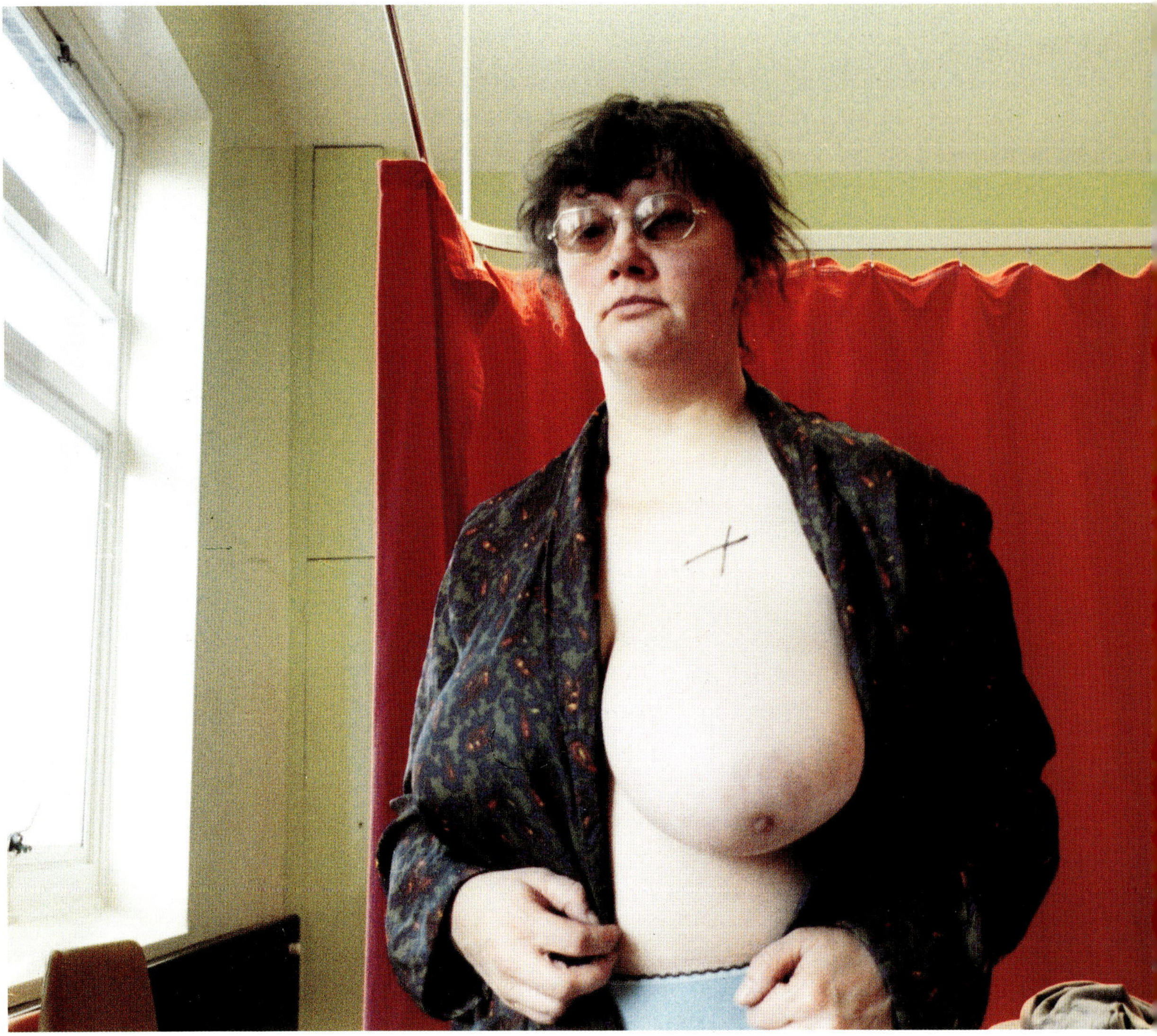

10 Jo Spence/Terry Dennett, 1982
Marked Up for Amputation (from 'The Cancer Project', Nottingham)

to try to put together a 'package deal' for yourself, which might consist of orthodox treatment, plus (say) acupuncture or diet, then this is relatively easy to do if you have an income of your own. It can be nigh on impossible for working-class women who are on low incomes or whose income becomes part of the family income, and who anyway are more used to 'doing what the doctor says', and are perhaps less articulate in a situation where they are in a subdominant position. . . .

I feel it is important to think about different holistic health approaches as *systems*. Western medicine treats all other systems as commodities, i.e. they will lift a bit off the shelf and insert it into their own system of medicine. There is a constant struggle going on for definitions of health care between orthodox and non-orthodox practitioners, as to who will have professional status, who can prescribe treatment, who can be employed by the state as part of the NHS – but e.g. India and China have their own philosophies of medicine, and medical subcultures. When looking for treatment for cancer I feel it is useful to know how other cultures have dealt with it – not all miracle drugs are seen as miraculous in other cultures, though some have revolutionized health care.

It is important to know where to get information about alternative approaches. . . .[1] It is important to know how to separate the disease from its treatment. Possibly getting in touch with others who have gone the alternative route will help. (I did it by putting a letter into the magazine *Here's Health* which brought forth dozens of replies. They also list health groups in various towns.)

HINTS FOR THE DAILY ROUTINE

How can you evolve methods of stopping people treating you as a victim or a heroine? Telling you shock/horror stories of other people's cancer and treatment? Initially when I was ill people were in full flight with their anecdotes before I could stop them. The images of horror and death piled up at an alarming rate and it was only when I went to Bristol Cancer Help Centre that I realized the importance of having positive (even utopian) images to aspire to. . . .

Think about the problems of meeting others who have the same or similar problems to you. Do you want to mix with people who are having orthodox treatment (this often happens in a therapy group), people who are trying to combat degenerative illnesses in general and have a good pool of information about systemic diseases (e.g. multiple sclerosis, arthritis)? Do you want to meet survivors or people already half dead with chemicals? . . .

There is a need for some sort of assertiveness training for those of us who feel totally intimidated by the medical profession.

CONSCIOUSNESS RAISING

How do we deal with the abject loneliness of the long struggle for health (the most boring of subjects to other people who are 'well')? How to present yourself as a subject in daily struggle? People are used to the 'narrative resolution' of illnesses like cancer (in the media's terms you are either 'dead' or 'better'. The actual *struggle* over many years to regain health is not good box office. It is more like soap opera with its continual peaks and troughs and minor resolutions for most of the time).

Cancer may mean restructuring your life *and* society, but when you as an individual have it, the struggle is usually on your own! You have to get your priorities sorted out – if you are a feminist or a socialist it probably means that you are involved in half a dozen struggles which are no longer *immediately* relevant to your day-to-day life. Cancer research and 'self-love' must take priority in my opinion at this stage. This can cause a lot of internal conflict if not sorted out from the beginning. (I lay in bed worrying that I could not go to a rally at the Greenham peace camp the day before my operation!) The amount of solidarity among people around cancer is very limited (and breast cancer terrifies most women) – and though people are 'supportive' they can't take on our burden for us. It is often up to very close friends and/or our partner to shoulder the main burden with us. But what do we do if a partner rejects us because our 'body image' is no longer tenable to us or to them due to our having breast cancer? Who do we turn to?

A basic problem for me as a socialist feminist was that I had a 'conflict' model of the world. How to mesh this up with needing to be more 'harmonious' in order to begin to be well again? For instance, initially I took on the medical profession rather than the illness itself!

How do you deal with the problem for us as 'new' women of 'over performance' in order to prove ourselves, often burning ourselves out? (Something I continue to witness to my horror.)

How do you deal with your own bravado/rebellion? Being the 'naughty little daughter' is all very well when facing up to doctor/daddy and nurse/mummy within the cancer field (where most top jobs are held by men) but what we need is knowledge of how to begin to take responsibility for ourselves and have a say in defining our own bodies. A well-trod path in feminism but not in relation to breast cancer.

The problem of love and sexuality for us in relation to this particular illness: how to redefine 'love' and move towards a less phallocentric type of sexuality? Many women see their sexuality as totally destroyed through mastectomy and hysterectomy ... a good prosthesis might help us to pretend to the world that nothing has happened, but for many women the scars will remain in memory long after the others have faded. Good counselling can help here.

Time scales? If it took twenty years to get your body in the state it is now, then how can you expect a few 'magic bullets' to sort it out? We need a different philosophy of our body's needs in relation to cancer therapies. It might take many years to get the body back onto an even keel – it might never do it. But, as has been said many times, the 'quality of life' may be vastly improved.

Not only is there a 'cancer industry' where (as in America) more people are involved in researching and treating the disease (and whose standard of living may depend on it) than are actually being treated at any one time, but it is important to note the continual orchestration in the national media of various 'breakthroughs', 'miracles', 'new discoveries' (always on the horizon), etc. The public relations of the British Medical Association is quite phenomenal, and this orchestration should be examined for its subtext in the ways in which it constructs 'the truth' of cancer. In an inverse ratio to this is the limited mileage given to alternative (less miraculous and more long-winded) treatments in their onslaught against the cancer orthodoxy.

Some people have theorized that cancer is just another form of slow suicide. Whilst this might be highly contentious I feel that for some people life might be so stressful and apparently unchangeable that legalized death is the only way out. However, in my own journey through illness I seriously considered my rights to suicide or euthanasia and found the literature of the Voluntary Euthanasia Society very useful.[2]

Finally, and on a positive note, I feel it is *important* to try to help others to share a new philosophy of health. My partner, David, asked if he could attend the same practice as me, which he now does. I am quite happy that our general health is openly discussed between all of us, and that he is taking the same long-term (good ecology, whole body, *mind* and body *integration*) route as myself.

13 · TIP OF THE ICEBERG

This was a proposal for a TV programme which was later taken up by BBC 2's *Arena*. Feminist writer and lecturer Ros Coward was proposed as joint scriptwriter with Jo; Litza Jansz from Pictures of Women production company was the proposed art director; and Christine Pearce was proposed as director.

The programme will be loosely divided into three sections. Visual and verbal links will be made across the sections.

SECTION 1: WHOSE BREAST?

In this section we examine the conflict between the male fantasies around women's breasts and women's experience of their own breasts. As our fantasies are influenced and informed by our childhood experiences we start by examining (in an accessible way) the infant's relationship to her mother's breast.

From the first moment of life the breast is the source of both nourishment and comfort. Whilst unaware of our general environment we are deeply aware of the presence or absence of the breast. Considering the psychoanalytic evidence prioritizing the role of breastfeeding, it seems surprising that as we develop from childhood we have a confused and dissociated relationship with our own breasts.

In the light of this we look at the way the young child is told to cover her chest whilst her brother is encouraged to proudly display his. We look at the way young girls are represented through Hollywood and television as being young *femmes fatales*, brides and mothers. The 'little women' toys offered young girls (e.g. Sindy doll with her 'keep fit' outfit) show clearly the shape they should aspire to (i.e. small-breasted and slim) and how that shape can be manufactured.

As we move on to adolescence we show how romantic fiction, advertising, pornography and the underwear industry dictate what we should do with our breasts, what shape they should be and to whom they should be offered. We experience how contradictory these ideas are. We are told that big breasts mean 'desirable', yet they are shunned by the fashion industry and become the butt of constant jokes and comments.

From here we go on to examine images of motherhood, we look at the conflicts around breastfeeding. Starting from a historical perspective, we look at the recurring image of the mother as being the woman with the baby at her breast. We consider the role and recurring fashion for wet nurses. Now that breastfeeding is back in fashion we are made to feel guilty if we don't or can't breastfeed our children. Undernourished babies and delinquent adolescents are our fault. When breastfeeding we become the property of the medical profession who expect us to prepare and administer the breast in a prescribed way. At the same time it is considered shocking to breastfeed in public.

The feelings generated that our body is merely a set of parts, and those parts are someone else's property, are intensified by the treatment we receive from doctors when something goes wrong.... If we detect a lump on our breasts we are expected to hand them over to the medical profession. The breast that we have learnt to associate with being sexual suddenly becomes utterly dispensable.

SECTION 2: FIT TO BE SEEN

In this section we look at the way medical orthodoxy treats parts of our bodies rather than the whole woman. From the testimony of women who have experienced breast cancer we find that the process of medicalization means that women have little or no control over their treatment. Not to comply with that treatment (often the subject of controversy amongst the medical experts themselves), we are told, is suicide. Against the increasing evidence that cancer is a systemic disease (affecting the whole body), the treatment involves war being declared on the specific tumour. We refer to the American doctor who compared the medical tactics of 'cut', 'burn' and 'chemically destroy' to the military tactics used by the Americans in Vietnam.

We question why the patient is pressurized to wear a prosthesis (false breast) after the operation of mastectomy, when it has no function other than a purely cosmetic one. Just as social and political injustices are covered up, so (with perhaps the 'honourable' exception of war veterans) are injuries, deformities and amputations hidden. This not only leaves the individual isolated, unable to recognize and share experiences with other survivors, it also conceals the high incidence of the injury. The tyranny of the one acceptable body shape is maintained.

We consider what it means to be 'fit to be seen'. We look at the cosmetic value placed on health – how we are encouraged to be healthy in order to look good. We go on to show how we conceal and hide images of ill-health from our lives. We examine ideas of health which see illness as the opposite of being well rather than part of a bodily continuum of health.

SECTION 3: TAKING CONTROL

... In this section we examine what it means to resume control of our bodies. Through the experience of women who have rejected orthodox approaches to the treatment of breast cancer we look at approaches to recovery and health in which the whole body, rather than bits or parts, is treated. We explore the role of women's self-help groups and clinics set up specifically to deal with women's health.... We consider how we have to restructure our own images of ourselves in relating to other people, in our work and in our lives.

TREATMENT

The programme will be visually linked by a surreal, witty representation of a woman taking her breasts on a journey from childhood through adolescence and motherhood to old age – a journey which ends in hospital. This will be visualized either through animation using cartoon characters or through a dance/mime set against a background of studio sets, animation and graphics (using back projection and chromakey*). Through this device we cut between the character and her background images allowing us the opportunity to expand and develop various issues through interviews and clips. The soundtrack will include music, voiceover, and different forms of sound montage.

The ideas will be linked with a simple spoken commentary. It will use popular visual imagery (particularly important around such a taboo subject as breasts when our ideas are built up through what we see and perhaps more importantly what we don't see), clips from popular light entertainment TV programmes and 'vox pop' sequences of girls and women talking about their experiences as an introduction to each section. Interviews with various experts and professionals (agony aunt, doctor, etc.) will then be used to develop and expand themes. The visual imagery which forms the basis for the programme will

* A video special effects technique called 'colour separation overlay' in film. Areas of saturated blue in a foreground scene are substituted by a picture from another source into which the foreground is 'keyed'.

be taken from advertising, fashion and health magazines, medical journals and textbooks and television programmes.

The cartoon or mime is here described in some detail to illustrate how the sections could be linked.

The programme opens with a mime artist in the character of an infant. She is fondling and sucking on a large breast. (If a mime, the prop would be a large inflatable beanbag in the shape of a breast.) Her enjoyment is evident as is her anger when the breast is denied her by being covered up. The lights dim and we leave her in an infantile tantrum. (The breast also serves as a screen onto which comforting and pleasurable shapes and colours are literally projected.)

As the lights mix up we find the mime artist in the persona of a young child. She is dramatically lit and reacting in character to the sound over telling her to cover her chest. As she stands up we can see that she is wearing joke breasts attached to her by a piece of string which hangs round her neck. She has to keep adjusting them so that they are the same height.

The lighting changes and we see that she is in a supermarket at the beginning of a long row of shelves. Throughout the programme we can cut back to her wandering through a labyrinth of shelves filling her trolley with the goods relevant to the breast, which women are meant to consume through their lives. Our character is joined by other characters who interact with her in different ways. For example, a group of boys pass her. They are scooting along on the trolley knocking things over as they do so. They laugh and point at our character as she is unsuccessfully trying to adjust her joke breasts to look like the model on the underwear display stand.

The programme will mix from the supermarket scene to film footage, interviews and rostrum graphics sequences by using the sales notice-boards as a linking device. The notice-boards will act as screens depicting popular images from romance to pornography to advertising. The programme will constantly leave and rejoin our character by zooming in and pulling out from sales boards, allowing us to show a range of related images whilst maintaining the visual theme.

In Section 2 we find the now adult woman queuing at the medical counter which is selling surgery (including cosmetic surgery) and drugs. At this counter the customer also becomes the commodity. It is the customer who is weighed and parts of her are packaged. Our character gives her breasts to the experts behind the counter.

Section 3 opens with our character visibly aged, laden down and struggling with full bags from the supermarket. She stops and empties the bags one by one, looking progressively happier as she is relieved of her burden. She examines the bags and starts to cut them up and stick them together. One by one, other women follow her example and join her in emptying their bags and sticking them together. They are making a screen which is blocking out the image of the supermarket. On that screen we introduce images concerned with patient-centred treatment (alternative medicine clinics, self-help groups, women's clinics and therapy centres). The programme leaves the women shutting out the supermarket, square by square, and using film footage, graphics and interviews to examine visually how we regain control of our bodies.

14 · IDENTITY AND CULTURAL PRODUCTION

Or deciding to become the subject of our own histories rather than the object of somebody else's

This article appeared in the US photography journal *Views*, Summer 1990.

In my writing here, I have chosen to slide between my emotions, description, and some degree of analysis. I don't want to be tied down either to making generalized statements about illness, or to airing disembodied, erudite theories of representation. I have written from inside my own history as a woman and as a cancer patient, while commenting upon that history as a photographer who employs critical practices from within psychoanalytic and discourse theory. In this context, my work may be useful to those interested in representations of the body, illness and subjectivity, and in the potential of photography as a healing agency. This is not a linear tract, developed out of a complex set of well-argued statements about identity politics, nor is it a list of techniques on how to use photography therapeutically. Instead, I have tended to loop around, and to create a montage of images and sentences which I hope will convey something of my journey, and also outline some resources.

I am currently working as a collaborative artist, as well as an art therapist and phototherapist. In such work, I have been able to develop much of the critical theory I studied with Simon Watney and Victor Burgin in London. Rather than merely illustrating that theory, however, I am now using it to foreground some of the structured and structuring absences and silences which dominate forms of representation. I am currently exploring the philosophy and techniques of person-centred therapy,[1] developing bridges between representations of the psychic, the social and the political; between fantasy and everyday life; and between materialist and psychoanalytic frameworks.

As the daughter of trade unionists, I grew up in a household where there was a constant fight for labour and human rights, where the networking of information was commonplace, and where self- and group help were common practices. Across the years of estrangement from my family through my own gradual 'social mobility', however, I had forgotten all about that part of myself and my history until I became despairingly ill with breast cancer in 1982. In my experience, very little orthodox medicine is patient-centred; although a range of charities and lobbying groups struggle to humanize orthodox medicine, they sadly often end up as its handmaidens. Self-help groups have proliferated, but they frequently lack a political perspective. Initially, I believed that I had somehow brought cancer upon myself, and only later looked at the broader environmental, political and economic profiles of illness.

Within the orthodoxy, I occasionally met with pockets of resistance, glimmers of hope, as people talked about and practised more holistic attitudes towards health. Yet it still seemed difficult for them to understand that, as a photographer, I might have something to contribute to *their* debates. Medicine and photography fragment the same human bodies, if in different ways. This separation of disciplines, of split identities – in this case, me as 'cancer patient' without any history except a medical one, versus me as 'artist' rendered unproductive through illness – at first seemed irredeemable. And if I was sick of medical people who viewed me as only an object of study or treatment, I was equally sick of academics within my own discourse who wrote theories of the representation of bodies without in any way seeming to inhabit their own. Was this a newly disguised form of surveillance?

When I learned that I had breast cancer, I went through a kaleidoscope of feelings. I moved from depression to despair, then into suicide fantasies, then into anger, then back into hopelessness. The pendulum finally stopped swinging, and my feelings of being out of control began to be coupled with a powerful anger. In the shadow of my fears came a kind of rebellion. Instead of following my usual pattern of pouring more chemicals down my throat, or of disavowing my state of health, or studiously poring over the latest theories of representation for answers, I decided to document the procedure of being 'processed' through the hands of the medical profession. I used my camera as a third eye, almost as a separate part of me which was ever watchful: analytical and critical, yet remaining attached to the emotional and frightening experiences I was undergoing. As a woman whose mother was euthanased for the same illness, I felt like an avenging angel as I took my thirteen rolls of film in the hospital, ostensibly for my family album. By the time I had finished, I had no clear idea what I had photographed.

Later, when I looked more carefully at the three hundred or so pictures I had made, I saw images of the consultant's ward rounds on the morning I was to hear my diagnosis, followed by a picture (taken by my setting the self-timer and putting my camera on the top of my locker) of my naked breast marked up for amputation. I then remembered that the entire consultation had taken less than five minutes. For me, this series represented moments of terror and a complete loss of dignity and power, followed by repressed rage at the ways in which I was silenced – professionally 'managed' from asking questions about my fate. Behind these thoughts lay my unspoken terror of suffering and dying as my mother had done. Somehow, I managed to refuse the proffered amputation, and it was later conceded that a section of my breast be removed, to be followed by radiotherapy and possibly chemotherapy.

After much research, I discovered that I (along with thousands of other women) had been included in one of many national 'trials' where I had been matched by computer with another woman showing similar symptoms. She had been allocated a lumpectomy, I a mastectomy. What remained of those events were my tiny visual markers, later to act as touchstones for reliving memories and taking first faltering steps towards opening my mouth even wider to speak. In recalling the trauma, I knew that, instead of showing the expected humble gratitude, I had to become assertive and to research what I still needed to know in order to help my survival.

I discovered that, in the United States, data had been available for years which indicated that breast cancer was seldom halted by removal of a breast and that less 'critical' methods of surgery were usually employed. Such research was not being heeded in Britain, however, where empirical reports still seemed to indicate that consultants ploughed ahead with their own gruesome 'specialities'. Other research indicated that, in comparing the fatality statistics of women who had been deemed 'inoperable' with those of women who had undergone surgical intervention, those who had undergone *no* surgical intervention showed better survival rates.[2] Still other research confirmed that income levels and access to resources and information clearly played a crucial part in the demography of world health. I also began to understand that there are many different cancers, that there is a crucial difference between so-called 'primary' cancers and 'secondary' cancers, and that such difference would usually be established only *after* the removal of a breast. Looking then at my family history, I came to the frightening realization that my mother had had a breast removed when in fact she was already dying of liver cancer. I have since learned that this probably shortened her life by at least a year.

After my sudden, major health crisis, the course of my life was changed drastically. The switch from agitating about political and ideological issues such as unequal pay, inadequate childcare and representations of 'the history of the nude',[3] to working on something 'personal' was far from easy. I was determined to use photography as a tool to foreground what I saw as the inhuman and infantilizing treatment of cancer patients. The representation and politics of cancer remain fairly taboo subjects, except within the sensationalist media. Given that one in four of us will experience the disease in our lifetimes, I wonder why it is considered to be of such little importance among photographers and artists.

I chose to situate my critique of what has been called 'the cancer industry' in the context of the nutritional and self-help therapy research which I pursued after leaving the hospital.[4] Given that holistic attitudes towards cancer in the UK were in their infancy in the early 1980s, this was not an easy task. I began to make my work available on traditional educational circuits, hoping that it would get picked up by groups who might benefit most from a discussion of the issues I tried to raise. I also wrote several articles for different magazines to help create a more receptive climate for the work.

In 1984, I reworked some of my research into an exhibition titled 'The Picture of Health?', a project which made it clear that there were alternative approaches to breast cancer, despite orthodox doctors' unwillingness to discuss options with patients. In Part One of 'The Picture of Health?', I created a double narrative, juxtaposing a critique of the cancer industry with enlargements of my hospitalization snapshots. I wanted to make visible self-help methods of caring, as well as details on how to detoxify, physically and mentally. To provide a sense of personal, historical context, I included such symbols as my mother's death certificate, presented against family snapshots which categorically seemed to deny any notion of illness in the family. I also included early phototherapy work, in which I had re-enacted the trauma of being marked up for breast amputation. This exhibition has since toured to schools, health conferences, hospitals and women's health groups under the auspices of London's Cockpit Gallery. Parallel to this exhibition, I have developed a slide show which I have used to talk to various groups about the politics of the representation of the female body, as well as the representation of breast cancer. . . .

In the last five years, the public/political climate has begun to change the ways in which it frames breast cancer, due in part to the increasingly holistic and patient-centred attitudes of some members of the medical and nursing professions.

There is also clear evidence of a shift in the ways in which cancer charities advertise to the general public. Three years ago, advertising campaigns showed a family wedding group with two women missing, emphasizing the women's deaths from breast cancer. A more recent campaign focused on a young woman's naked trunk with a dotted line drawn around the outside of a breast, marked 'old treatment', and a tiny circle drawn within it at the site of the trauma, marked 'new treatment'. The former image suggests that women are literally wiped out by the disease; the latter sets the body up for target practice. As examples of health education, the former works on the fear principle (get screened, give money); the latter suggests that drastic advances are being made. However, the latest statistics show that fatality rates and recovery rates have scarcely changed; these ads give little indication that the new technique is still so controversial.

Over my years of research and image-making, I have generated an enormous image and information archive, with which I approached BBC television in London several years ago. I suggested to them that such an archive could form the basis of an arts programme on the cultural and ideological meanings of women's breasts across such diverse discourses as pornography, religion, fashion, motherhood, health and humour. After much vetting of my outline, it was decided that two filmmakers would produce the film, and that Rosalind Coward and I would be engaged as programme consultants. The programme, called *Tip of the Iceberg* [see Chapter 13], was transmitted last year, and we received good critical feedback from radical health and cultural workers (who videotaped it for further use). By and large, however, the critics couldn't understand the point of bringing different discursive representations of the female breast together in such a witty and complex manner. Indeed, some seemed appalled that we had dared to question what was obviously a fetish to many of them.

My current work could be called 'photography plus therapy'[5] – for myself as well as with a cross-cultural range of clients – unpicking the threads of our own repressed histories. I facilitate this process by setting photographic 'mapping' assignments for clients, using existing family albums and documents as starting points and creating staged studio works as methods of social and psychic storytelling. I am particularly interested in the political and therapeutic power of personal storytelling, moving across techniques from different discourses such as oral history, education, politics or therapy. Some of my clients are – like myself – part of the 'invisibly ill', coping with MS, ME, diabetes or cancer. Others are suffering post-incest trauma, or come from alcoholic families; many were grieving over abortions, deaths, suicides or even murder. Still others needed to reconnect with the repressed pain of racial, sexual, gender, class or institutional discrimination or harassment. Some of us have begun to unlearn our deeply internalized shame about sexuality, or about our racial and cultural backgrounds. We are beginning to come to terms with ageism and ageing, and are acknowledging that we are caught up in a range of psychic or chemical addictions. Healing often means getting in touch with parts of ourselves which we have had to sever or disavow from childhood.[6]

Work is enacted in a private space whereby, with the joint production of visual and verbal signs, fantasies and memories (through snapshots, studio camera work and client drawings), it is often possible to recall and to rework painful, repressed material from the 'unconscious' mind (to use a Freudian term) or from our 'shadow side' (to use a Jungian term). Such a process is not merely archaeological; it can render visible defence strategies for survival by examining unstated losses, abandonments, angers, hopes and desires. . . .

Four years ago, I began a fruitful collaboration with Dr Tim Sheard, a trained psychotherapist who works with a British cancer charity. We shared numerous phototherapy sessions about his life until we reached a point of stasis. Tim then suggested that he could become my phototherapist, so that we might work on my still deeply repressed anger. In a very stimulating four-hour session in 1989, I was able to re-enact major threads from the years since I was diagnosed with cancer until the present day. The results were very painful, particularly those prints which showed the ways in which my body is not only badly scarred and damaged, but also ageing, overweight and deteriorating. Ironically, I now reflect that the body I hated so much as a teenager has become the one I've always wanted. This and other such work brought with it some kind of catharsis, and it began to acclimatize me to the visible aspects of my ageing process so that I could learn anew to love myself. I am not only 'ageing' or 'damaged', I am also the sum total of all the other fragmentary selves which have come to light in the therapeutic process.

Later, I was invited to submit work for a major show, modestly called 'The Great British Art Show', to be held this year in Glasgow's premier art gallery (1990s proclaimed cultural centre of Europe). I decided to take the risk of showing some of the work that Tim and I had made together, selecting five images, and had them blown up to 36" × 24". These five images each form fragments of stories, and in their juxtaposition create a metanarrative which represents eight years of my life. They were accompanied by text, including the following statement:

Narratives of Dis-Ease: Ritualized Procedures

In these photographs is the beginning of a 'subject' language, one which allows me to start the painful process of expressing my own feelings and perceptions, of challenging the 'ugliness' of being seen as Other. In so doing, I cease to be a victim, becoming again an active

> participant in life.... Breaking out is not a painless process for anybody. In cracking the mirror for myself, I am automatically challenging your view too.... By giving expression to this part of my history, I stand in contradiction to those who have the power to repress or deny the experiences of others. In so doing, they make our experiences appear ordinary, robbing them of any importance or potency. If I don't find a language to express and share my subjectivity, I am in danger of forgetting what I already know.

These kinds of projects confront the neurotically induced notion of an idealized self, seeking instead to represent the multiplicity of split-off fragments which go to make up an apparently coherent identity. In such work, different gazes between the photographer and the client are enacted: the gaze of the photographer as surrogate mother, most feared or most revered, followed by a range of other gazes which are either judgemental or confirming. These dynamics can evoke feelings of shame or punishment, or can celebrate and affirm. Across my body of work, it is becoming clear to me that racial, sexual, familial and class gazes are also enacted, so that homophobia or racism or classism are also often challenged both by my clients and by myself in continued self-monitoring. There are no neutral gazes.

In my eight years of working this way, I have learned the importance of linking the representation of experience (the materiality of subjectivity in process) with theory and politics. My 'unofficial storytelling' is always concerned with health: with damaged and potentially healable bodies and psyches; with definitions of identity and the construction of our subjectivities. But if my work is about deconstructing visual signs and symbols, it is also concerned with the continual reconstruction of such signs in ways which are more in the interests of those they signify than those who traditionally control signs' production and circulation. Such work is a form of cultural sniping.

I can't say in all this that I ever expected to 'save my life', but rather to learn to live with myself and be ready for my eventual death.... I learned to listen for the first time to the signals of distress which my body manifested, rather than seeing her as the enemy. But I must state: I would rather have travelled the journey without cancer as my companion. I see, in retrospect, that I have not 'arrived' anywhere, but am at least more at peace with my perceptions of the processes of ageing and illness. Life is so much more than illness, and I am now actively and creatively angry.

11 *overleaf* Jo Spence/Dr Tim Sheard
Crone

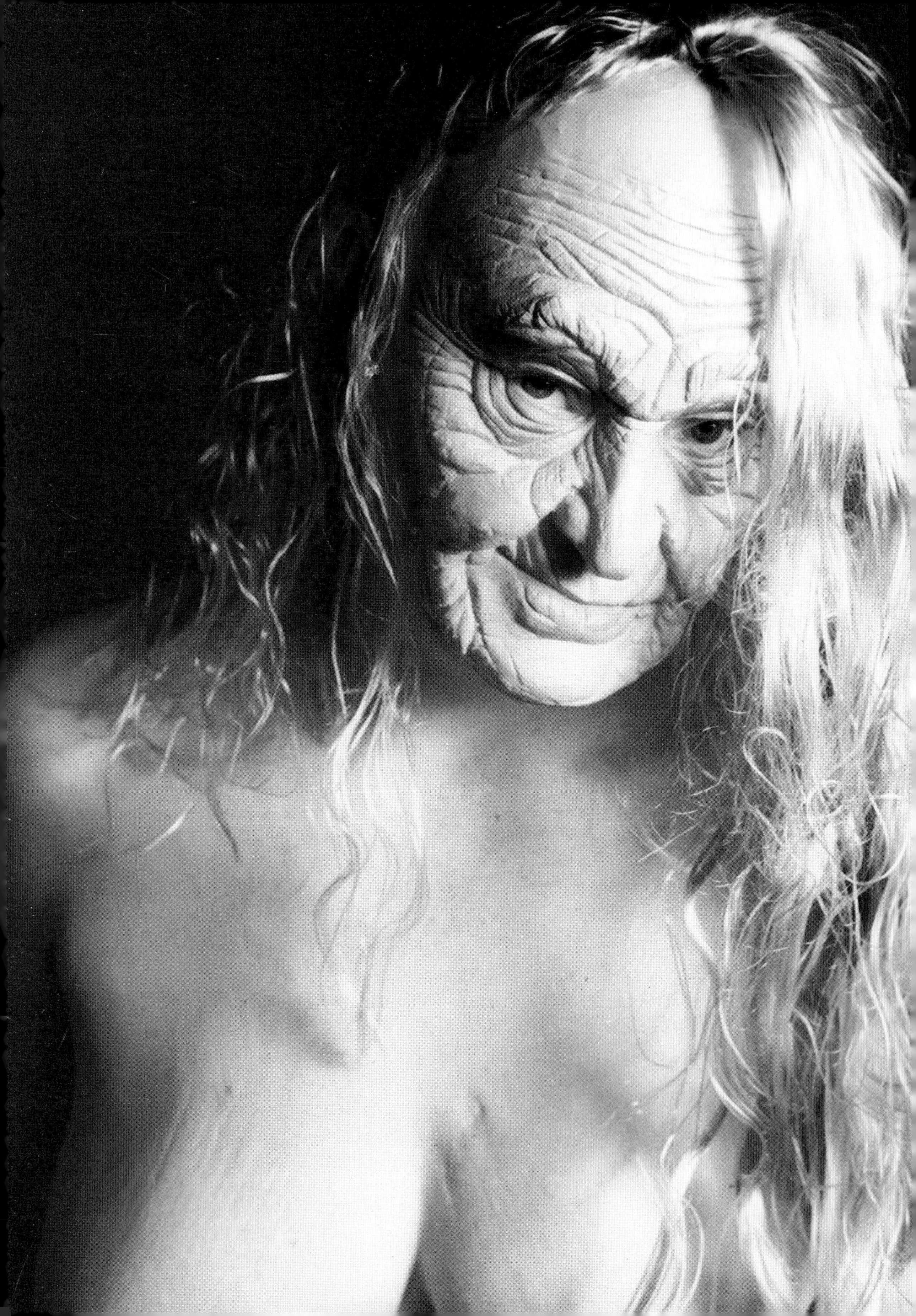

15 · BODY BEAUTIFUL OR BODY IN CRISIS

A fuller version of this was given as a keynote paper for the Women's Surgery Conference in Melbourne, Australia, in 1990. Being jetted to and fêted at an international conference was important to Jo's sense of being properly respected at last. But the experience exhausted her and made her finally reappraise what she wanted to put her energies into. The symptoms of what was later that year diagnosed as leukaemia were beginning to show. *Open Mind*, the journal of the mental health organization MIND, published an earlier article of the same title in April 1986.

Grin and bear it.

Suffer in silence.

Stop nagging.

Put the needs of others first.

Familiar themes? But what happens if you abandon these scenarios and speak about what's on your mind? Or try to define your own needs?

At the heart of my talk (which loops about in all directions and is fairly global but has a central core) is my experience of beginning to speak out about something which others would rather not hear about. As part of this speaking out, what I am offering today is partly what has been called psychohistory, partly social history, partly analytical, partly oral, partly visual. For me, learning to speak about my conscious and unconscious history has become part of a healing process which I want to share.

BREAST CANCER: WHAT IS IT?

In the United Kingdom, one in four people will be diagnosed as having cancer in their lifetime. One in eleven will get breast cancer and annually 18,000 will die of it in its advanced stages. But we don't just die of a 'lump in the breast' as the state's health literature seems to suggest, but of an illness with many variants, developing from primary to secondary stages. The huge chasm between two groups of women ('the well' and 'the ill') leads to all sorts of problems for health education. This is compounded by the ways in which cancer charities have, until recently, tried to terrify us into donating money, using visual modes of address which assume that all readers are well.

A CONTEXT FOR SPEAKING: WHO AM I?

As I don't know any of you, and you don't know me, it might help to begin with some autobiographical details.

Long before I became a person living with cancer I had an identity of my own. As a photographer and as a feminist I used photography to be critical of the status quo within the art galleries.

During the years 1979 to 1982 I studied as a mature student, looking at the history of sexuality and of the female nude. I then worked to make visible the ideological work of the nude.

In the early 1970s I was involved in various campaigns for contraception, abortion rights, childcare facilities, equal pay. I was working in a women's photography group making campaign photographs for unions and community groups, where we found it useful to continually point out the contradiction between the media's images of women and the often distressing reality of people's lives.

One of the things which I feel is lacking in relation to health education is any notion of how breast cancer could be visually represented better. I mean beyond an image of a woman palpating her breast or 'living with one breast'. Perhaps we could begin to make more sense of it, and to ask pertinent questions about how it concerns our lives and what to do about it as women; helping us perhaps to see that the whole canvas of our lives as women is integrally linked to health education in its broadest sense. And most especially how to move beyond the fear generated by the various charity campaigns.

After I left college in 1982 I was diagnosed as having breast cancer. In a sense, through the type of work I was doing, I was already prepared for the contradictions of being a patient – and thus I was aware of them as they happened. . . .

Outside the hospital I had a complex identity which had taken forty-eight years to form. I had a profession, a set of life skills, a network of relationships with friends, colleagues and family. Inside the hospital I was reduced to my disease, to the part of my body where it was apparently located. . . .

Because the two worlds of inside and outside the hospital seem so totally cut off from each other, I have come here today to share with you who are from within health education some of the concerns from within the professional discourse of photography to which I belong, where I am seen as having a value and am sometimes listened to. . . .

Women who are health workers and women who are cultural workers need to talk to each other more because the discourses of art and medicine use as their essential raw material the human subject and the human body. To try to bring these into a dialogue in my work I became interested in how our identities are formed, and what part images and the media play in building up these identities. We are constantly bombarded by the media into an imaginary view of what we should ideally be like as women, a view that most of us feel we cannot match up to, living instead with the anxiety of body size, beauty culture and 'fitness' at one end of a spectrum, and tiredness, ageing, illness, drugging, mutilation and death at the other.

Given that the breast is continually and banally represented in the media, and emphasized as our most important asset, it is not strange that we would find a journey to try to include the rest of our bodies hard. . . .

TOWARDS A DIALECTICAL VIEW OF OUR BODIES

I want to ask you to concentrate on the idea of bridge building. As a cancer patient who was also a photographer this became possible as part of my everyday life. As well as documenting my own life, I also collected images of bodies and began to use them. I have used the slides showing this representation to lecture not only to postgraduate medical students but also to women in 'breast care' groups and students in arts and media courses. I feel it is important to begin to challenge the images produced by both the fashion and advertising media as well as the medical profession. It should be possible to talk about health and aesthetics as a duality. Women who are involved in illness should think more of documenting the processes, not as 'personal problems' (though they are) but as a way of making visible what is done to people and is never talked about openly. It might then be possible at least to discuss things more within one's own family, at most to go public with them.

It is not easy to make your journey through trauma and dis-ease the subject of your own camera. And certainly I needed to be counselled or in therapy before I released anything into the public world. I also needed to have separated from the work so it no longer has any emotional charge for me when people are critical of it.

I am now running workshops on identity and autobiographical work for groups of eight to ten people. We use family albums and snapshots as starting points for counselling each other, then people start to keep journals with pictures (either drawn or using snapshots) and to do 'body and life mapping'. They also produce self-made masks, write on themselves, or stage tableaux for the camera, all as ways of having an internal dialogue. Such work is never for anybody else but is 'raw material' to work on. We work fairly cheaply, using cheap processing houses and instamatics, or using my professional camera.

The work is about having different ways of storytelling and becoming the subject of our own histories rather than the object of somebody else's. It seems we have lost the art of an oral tradition, passing stories from generation to generation, but it is possible to revitalize this. This might seem a far cry from where I began but for me it has been important to share my work with others and to suggest that it is possible for anybody to do this work – but you need a safe and private space to work in.

My paper is a call for a continuing interchange between dissenters or critics from different disciplines. We live in a culture which flourishes on the inculcation of inadequacy and shame, so it is hardly surprising that people find it difficult to speak out except in the most politicized situations. This means we often end up internalizing subtle violence done to us as 'our fault', part of a victim culture. In contradiction to this, people all over the world are beginning to build support networks and services, collecting important information, taking political action about health issues and instigating educational programmes. This needs to be linked to cultural production. We need emotional and physical education which crosses from the personal to the political, from the social to the imaginary, and from the ideological to the political.

As an ageing/older woman, I hope that sharing my experience will be seen as an act of solidarity. I have learnt that by sharing my wounds in my teaching (and therefore my vulnerability) I can help to open up some safe spaces with others so that risks can be taken to open our mouths, show our images. We need to use our cameras, tape recorders, diaries, poems, videos – whatever cultural resources we have – to witness our own histories, to learn to protest and share, and to learn to nurture ourselves. Don't wait for somebody else to do it for you, for they may define you in ways which are not in your own self- or group interest.

NOTES TO PART TWO

12 THE PICTURE OF HEALTH? PART 3

Editor's note: Jo listed no references but recommended the following books:

Brohn, Penny, *Gentle Giants*, London, Century Publishing, 1986.

Davis, Adele, *Let's Get Well*, London, Unwin, 1979. (See also their other titles on vitaminology, diet and health.)

Doyal, L. and others, *Cancer in Britain: the Politics of Prevention*, London, Pluto Press, 1983.

Faulder, Carolyn, *Breast Cancer: a Guide to its Early Detection and Treatment*, London, Virago, 1982.

——— *Whose Body Is It? The Troubling Issue of Informed Consent*, London, Virago, 1985.

Forbes, Alec, *The Bristol Diet*, London, Century Publishing, 1984.

Foucault, Michel, *The Birth of the Clinic*, London, Tavistock, 1973.

Gorbach, S.L., Zimmerman, D.R. and Woods, Margo, *The Doctors' Anti-breast Cancer Diet*, USA, Simon & Schuster, 1984.

Grossman, Richard, *The Other Medicines*, London, Pan, 1986.

Kidman, Brenda, *A Gentle Way with Cancer*, London, Century Publishing, 1983.

Lorde, Audre, *The Cancer Journals*, London, Sheba, 1985.

Phillips, Angela and Rakusen, Jill, *Our Bodies, Ourselves*, London, Penguin, n.d.

Richards, Dick, *The Topic of Cancer: When the Killing Had to Stop*, Oxford, Pergamon Press, 1982.

Ross, Ralph W., *The Cancer Syndrome*, New York, Grove Press Inc., 1980.

Sontag, Susan, *Illness as Metaphor*, London, Penguin, 1983.

Thunhurst, Colin, *It Makes You Sick; the Politics of the NHS*, London, Pluto Press, 1982.

Walton, Jean, *Orthodox Cancer Treatment: a Critical Analysis of Results, Research and Clinical Practice*. (Most of the data referred to are from research done on breast cancer and the writer has gone back to original data on survival figures for women who *have had no treatment at all*. She reinterpreted the survival figures and came to some astonishing conclusions. The report has been examined by the Director of the South Western Metropolitan Cancer Registry who has been unable to come up with any unfairness or bias made in the new interpretation of the old research. Jean has given me permission to supply xerox copies to anyone interested.

Jo Spence gave no publishing details of this but it is hoped that a copy will shortly be found and placed in the Jo Spence Memorial Archive, for public use. She also offered anyone who sent an SAE a resource list of organizations and reading material relating to cancer and alternative treatments. That too will be in the archive. The following may be useful starting points:

1 CancerLink, 17 Brittania Street, London WC1X 9JN, tel: 0171 833 2451. Bristol Cancer Help Centre, Grove House, Cornwallis Grove, Bristol BS8 4PG, tel: 0117 974 3216.

2 The Voluntary Euthanasia Society, 13 Prince of Wales Terrace, London W8 5PG, tel: 0171 937 7770.)

14 IDENTITY AND CULTURAL PRODUCTION: OR DECIDING TO BECOME THE SUBJECT OF OUR OWN HISTORIES RATHER THAN THE OBJECT OF ANYONE ELSE'S

1 See especially Carl Rodgers, *Client Centred Therapy*, published continuously by Constable, London, since 1951.

2 See *Spare Rib*, 163, 164, 165 for in-depth articles about the personal and political ramifications of being a cancer patient.

3 Editor's note: See especially 'Remodelling photo-history', made collaboratively by Jo Spence and Terry Dennett, Chapter 9, p. 76 of this volume.

4 After much research I chose traditional Chinese medicine. TCM is not a form of complementary medicine, but a system in its own right.

5 The techniques of phototherapy which Rosy Martin and I developed are discussed in a number of articles.

Editor's note: See the list of articles by Jo Spence, p. 234 of this volume. See especially 'Phototherapy – psychic realism as healing art?', this volume p. 164.

6 Other examples of exhibitions directly addressing phototherapy include 'The Minefield of Memory', 'Tales My Father Never Taught Me' and 'Jo Spence'. Other works produced in collaboration with colleagues have been presented in a range of exhibitions both in the UK and US, such as 'New British Photography', 'The Body Politic' and 'Through the Looking Glass'. [See exhibition list on p. 237 for details.]

PART THREE

IDENTITY, PHOTOGRAPHY, THERAPY

16 · NEW KNOTS, 1983

Unpublished poem written in 1983, referring to radical psychiatrist R.D. Laing's work, *Knots*. Jo's other short stories, poems and journals are yet to be published in an anthology. They are available in the Jo Spence Memorial Archive.

Questions of autobiography and authorship: recounting one's own history and professional practice. Reworking those accounts

The question of political commitment, differing psychic, social and economic formations within which we are formed and struggle: the denial of a need to belong, to belong to something greater than a set of conflicting ideas or incoherence; the denial of the role of 'the family' (our families) in our unresolved needs; the problem of love

The problem of not wanting a god

The problem of a dialogue with our families (social mobility, change of language, change of concepts in the now, but still a re-living in and through the past)

The denial of continuing conflict between family members (removing ourselves from the battlefield does not end the war) (Death does not end the war)

The problem of christmas

The question of being de-centred (that is having lost the idea of a coherent and autonomous self); how are we constructed across and between discourses (what about the bits in between?); making new spaces

Being allowed to speak, allowing ourselves to speak; learning to act

The problem of being too articulate (frightening to others): of encouraging others to speak and act; impatience at the slowness of it all. Still not being able to speak for ourselves as there is no coherent self; not wanting to speak for a movement; the problem of being theoretically correct

The problem of moving from over articulacy (honesty) back into silence. New anger. Decentring completed (is it ever?), fragmentation acknowledged; chaos of signification, crisis of representation; theory perfected (but always already out of date!)

The problem of silence; the playing out anew of unresolved and unconscious drives and desires onto new authority figures; pretending still to work collectively

THE PROBLEM OF NOT KNOWING WHAT THE PROBLEM IS

The problem of knowing there is a problem but that nobody else will acknowledge there is a problem

The problem of the past (family breakdowns); desire for the lost (in)coherent family; the problem of being out of control in the present (destruction and rebellion within various discourses)

The problem of waiting to receive permission to stop work and to rest. Who do I ask? Will she listen?

The problem that nobody understands the angry language used in the articulation of this preliminary request; the manifestation of a new crisis of representation. How do I now represent myself? How to speak when you are not spoken to? The problem of being polite

Who am I? How do I know that?

The problem of knowing when an internal request is really a request and not just a new power struggle, newly articulated

The use of illness as a way of solving intractable problems (just like I used it to bait mummy to get some attention, to avoid school, work and sex!)

The problem of feelings of guilt when we know we are manifesting such behaviour

The problem of love

The problem of final and total silence (no family, no coherent discourse, no language, no future)

Illness: the ultimate crisis of self-representation

Illness: how to represent this crisis? Who is listening?

Am I listening?

Re-remembering and re-reinventing the family

17 · THE POLITICS OF TRANSFORMATION

The female gaze

This paper was written in July 1986 as a possible contribution to *Photography/Politics: Three* but has never been published. Jo was in the process of revising it for publication as a small pamphlet in the Working Press series. Her revision notes suggest that she was also going to deal with unconsciousness raising, the role of women photography students, women in families, implications of race and class in the gaze of the child.

'The eye is the most frequently used symbol in psychiatric art.'

(Edward Adamson, *Art as Healing*[1])

THE BACKGROUND

Many millions of words have now been written about the deconstruction of texts, or the unconscious processes of the interpellated viewers therein.[2] Because this has privileged only particular aspects of representation, it might perhaps be useful to try to shift our focus to another link in the chain of the ways meanings are produced within the signifying process: to the time of taking the photograph, and to the relationship between photographer and subject. In this way we can shift the emphasis from the process of viewing to the process of being photographed, the meanings generated there, and how they are negotiated. We need to investigate ways of showing how, as 'split subjects', we can and do inhabit different (and often contradictory) positions within different discourses at different times.

Similarly, any theoretical work that has attempted to demystify professional relationships has been done through a critique of the dominant discursive practices of the institutions within and surrounding photography, and of news, documentary, advertising and fine art practices; not forgetting of course the ways in which this is engaged with through the (dissonant) discursive practices of the avant-garde. News and advertising have proved remarkably adept at listening to criticism and changing, whilst subtly remaining exactly the same. In opposition, 'community' photography has endeavoured to evolve practices which move towards a democratization of the image, by involving the 'community' (the subjects) in the taking and using of photographs, film or video. Practices now exist which are both celebratory and validatory to the groups concerned, as well as work which has a valuable use for specific petitioning and campaigning purposes. Work has also evolved which deals with identity and socialization processes within discourses of employment, school, the family and the media, dealing also with peer group 'style' (I am thinking here, for example, of the work of the Cockpit Cultural Studies Department). Within these contexts, however, very little has been theorized about 'amateur' or 'personal' photographic practices. And whilst most 'alternative' practice does have a certain rallying call towards the idea of social identity, shared between members of groups, it takes very little account of unconscious thought processes, and has never set itself the task of dealing primarily with the 'private' domestic sphere of the family or the inequality of power within certain groups. This arena still remains therefore to be 'opened up' for theoretical discussion, and this paper is by way of an attempt to do this.

The most important place to try to map out visually power relationships both within, and in connection with, the family would seem to be the family album.[3] However, there is ample evidence from sociologists to suggest that the visual images kept by most families in western culture stubbornly remain remarkably similar across the generations, locked into a narrow aesthetic range. The only major change which is apparent is that as tourism has expanded, so people travel more and take pictures wherever they go, and that processing houses now accept 'domestic soft pornographic' images for processing, for which there is a flourishing literature. So whilst electronic flash, miniature cameras, colour film and cheap processing might have widened the audience of users, the actual 'content' of most snapshots remains remarkably similar; so similar in fact that all bulk processing houses have been able to classify snapshots into a depressingly small range of categories which are used to trace films 'lost' somewhere between camera user and processing house. Thus we effectively remain locked into an unspoken agenda wherein only certain (imaginary) scenarios, e.g. 'snow scene', seem possible as subject matter for our cameras. And so we remain positioned within a series of structures (and structural absences) – within 'private' imagery, telling ourselves the same old fairy stories, with the encouragement of companies like Kodak. Clearly the family (however benignly it may represent itself to the 'outside world') is a battlefield of emotions and varying power struggles between men and women and between adults and children which is totally invisible within family archives, and I feel we should strive to find ways of 'talking' about this 'dark side' of our lives. Women especially, as the keepers of family memorabilia, could play a significantly different role as social historians if only they had a value for what has been termed 'the archaeology of everyday life'.

In the past few years another sphere of photography has begun to be developed, most particularly in North America. This involves the use of photography in counselling and therapy.[4] There is now a thriving community of therapists there, using photography in a variety of ways, who have regular conferences and symposiums, and publish the *Photo Therapy Journal*.[5] In some respects their body of work can be seen to be in alignment, in this country, with that of the growing discipline of art therapy though this has not, as yet, given any significant attention to the uses of photography within training courses.

A recently published book *Art as Healing*[6] is a useful guide to one aspect of art therapy and deals with the artworks of hospital and psychiatric patients. Much of the imagery contained therein deals with power and powerlessness. Such work is clearly operating within the twin discourses of art and 'mental health' (the book won the Book of the Year Award of the National Mental Health Association), so perhaps here we have a clue as to why British cultural journals have largely chosen to ignore this sphere of activity, in spite of 'readers being present in their texts' at every stage of the production of meaning processes. In the British photographic press, for example, there has been no interest in these developments or in their potential usefulness to us in debates about the importance of visual representation. I wonder why.

PHOTOTHERAPY – A HEALING ART?

All this is by way of scene setting, for I want now to move to a more specific account of my own experience of phototherapy. Being 'taken ill' in 1982 was possibly the most eye-opening experience of my life. In retrospect, I can now see that it took me on a journey from which I finally emerged with a 'new' practice in photography. During this journey I sought out and experienced many different kinds of therapy, as a way of trying to come to terms with the physical and mental crisis I was experiencing. Some of these therapies I used intermittently, some only once, some I have an ongoing commitment to within my own struggle for health. . . .

I learnt a lot. In retrospect I came to realize that each of these frameworks or disciplines had different (though sometimes overlapping) systems of conceptualizing the psychic and the social, both theoretically and through visualization, dreamworks, visual fantasies, body and mind mapping and image making. It was a short step then to realize that as a photographer I could apply some of these techniques to photography.

Whilst I was a student in higher education we were offered a vast number of theoretical texts on Freudian and Lacanian psychoanalysis, related to ongoing debates within film theory, which we were then encouraged to integrate into our photographic practices. The work of women in the same field, for example Melanie Klein and Anna Freud, was never referred to (even though it was present in feminist studies). The work of Jung was ignored entirely. Some students took to this like ducks to water and produced excellent work. But because I was interested in the ways in which, in a patriarchal and class-based society, family relationships are contradictorily and unevenly lived out through the grind of fantasy and experience, I found it impossible to apply theory to existing 'public' or 'mass-produced' imagery in an endless round of deconstructions of texts – important though this may be. What was missing for me was any notion that psychoanalytic theory and its application to photography was integral to an understanding of my personal past (and that of millions like me) and to the images made and kept by families – a subject I have worked on continuously since 1975.[7] No theory of 'the subject' can merely deal with the image-making process 'out there'. Nor, if we are working with an analyst or therapist and being involved in the linguistic aspects of memory, should we exclude the reworking and reinvention of family photographs. Clearly if psychoanalysis is the 'talking cure' then phototherapy could conceivably be the 'seeing cure'. It should become a priority to work to find ways to produce new photographs which can begin to address the silences, absences and disavowals that are continually being dealt with in therapy. After all, the 'family photograph' is a well-exploited genre within news and advertising photography, where psychologists and visualizers are employed to work on ways in which our unconscious processes can be engaged with. So why not re-appropriate, turn on its head and deconstruct their techniques back into the family itself?

THEORY AND ACTIVITY?

It was only in the safety of the *activity* of therapy, crying, screaming, shouting, sweating, trembling, dredging up and engaging with repressed feelings, acting out and being acted upon in psychodramas, touching and being touched, moving and breathing differently, playing trust games, in solo and group work, that I began to get in touch with all my senses, and make the connections as to how photography and some forms of such therapies could come together; and how, at last, I could begin to apply my hard-won knowledge from higher education in a different way. . . .

'YOU DISPLAY . . . ME WATCH'

Drawing upon my experience of working jointly with Rosy Martin, I began to work as photographer/therapist with two different men, both of whom were in therapy and working on aspects of their masculinity. In this work I have now begun to experience what perhaps could be meant by the positive connotations of the term 'the female gaze'. In the safety of a phototherapy session based on mutual trust, with no value judgements, no interruptions, no interpretations of what is going on, it began to seem possible that whilst I was in the position of the therapist (and therefore possibly in a surrogate 'mother' position), my 'sitters' could begin to give visual expression to how they felt about aspects of their own sexuality: either to live out that which they felt had been repressed, or to try to broaden their own definition of a range of visible sexualities. This immediately foregrounded for me these two men's totally different visual approaches to their sexuality. One, working within a Jungian framework, presented himself in each session in a symbolic fashion (what in psychotherapeutic terms is called the 'transpersonal'). In giving expression to deeply felt longings and anxieties about the fixity of his own masculine construction, he felt it would be productive to try to work through how it felt to become female (the Jungian concept of the bringing together of the male and female 'halves' within the one greater self – a formulation which in itself is highly significant; there is perhaps more clearly a Jung for men and a Jung for women, than a sexually divided Freud). One way this was done was by making huge symbolic drawings of an archetypal mother, then entering the sphere of the womb and becoming the growing foetus, finally emerging to be born 'female'. A series of tableaux was then produced which follow a transformation through symbolic childhood into puberty and menstruation. Another session dealt with a 'regression' backwards through a symbolic devolution of humankind into a 'freer' and more primitive or animal-like state, in which the sitter felt free at last to enjoy his own body, to masturbate (at first fearfully) and to try to renegotiate the narcissistic phase of his own history.

My experience of the other 'sitter' has been more from within a Freudian framework in that we re-entered the realms of his specific family history. Using

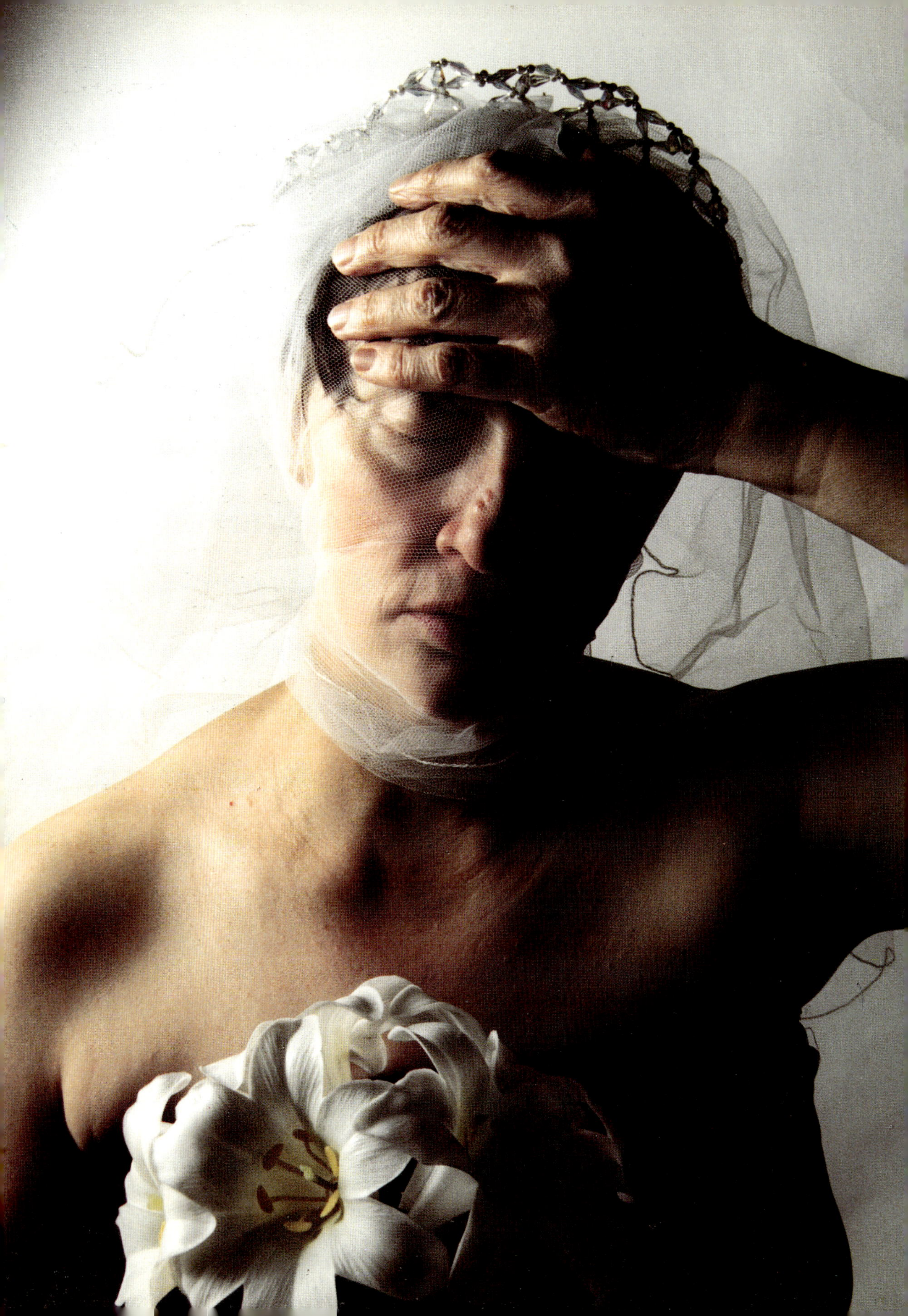

techniques borrowed from Neuro-Linguistic Programming (NLP),[8] and through the playing out of all the familial positions (mother, father, child) within specific scenarios we were able to establish that he could take up all these different positions one after the other in visual and verbal form.

Within the safety of having explored himself in the 'victim' position of the child in relation to the mother, and then remembering that his mother would be in the 'victim' position in relation to his father (i.e. she would get the blame for the child's misdeeds), we could then take more risks. Here the female gaze seems to be of paramount importance. In his re-enactment of aspects of male childhood I could not avoid being positioned as surrogate mother. But by being, in that instance, a non-punishing, non-evaluative mother (i.e. a 'good' rather than 'bad' mother), it became safer to enter the realms of sexual fantasy, and sexual difference. Thus we were able to see visual evidence (through body positioning and gesture) of the potentially bisexual or androgynous child blocked off within the adult. In each instance with these clients I have been able to witness, and help give visual expression to (no longer as a mere voyeur), aspects of their childhood sexuality without interfering, punishing or passing judgement. They, for their part, were both able to display their bodies to the maternal camera in a sexually ambivalent way. Such ambivalence held out the promise both that one day they would grow up and take the positions of their fathers, and that they could move beyond the realms of merely pleasing or possessing mummy. It also offered a space for the expression of all those signs of body movement which signal 'feminine', which are normally blocked in early childhood. There was also safety to explore their own narcissistic auto-eroticism without fear, shame or guilt. In this sense, then, such sessions are 'enabling' processes to open up their own potential for exploring sexuality in all its polymorphous 'perversity' and roundedness.

I maintain that initially none of this would be possible to explore with a male photographer, who would represent a double threat to the sitter – of paternal punishment both for desiring, pleasing and showing off to the mother, and for the potential of the transgressive revelation of homosexual desire (or even the desire to be female?). In both instances this work was part of a transitional phase to other understandings of more generalized potential within themselves, and an examination of power and powerlessness, between the rigidity of polarized masculine and feminine positions. . . .

12 Jo Spence/Rosy Martin, 1984
The Bride (from a phototherapy session on powerlessness)

DEALING WITH HOMOPHOBIA AND THE CONSTRUCTION OF HETEROSEXUALITY

The female gaze was always foregrounded in work with Rosy, when I was in the 'client' position. In working with her and going back to a revisioning of my adolescence, the major area of family 'silence' became apparent. . . . In working with Rosy (who was again positioned as the all-seeing eye of the surrogate – and unconditionally loving – mother) I felt fear rising inside me as I presented myself to the camera coded as a 'sexually active' teenager (this could be something as simple as undoing buttons, or giving a knowing look to camera). The taking of these pictures was for me a watershed in which I no longer felt ashamed at what I desired or what I 'lacked'. The maternal gaze was a healing gaze.

Possibly the fact that I have worked in therapy on my own homophobia and that Rosy is a lesbian made this journey safer. To be afraid of intimacy with members of one's own sex, irrespective of whether or not they are the object of one's sexual desire, is a way of severely limiting the range of unfamiliar responses, feelings and sensibilities. Working with someone who has fully explored her own sexual choices offered a safety not always apparent between heterosexual people. Working through (and accepting the pain of) the reconstruction of our individual heterosexuality was an astonishing process. To begin to unpick tiny details which before had seemed irrelevant made it possible to bring major patterning in our lives into focus. Phototherapy is not about the denial of desire or trauma but a way of opening up and learning to accept the pain of our failure to live out the reality of the images we desire to become or repossess.

Instead of talking in generalized terms of 'masculinity' and 'femininity' we came to see and feel how our formative years had been a very specific construction of very specific aspects of heterosexuality. For Rosy this meant trying to cross as quickly as possible from being positioned as 'child' to 'being adult' (I am not at liberty here to give an account of this work[9]); for me it meant trying to hang on to 'childhood', perhaps because I was afraid to lose my playful, less responsible side, fearful to take the plunge into openly active sexuality?

For both of us it meant, too, tackling head on that painful transition of trying to 'pass' ourselves off as 'middle-class' children/girls/women in certain areas of our lives, because we were both encouraged within our own families to 'see' ourselves as potentially socially mobile; 'beauty' and passivity being the path to romance with the 'right' man who would offer us the ability to 'transcend' our class backgrounds. (Easier to carry off in fantasy when one is 'an image to be looked at' than when one opens one's mouth.) Once I had worked through some of my material with Rosy on adolescence, specifically using NLP techniques of 'part work' and 'reframing' and felt the safety of her acceptance in a non-critical way of what I presented to camera, it became easy to move backwards into reinhabiting scenarios of my so-called oral, anal and genital and 'mirror' phases for the camera. This is something which I would find unthinkable with a male photographer/therapist. . . .

EMPIRICAL WORK VERSUS THEORY?

Clearly these are all empirical accounts taken out of the flux of ongoing work, but they are grounded in our theoretical knowledge. For Rosy and me, they represent a tiny ray of hope for us as women, and feminists, using the camera. What the potential is for homosexual photographers generally remains in the realms of speculation. I feel I am no longer an onlooker or critic of patriarchal theory, but have become a participant within developing aspects of feminism in relation to the theory and practice of psychotherapy. . . . Out of the broken pieces of the self will come a subjectivity that acknowledges both the fragmentation process and the 'part work', but which encompasses and embraces such parts and allows them to have a dialogue with each other. Out of this, for me, has come new activity, new acceptance, and changes I never considered possible, both sexually, socially and politically. And speaking for myself alone, a new view of my sexuality is gradually emerging: one in which I feel happier to 'see myself' as potentially able to make use of a whole spectrum of 'masculine' and 'feminine' behaviours, but in which I still seem, as yet, to be positioned as a heterosexual woman.[10]

18 · 'COULD DO BETTER' . . .

Towards a personal and political theatre of the self?

This was published in *Practice*, 1990, and also in *Variant*, no. 8, 1990. The blurb noted that Jo 'was recently honoured as one of Britain's most significant contemporary artists at "The Great British Art Show" in Glasgow' that year.

Shame: ... a painful emotion caused by consciousness of guilt, shortcomings, impropriety, or disgrace.

(*Shorter Oxford English Dictionary*)

Imagine looking into a mirror. Instead of an act of pleasure, or confirmation, or vanity, think of it as an act of anxiety. Imagine then that every time you opened your mouth you were aware of the potential for 'giving the game away', knowing you might be 'found out', 'seen through'. That you faced the world as a masquerader. This was the story of my life from as early as I can remember as the daughter of working-class parents: pushed to be socially mobile through education, fashion, social contacts, love affairs, work. Unconsciously encouraged to assimilate, to 'pass' into middle-class culture – yet underneath still remaining somebody else. But who? All that wasted energy in denying my own realities, my own needs, my own shared history. Think then of family snapshots as those partial mirrors where the masquerade of *appearing* to be something which you know you are not is viewed as a high achievement.

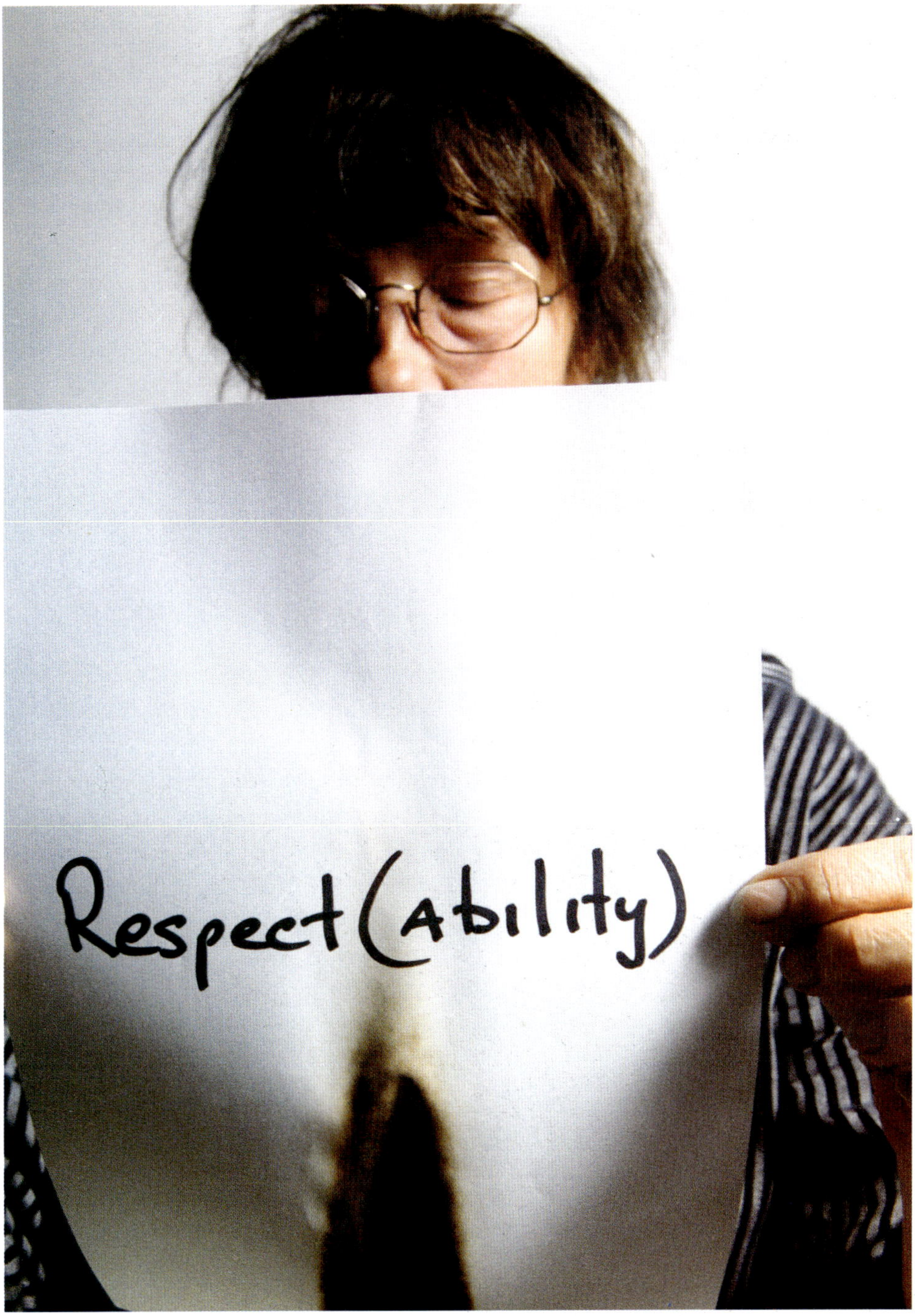

13 Jo Spence/Dr Tim Sheard, 1987
(Untitled, from a session on powerlessness)

The final phase of my ongoing identity crisis happened when I was 46 years old. I finally got my act together, took my intellectual 'chip on the shoulder' and enrolled at the Polytechnic of Central London to do a degree in the theory and practice of photography. By that time I had already been a professional photographer for nearly twenty years, but nobody seemed to be very interested in that, or in my political achievements within photography. Within weeks of the term beginning I was already filled with shame of what I didn't know, what I lacked. This has never fully gone away in spite of all the work I have done since. In this respect, I come from a background where, within state education, I was systematically treated as if I was stupid. Even if, rationally, I knew that to be untrue, nonetheless I persisted in my irrational belief that because that was the way I was treated, it must be true. Entering higher education for working-class people is problematic if it does not address the realities of our lives, or the ways in which our particular subjectivities were formed. . . .

In view of my early experience it is hardly surprising that the area of cultural practice to which my work relates is most usefully described as 'unofficial storytelling' – both in the sense of lying and of narrating. . . .

When I fell ill in 1982 I began to make my own life an object of study, to understand my psychic formation and my social and economic history. I was already immersed in a study of theoretical considerations of representation and now tried to bring them all together. How could I be useful to myself for once? Coming from a workaholic and highly repressed family, forever pushing poverty to arm's length, clad in a cloak of 'respectability' and 'self-sacrifice', I found it difficult to play and explore my emotions and feelings, to 'expose' myself to myself. In working on 'The Picture of Health?'[1] I discovered that one of my major defensive strategies was to hide my overwhelming feelings of shame. Shame of my 'ugliness', of my deformed and injured body, of my inability to carry on 'being successful', shame of my inability to perform while I was ill, shame of my poverty (I got behind with the rent, had the phone cut off, sold my car), shame of my inability to form the perfect relationship, shame of not being the daughter my parents had hoped for, shame of not being the intellectual my tutors had expected. 'Could do better. . . .' As the year progressed I began to be in touch with a deeply buried structure of shame in relation to my class and background. I found in my therapeutic explorings that, in spite of all my parents had done for me, when I had become socially mobile I had become a monstrous daughter, looking upon *them* with shame. I had forgotten the history of my subjectivity because it was just too painful to remember. . . .

ART EDUCATION?

As a 'post-education' working-class woman now lecturing within higher education, I am constantly aware of the contradictions and ambivalences of many art students who want to articulate their (our) class realities/fantasies while at the same time needing to be validated by people/bodies/institutions/discourses which invariably disapprove of, or have no value for, or see as inappropriate or inadequate, the utterances we might be groping towards. As somebody who has trodden down the same path as countless other students from my background, I am conscious of the double bind of this situation: i.e. 'Please validate me for being critical of your class and your power.'

Moving across the boundaries of being in therapy back into working as a visiting lecturer on arts, I have become aware of the different (hidden) agendas working in both sectors. I am aware of my own taboo thresholds, of how I have constantly censored myself for not wanting to be perceived as 'too powerful' or too 'middle class' – depending on who I am speaking to and how 'safe' it feels to reveal myself. Every day, in a variety of different situations, I carefully choose my modes of address, whether or not to signal my 'authority' or 'knowledge' or 'superiority'. On the other hand, when in an amenable or 'therapeutic space', I am less guarded, more vulnerable and in consequence I am able to speak in a more fractured, tentative, incoherent way.

Because the theoretical debates within higher education (in particular on arts and media studies courses) have begun to engage the representation and deconstruction of racial and sexual differences, many students are now opening up these areas in a range of works on 'identity'. This, however, brings up a rather paradoxical situation. Despite this apparent encouragement to open up cultural agendas, instead of *blossoming* in their work, many students are rapidly encountering their fear and taboo thresholds. Working on one's identity is not merely a theoretical exercise: it means engaging the fantasies of an actual past which is perhaps better hidden from institutional scrutiny, especially if such work is being evaluated and assessed by tutors who are not doing parallel work on their own social or economic histories, or on their psychic or subjective processes. Very often in such courses a major component (and crucial factor) in the lives of those of us from working-class backgrounds is rendered absent: namely a theorization or discussion of class and power *differentials*. Social or socialist realism or documentary practice is ridiculed in favour of post-structuralist image/text work, leaving the rest of us with fewer and less-sanctioned ways of dealing with the overlap between the personal and the public, the psychic and the social. I would argue we still need forms of realism which bring together the psychic with the social, the unconscious with the material, the construction of desire with the experience of fear.

Jo Spence's Cultural Conundrum List

Splitting the self – assimilation, masquerade or rebellion?
A need to re-construct and affirm my roots.
Or did I assimilate so well that no one would know?
Secret/unofficial/naughty/wrong/undercover/pretence/shame.
Low class/inferior/ashamed/stupid/bad taste/underprivileged.
Whose words are these?
How did they become so important to me?
Labels: artist/photographer/cultural worker/fine artist/artworker?
Who am I?
No role models – only a history of great names.
No visible spectrum of practices – only a history of limitations.
New orthodoxies/avant-gardes to be aspired to?
Artwork viewed not as part of a general process of living?
Viewed as something separate?
Only valued for our final 'performance'?
Who is it for?
Complex questions.

PERFORMING FOR WHOM?

If we were to take account of unconscious psychic processes, most of us would discover that we are still performing for internalized parents or superego figures (now embodied in tutors, bosses – the last of a long line of authority figures). In contradiction to this, work on identity might also show us trying to speak to ourselves about something that is 'unspeakable' or 'unrepresentable' – trying to explain something but never quite getting it into focus – too afraid, too ashamed to look, too scared of the pain of knowing, too apparently alone?

We might also be performing for/speaking to the group with whom we align ourselves: socially, familially, politically or economically. Work might be around 'issues' or around 'crisis' (e.g. the poll tax in England, Clause 28, homelessness or drug addiction). It might be about the complexity of a fragmented or diversified cultural identity, never fixed or stable, always sliding about. Other starting points for such work might be rooted in the history of our victimized or damaged lives. It might also be that we can't deal with the 'personal' but need to seek refuge in theories or abstractions or politics as a way of having some control in the world. Or that we feel so powerless that we are unable to place any faith in theoretical work and want to be left alone to paint landscapes. We might merely see our work as a career structure. Or, if we are students, our primary objective might be cynically to get through the courses, get our degrees and get out. It is a juggling act to conjure with, for these are not necessarily compatible frameworks for study or the production of work. Within educational and art institutions, these external structuring presences are always around us, whether we are students or artworkers. Yet they are seldom addressed.

SO WHO AM I WORKING FOR?

When I ask the question of my work, 'To whom am I speaking?' followed by 'Whose interests does this serve?' I need to be honest with myself and work out strategies for dealing with unfamiliar and possibly alienating situations. For example: upon entering some arenas of the art establishment I often try to garner my psychic resources by appearing to be something I am not. I still masquerade, pass myself off. In so doing I speculate on whether my identity is perceived in such a way that I am in collusion with something I disagree with by my passive participation. How do I inhabit the categories offered in the world of art? How does anybody with my background proceed unproblematically to be an 'artist'? As a partial solution I decided years ago that, coming from a political family, the term 'cultural worker' was more appropriate, offering a category that embraced the notion of work or of cultural production. Within this category I have tried to make visible the processes involved in my work rather than expecting to be understood merely by the fetishized products of my labour, cut off from its own history, elevated to object status. Later, I styled for myself the term 'educational photographer'.

So what models were available to me as a working-class woman involved with a range of cultural practices and working in a diversity of cultural venues? For a start I do not easily inhabit the bland label of 'woman' (it has to be further subdivided – I am both similar to and different from other women). I do not inhabit the category of artist – therefore who am I? (My work has been consistently ignored by both the new feminist orthodoxy and most of the post-structuralist avant-garde as 'too popular'.) My work fits well into the concept of 'popular culture', yet where are the venues for such work except the odd spot on television? In mulling on this question I decided to do a piece of autobiographical work to try to tell myself the story of who I am. Done over a period of two years, this culminated in the image of the cultural sniper.

As soon as I knew I was telling myself a story that made sense to me I felt I had discovered a major structuring absence, a frame in the middle of my

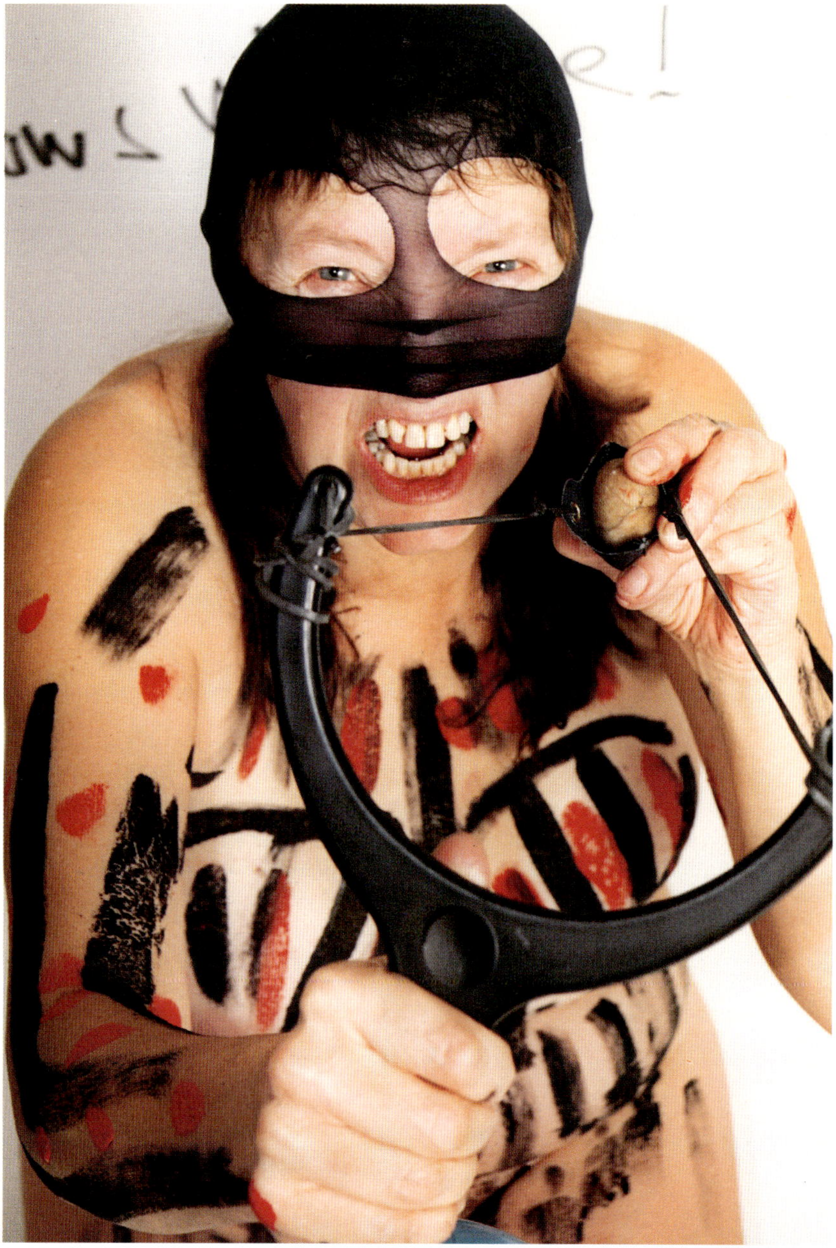

14 Jo Spence/David Roberts, 1990
Cultural Sniper
A crisis of identity culminating in my trying to tell myself a story of who I thought I was. I finally came up with an image which had evaded me, one which was structurally absent from my previous photographic discourse, the image of myself as a Cultural Sniper, capable of appearing anywhere, in any guise.

identity. There are no categories for artists who invoke notions of class. By taking a metaphor from outside the art world, the sniper, terrorist, freedom fighter (a metaphor for anti-oppression and for solidarity), I was able to understand that there are many others like me. We must now continue to identify each other so that we can form alliances and create cultural groupings which are more complex than simply being 'black' or being 'women'. Now when I lecture, teach or lead workshops, instead of my previous confusion over my identity (I've dropped the masquerade of being in a position of 'knowledge' and work rather through the shamanistic idea of visibly 'sharing my wounds', thus offering the framework for an egalitarian relationship), I see that I am no longer an ugly duckling trying to be a swan but that I belong to a very specific and previously unlabelled group. When I go back through the histories of art I can now see that I *am* aligned with other oppressed groups, including working-class artists. I am not talking about being social workers with cameras or paint brushes, or appealing on behalf of oppressed people, but rather that within the theoretical debates about identity and the ways in which our subjectivity is constructed, how we represent our inner world and connect it to the world of the social, the economic, the ideological and the potentially political must be discussed as a more complex model of identities.

Of course I am outraged as I have learned my history, as I have taken off the mask of being someone I was not. I am outraged at what was done to working-class peoples. I am outraged at what the dominant culture (which produced me) has done in colonizing and destroying other cultures, other economies. I am outraged at how we still differentially continue to benefit from this. Yet I cannot fully engage with these struggles until I fully understand what I am still trying to work through and make visible – i.e. the shame of who I was told I was/what I lacked. In this way I am beginning to be more congruent within myself so that all my energies can be directed outwards in a pro-active (rather than re-active) way. I can't go backwards to any physical roots. There was never any pure state left behind to be recovered, only half truths, evasions, fabrications, fantasies, memories, hypotheses. The best I'll ever be able to manage will be a montage of fragments of reconstructed histories in which I can gain new knowledge and wisdom and perhaps begin to share it. Not merely a history of victimization and injury, nor a shift into a utopian world of 'positive images', but one which represents the continuous struggle to speak, to redefine, to name, of coming into being. Where I become the subject of my own enquiry rather than the object of someone else's, where I act rather than being acted upon.

19 · PHOTOTHERAPY
Psychic realism as healing art? (with Rosy Martin)

This appeared in *Ten. 8* magazine, no. 30, 1988. Originally, Rosy and Jo were asked to write an article for the Institute of Self-Analysis. That formed the basis of this key text. They worked on it extensively in late 1987 and it shows how eclectic their practice was, as they brought together ideas from a range of different discourses.

The victim who is able to articulate the situation of the victim has ceased to be a victim; he, or she, has become a threat.

(James Baldwin)

WHY THERAPY?

Since the 1950s there has been a massive development in private-sector counselling and therapy in this country. This is a response to the overwhelming unmet needs of people, and is often in opposition to the official agencies of medicine, psychiatry and social welfare work which, however benevolent they may appear, still aim to confine and control. Institutionally, and particularly if we are women (especially working-class and/or black women), we are encouraged to accept situations which we should resist. Women's working and domestic situations are often awful, but the resultant depression or anger is often so well contained that eventually many of us become silenced or ill. Rather, we need forms of assertiveness training to assess our needs better and to try to get them met, individually and collectively. Our work is an intervention into the field (and a redefinition) of 'health education', since it engages with the institutionalized mind and body split of western culture.

Many therapies offer ways in which repressed memories and feelings can be acknowledged and worked upon. They do not rely entirely upon words, but also upon smell, touch, sight, body memory, bodily reflexes and so on. As two women who have experienced many of these therapies, and because of our histories in the field of play and visual arts, we began to consider the use of photography within this sphere. Our work over the past four years, together with others, has indicated that photography is valuable and could be called one of the healing arts. Photographic technology is so highly evolved and relatively cheap that we now have a potentially revolutionary means of production in our hands.

WHY PHOTOGRAPHY?

We do not claim that taking photographs in a therapeutic way will enable you to meet bills, deal with sexual or racial harassment, unemployment, illness or any of the range of present-day afflictions. But we view such a developing practice as a way of reinventing the family album (that much-loved collection of photographic clichés). As such it is allied to other emergent practices in professional or community photography. Our experience has been that in developing phototherapy as 'serious playing' we have managed to bring photography into our lives in various ways. These range from creating personal icons to carry with us at a time of crisis (for example in Jo's work on breast cancer), producing photographs which enable us to have a better dialogue with ourselves within the world, or getting involved in collective campaigning work (as with Rosy's Clause 28 work).

The process of phototherapy is essentially collaborative; it is not something which is either done to you, or for you. Our introduction to therapy was through co-counselling in which when working in pairs we give each other complete attention and an equal amount of non-judgemental listening time. This has been carried through into phototherapy. The easiest way to understand it is as a form of phototheatre of the self; it is basically about the making visible of psychic reality. It is not documentary photography because everything is stage-managed and deliberately placed in images, though it could be called 'self-documentation'.

Initially our work was deliberately experimental and empirical. In order even to begin, we had to put aside theoretical approaches from our professional and political backgrounds such as feminism, photography, Marxism, sociology, media and cultural studies. From a synthesis of co-counselling, other practical therapies and some aspects of psychoanalysis, having created a safe space, we then chose to move more into permission-giving, playing and feeling.

'We hoped that by making the unconscious conscious we would reveal the ways we had absorbed and internalized the prevailing ideology. We could then uncover, root out and deal with those recalcitrant feelings, to gain control of our emotional lives and direct them more effectively. Our experience showed us that real change would come from combining our political activity in the world with the ideas and experience coming from discussion and consciousness-raising groups and with the feelings and emotional energy we can tap through therapy.'[1]

WHY PLAY?

In adults the facility to play has become blocked – yet the mechanisms for self-exploration remain potent if we can reconnect to our ability to 'play' through our feelings of fear, trauma, desire, etc. We can then integrate our insights. We brought to the phototherapy process our knowledge and experience of children's play: play has been defined as 'the active and creative process for the young child'. Play is also primarily the activity which enables a child to reach psychic equilibrium. In playing, the child externalizes and works out the differing trends of her internal psychic life. Children act out their own roles and those of their parents, moving across subject positions. Children gather objects from the world and use these in their fantasies, 'playing out' fragmented experiences, which are transformed and become *under their control*. Working through these deep feelings, from the position of power and control, as opposed to being acted upon, a child can resolve the conflicts of powerlessness within the family, and learn how to become a social being.

Although its use for us is to make visible our individual histories, when this began to be publicly shared, when we discovered that there were resonances in our histories for the viewer, then the photographs became part of a collective consciousness-raising process. This has been confirmed when we have used our own material as the basis for teaching workshops. When we are working on psychic material which has previously *not* been in consciousness, then we would argue that we appear to be involved in 'unconsciousness-raising' processes. In getting involved in the processes of phototherapy it is important to understand that all work starts from a position of safety and privacy. If it is later deemed to be *useful* for sharing, then any work can be lifted out of the ongoing flow and used in campaigns, for educational purposes, or as 'artworks', where they will take on very different meanings depending on the context in which they are used.

AN IMAG(IN)ED IDENTITY?

It has been argued by such differing theoreticians as Winnicott and Foucault that there are various 'gazes' which help to control, objectify, define and mirror identities to us. Sometimes these gazes are loving or benevolent, but often they are more intrusive and surveilling. Out of the myriad fragments thus mirrored to us, first unconsciously as babies, then as we are growing into language and culture, aspects of our identities are constructed. Through the internalization and synthesis of these powerful gazes we learn to see and differentiate ourselves from others, in terms of our class, gender, race and sexuality, thence into other subgroups. We learn the complexity of the shifting hierarchies within which we are positioned.

The mother represents the primary gaze, which is then transformed into the gaze of mother/father, within their conflicting power relationship. Yet the 'family' is itself positioned within the various discourses of society, which each sets up its own gaze of definition, power and control. (For example, when the powerful-to-the-child mother takes the child to the doctor she introduces the child to, and mediates between, the child and the discourses of medicine, in which situation she herself is relatively powerless.)

We discovered that we can re-enact these discursive gazes, which are not separate but overlap and reinforce each other. In particular we have reconstructed the gazes of mother and father (family); aspects of the communications industry; and various institutional discourses, for example medicine, fashion, education, law. Revisiting each of these has made it clear that they could be described as 'mirrors' in which we as individual children or adults saw, experienced, internalized (often in a self-oppressive way) what those who were/are doing the mirroring or surveillancing were offering, constructing or defining from within their belief systems....

'Psychotherapy takes place in the overlap of two areas of playing, that of the patient and that of the therapist. Psychotherapy has to do with two people playing together. The corollary of this is that where playing is not possible then the work done by the therapist is directed towards bringing the patient from a state of not being able to play into a state of being able to play. Playing implies trust, and belongs to the potential space between (what was at first) baby and mother figure.... It is in playing and only in playing that the individual child or adult is able to be creative and to use the whole personality and it is only in being creative that the individual discovers the self.'[2]

'Individuals can only identify their own interest in discourses. Individuals are both the site and subject of discursive struggle for their identity. The individual is always the site of conflicting forms of subjectivity.'[3]

... Strong emotions are involved because the photographs allow viewers to have access to 'private' information about their own subjectivity. For many people distance seems to be impossible, and the voyeur position is challenged. Rather than being offered as 'dirty linen being washed in public', the work is a deliberate provocation so that the viewer can recognize her resistances. We ourselves use our own 'material' to bring to the surface and open out the discussion of ideas and issues. Our aim is to shift the agenda of 'legitimate' struggle. Areas of structured absences within image production can be addressed, both individually and collectively.

THE IMPORTANCE OF THE FEMALE GAZE?

In phototherapy work we are often trying to represent what has hitherto been conceived of as unrepresentable. At other times we are working on the 'everyday' or what has been deemed as irrelevant. We have learned through phototherapy that nothing can be taken for granted or considered irrelevant – all images offer important clues.

As women, when working in the photographer/therapist position, we are initially positioned and projected by the sitter into the 'umbrella' position of 'mother' (though initially gender seemed to be important, it became clear that it is not the gender of the therapist herself which is at stake but rather the gender *played out* by the therapist). As phototherapist we are never fixed but oscillate between several positions. . . .

Whilst this work clearly does not change the outside world, once our inner or psychic reality begins to change we feel less powerless and can act differently. This is not an act of 'free will' but rather is a way of transforming our psychic resistances and defences, which results in changes within our conscious and unconscious selves so that we can literally begin to 'see – and then experience and act upon – the world' differently.

For us, in our joint work, the therapist's gaze does not attempt to control and objectify, but rather to unpick meanings and memories from the base-line of a shared experience of being women. We also share other base-lines in relation to the reconstruction of experiences of class and race. Phototherapy does not have to be practised between people who share such base-lines, but feelings of safety and trust are more easily established across common experiences. The therapeutic gaze is one of nurturance and acceptance of all aspects that the sitter/client chooses to show, the aim being to share insights and promote healing. The phototherapist can soon be positioned by the sitter as *any* authority figure.

Confidentiality is fundamental to our working practice. We have chosen to go public with some of our private work because we believe that it offers a useful exploratory and therapeutic tool to others, especially in relation to work on history, memory and identity. However, before anything is made public we always check with each other or with our sitters/clients whether or not any image may be shared. We always respect the decision and thereby remain within the barriers set by the sitter/client, who always retains the control, the right to say no.

A CULTURAL CONTEXT?

The images in circulation in a particular culture act to mould and set limits upon how each of us will 'see ourselves' and 'others'. Although we are never totally fixed by these images, they do shape our sense of reality. They are a major constituent of the dominant culture as well as being used continually to construct 'official histories'.

For some people, who are positioned by and identify with such all-pervasive imagery unproblematically, phototherapy would seem to be superfluous activity. If, however, you are not acquiescent with the positions assigned to you, if you are constructed or labelled as one of the various 'Others' *vis-à-vis* your sexuality, disability, age, gender, race and class in this society, and in receipt of the negative projections of those with power, then you might wish to engage in work on identity to redefine yourself. You then become the active subject of your own dissonant history. Photography seems to be an ideal tool since in contradistinction to the rest of the communications industry, most of us already have personal practices with our own cameras in the form of snapshotting and the *family album*. All we need to do is to redefine and reinvent such practices....

REINVENTING THE FAMILY ALBUM?

We can conceive of three overlapping spheres of activity with which individuals and families can engage in order to become more aware of the contradictory workings of their own subjectivity and of their histories. These can best be described as follows:

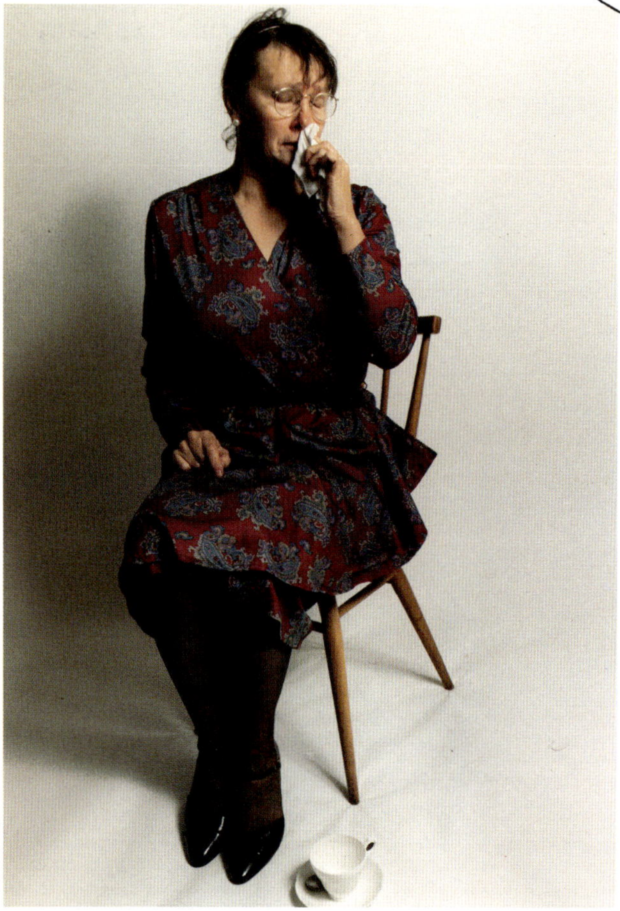

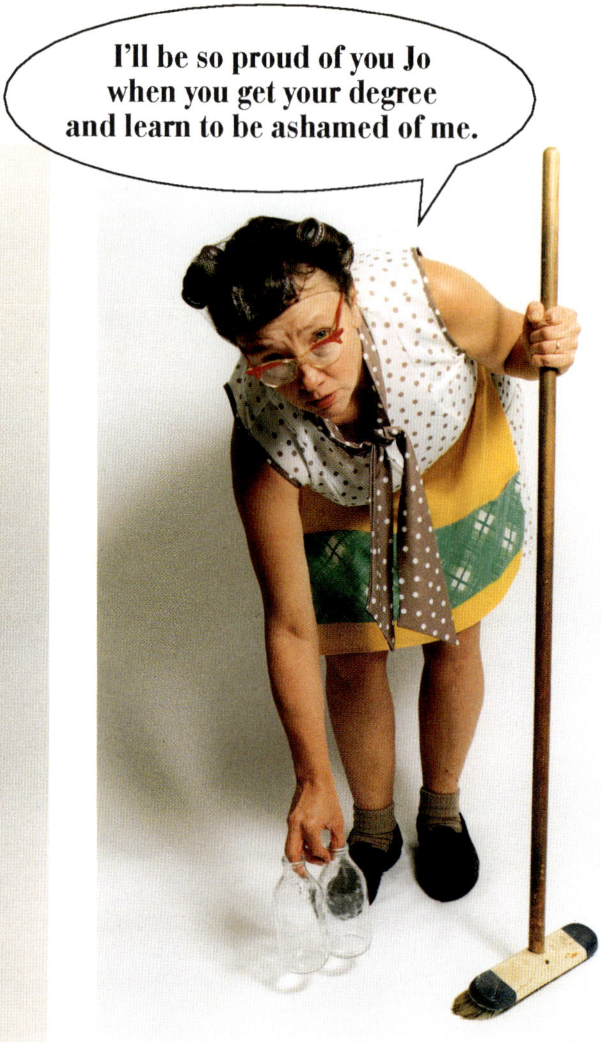

15–16 Jo Spence/Valerie Walkerdine, 1988
Mother and Daughter Shame Work: Crossing Class Boundaries
It's such hard work shedding a theoretical tear.

With some guilt I enact my personal stereotype of the mother I was ashamed to be associated with while in the social flight from my class roots.

17 *opposite* Jo Spence/David Roberts, 1988 (inset image: Jo Spence/Rosy Martin)
Mother and Daughter Work: Saying Goodbye to my Introjected Mother
In a photography session I try to come to terms with my own potential death. I enact a ritual for the camera to mark my willingness to say goodbye to my introjected Working-Class Mother, a person of whom I was taught to be ashamed. I deconstruct and reassemble, in order to reintegrate her into my history. A personal ellision of the psychic, the social, the economic and the aesthetic in a death ritual.

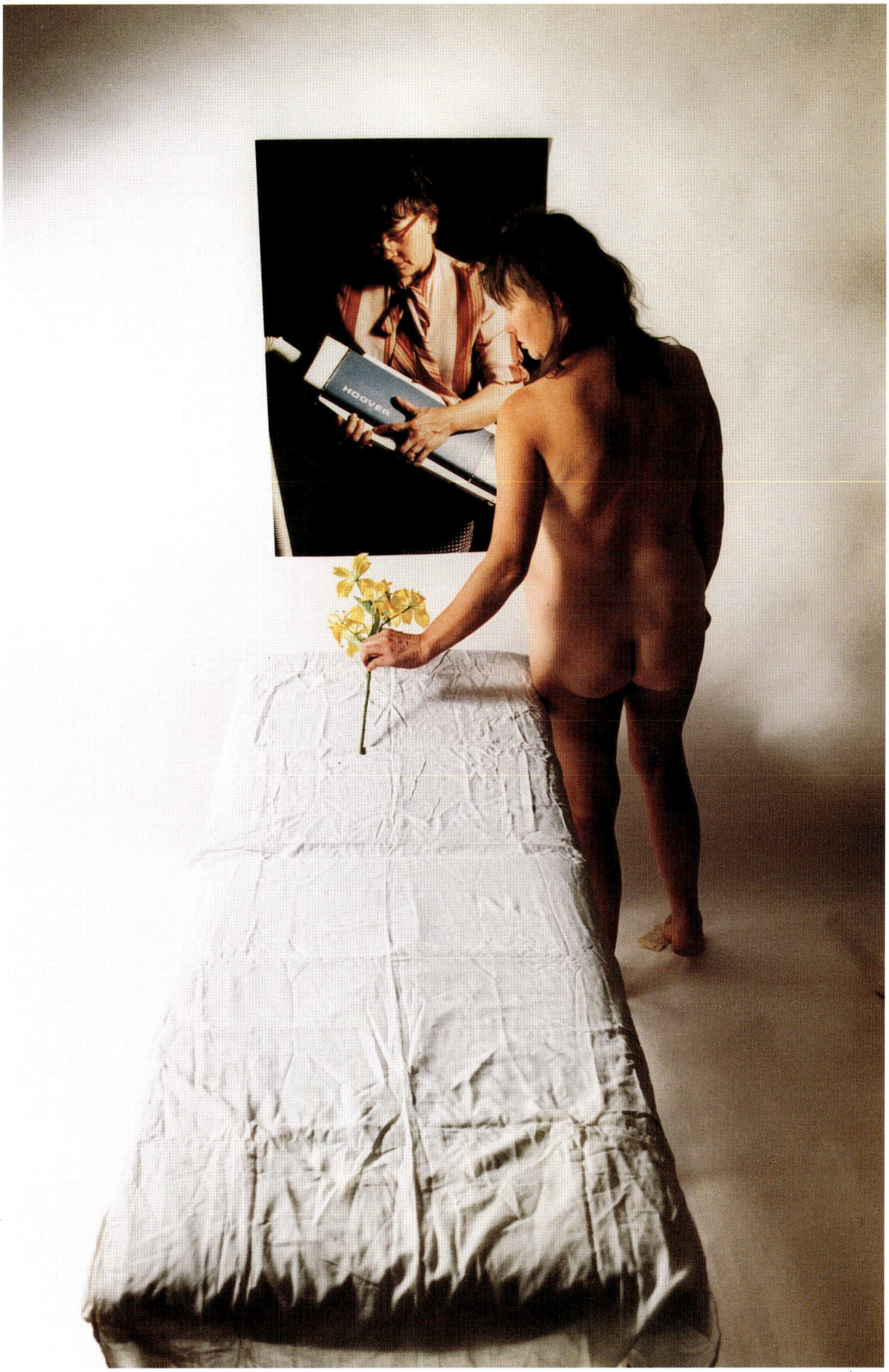
HOOVER

1 By using existing family album photographs as a basis for telling stories, and beginning to unmask memories with a sympathetic listener or in a workshop or collective situation. The agenda for this is always set by the context, the degree of trust and the underlying goal of the process. Whilst the oral historian may be attempting to retrieve, record and give back a dissenting history to the speaker/s and their subject positions *vis-à-vis* class, race, gender or a range of institutions, the therapist is more concerned with the psychic interpretations of individuals.

2 Taking things further by creating a *new family album* through snapshotting and documenting that which is absent or customarily ignored. If we train ourselves to 'see' differently, visual markers of various rites of passage which are socially tabooed within the family album can be made: for example, divorce, illness and death; undervalued everyday events such as signing on for the dole, childcare, schooling, housework, visiting the doctor. (The experience of those who have tried to take snapshots within institutional contexts immediately foregrounds the problem of the institutional gaze, as permission is often hard to obtain, or limited access only is offered. This in itself offers a useful learning process in relation to forms of external censorship and self-censorship.)

   Events which could not be photographed at the time can be remembered through the photography of objects or places which 'stand in' for the person/s or objects involved. In this way it is possible to break down ideas of universalized experience and to provide a spectrum of markers of race, class and gender through the photography of work, conflict and 'less-than-ideal' aspects of self and family. These areas of life are often photographed by 'professionals' who make a living out of the misery of others, while they help to label and position people as 'victims'. By recording such events ourselves, particularly those of us who are powerless and marginalized by the dominant stories in circulation (e.g. in contradiction to the 'happy family') a new form of social autobiographical documentation can be put together.

3 By the creation and use of images of 'the theatre of the self' as practised within phototherapy. This practice can be especially useful for exploring the contradictory visual markers of sexuality, of power relationships, and expressing *our own* desires.

PHOTOTHERAPY: 'THEATRE OF THE SELF'

Fundamental to our approach is the ideal of being non-judgemental, active viewers and listeners. As Patrick Casement has noted,

> The therapist's presence therefore has to remain a transitional or potential presence (like that of a mother who is non-intrusively present with her playing child). The therapist can then be evoked by the patient as a presence, or can be used by the patient as representing an absence. This is the world of potential space which is part real and part illusory.... The patient needs to be allowed opportunities for optimal experience without interference from the therapist.... The therapist has to discover how to be psychologically intimate with a patient and yet separate, separate and yet still intimate.[4]

Our own practice has always been client-centred and client-directed, and unlike most other therapies, has been done mostly on a reciprocal basis, exchanging the power positions of therapist and client. We have also drawn on a range of therapies; for example in psychodrama the sitter/client can act out with others past scenarios or patterns; in gestalt the sitter/client can role-play or take up different positions within a family scenario or any other power dynamic, try them out, be heard and seen; in Neuro-Linguistic Programming the sitter/client can 'reframe' past experience and examine the present limiting factors arising from it; and as in psychosynthesis, the sitter/client can work on various sub-personalities, personal or archetypal symbols, or visualizations. What phototherapy enables is visual markers of such work, and is a form of self-documentation unlike anything possible via snapshotting or naturalistic documentary modes of photography....

> 'the child's voice of protest may be repressed and may continue to be persecuted by the internalized parent ... which is not dead but remains in the unconscious.'[5]

WHY ARE PHOTOGRAPHS OF VALUE IN THERAPY?

Apart from the interactive process of phototherapy itself, we have found that the photographs which result from sessions greatly enrich the ongoing therapeutic dynamic for the following reasons.

1 Whilst we know, intellectually, that photographs are not 'real', do not 'tell the truth', but are specific choices, constructions, frozen moments, edited out of time, yet we invest them with meaning. Still, most people believe that

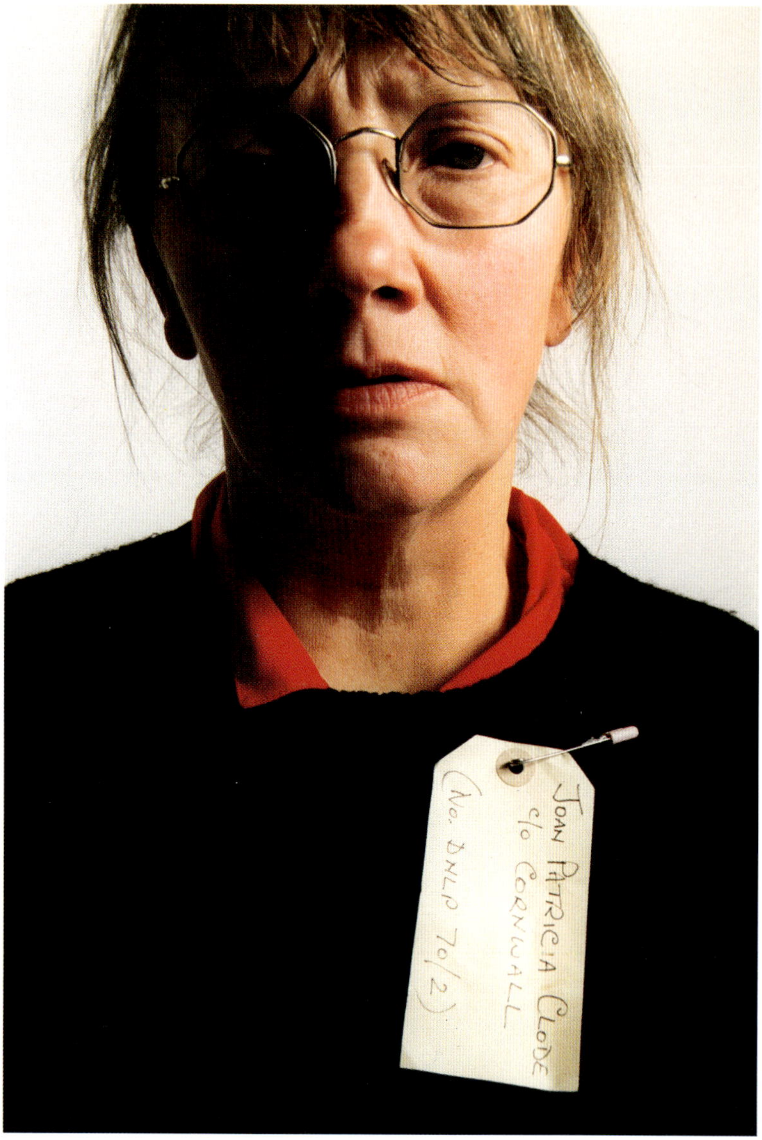

18 Jo Spence/David Roberts, 1988
Evacuee (a panel from 'The Crisis Project: Scenes of the Crime')
A collaborative work on the theme of public and private crisis. A contribution to the touring exhibition, 'Real Stories', curated by Jan-Eric Lundstrom, for the Museet for Fotokunst, Odense, Denmark, the last exhibition Jo completed while alive. It opened four days after her funeral and toured for two years.

19 *opposite* Jo Spence/Dr Tim Sheard, 1989
Love on a Plate (from the 'Unbecoming Mothers' series)

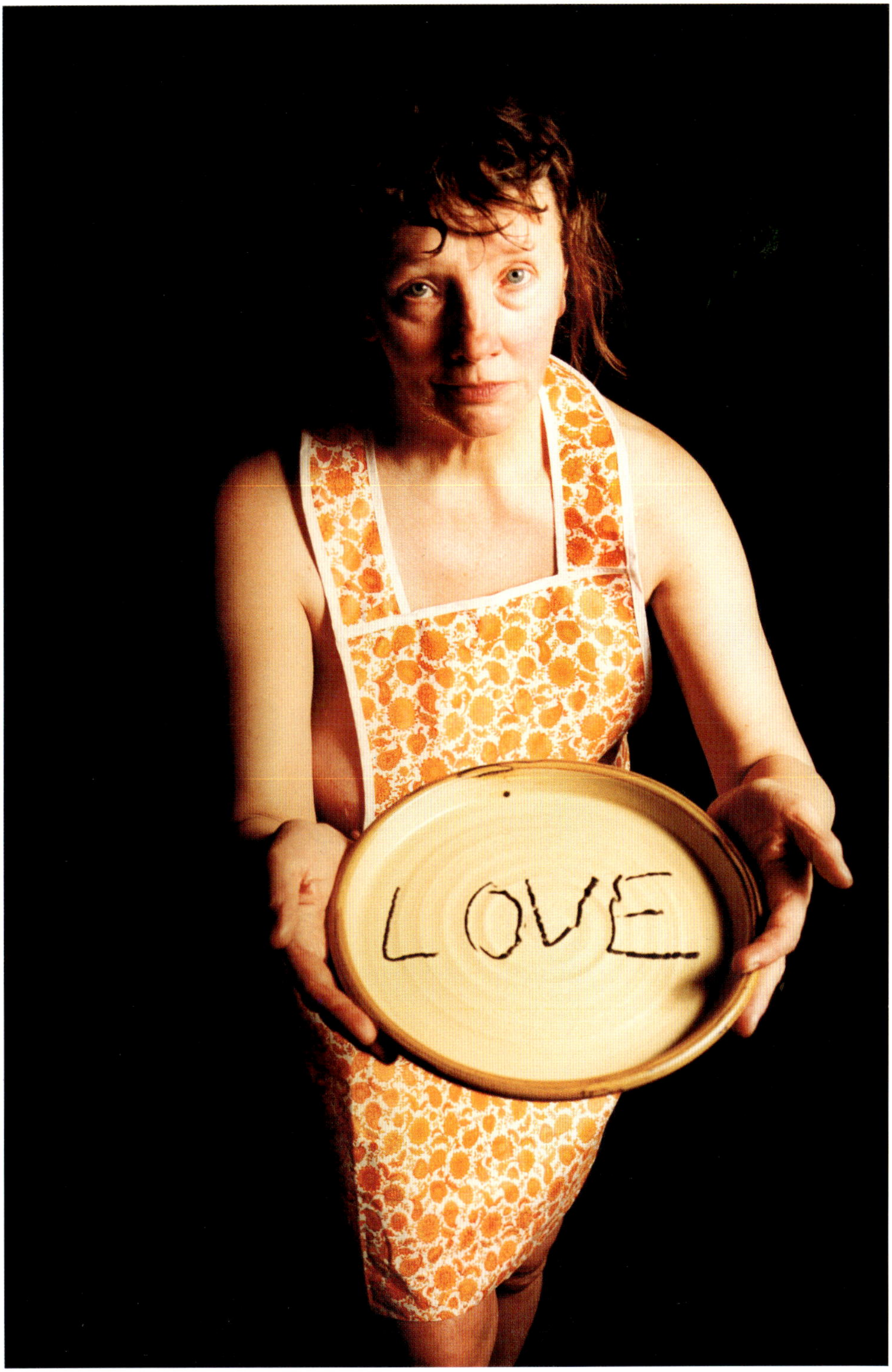
LOVE

photographs have the power to signify 'truth'. It is this contradiction and tension that is so productive in the therapeutic process. As we view the images and witness their mutability it becomes apparent that 'truth' is a construct, and that identity is fragmented across many 'truths'. An understanding of this frees up the individual from the constant search for the fixity of an 'ideal self' and allows an enjoyment of self as process and becoming.

2 They act as a record, a mapping out, of the process gone through in a session, and the making visible of psychic reality. They act as a tangible marker of something which could otherwise go back into the unconscious and remain dormant for a long time.

3 They offer us the possibility to objectify and see a separate part of ourself which can then be integrated back into the overall subjectivity, or core self, as and when we are ready for it, as in psychosynthesis. Although photography objectifies, because phototherapy is process-based photographs can act as 'transitional objects' (as theorized by Winnicott) towards another reality. In this sense they can be seen as stepping stones.

4 Photographs can potentially provide unfiltered contact with the unconscious, transcending talking and making possible the direct use of images and symbols. For example, as Assaglioli has said of psychosynthesis, symbols are seen as 'accumulators', in the electrical sense, as containers and preservers of a dynamic psychological charge.[6] This 'charge' or psychological energy can be transformed by the use of the symbol, channelled by it, or integrated by it. Symbols are especially powerful for transforming the unconscious which does not operate with the language of logic but with images.

5 They can prompt a cathartic release in that they are able to work directly on gut feelings without the interception of the intellect.

6 Transcending the single image, it is possible to order and reorder the photographs into a variety of mini-narratives, which in themselves can be moved around, providing an infinity of matrices or montages. There is never a fixed story being told, no narrative closure. Transformation of fixed or screen memories thus becomes possible through such forms of visual montaging. By adding actual objects, or aspects of other media to photographs, we can make collages. These are effective methods of taking things to pieces and putting them together again differently.

7 Phototherapy can make visible different 'parts' or 'sub-personalities' of our subjectivity, as well as enabling us to explore different positions within a dynamic. Thus we can play cyclically with positions of authority and victimization, power and powerlessness and so on.

8 They can be used as a tool within other therapeutic practices – for example, as a starting point for further sessions.

9 Photographs can help us to 'unfreeze', acknowledge what has previously been resisted and repressed, then let go and move on from the material being worked through.
10 As well as enabling a coming to terms with 'negativity', photographs can be markers of triumph, a celebration of integration, and the successful exploration of an issue or pattern.

'It has taken a long time for people to accept that we need and can have a therapy which we control ourselves. Critics within the women's liberation movement point to the growth movement's emphasis on self-absorbed individualism and the adjustment role played by conventional therapy. Many women fear that therapy, with its focus on the inner world, could immobilize us from taking action in the material world. Yet misery and so-called mental illness already immobilizes one in nine women in western countries within a mental hospital for some part of her life. Therapy which can preserve our sanity in a crazy world is actually helping us to remain active, enabling us to keep and extend the control we have over our lives. We do not see therapy as a substitute for political organising. We do think there is a level at which therapy can be an integral part of the process of revolutionary change. Therapy can help us to reach beneath our conditioning, to contact the power locked in ourselves and the deep love which energizes us to act in our own and common interests. The revolution we want seeks a change not just in the ownership of production but in the reclamation of our sexuality, our feelings, our relationships, our working and living conditions, our creativity.'[7]

OPENING UP NEW ISSUES?

It has become clear to us during the production of our large body of work, with each other and with individual clients, that we are often dealing with internalized shame.... This becomes a form of internalized self-oppression which blinds us and prohibits us. This shame is experienced either because it has been impossible to match up to the ideals offered as models, or because, in a hierarchical society which needs 'inferiority' in order to flourish, we recognize ourselves as one of the many 'Others'. Shame work is not simply reversed by the enactment of 'positive

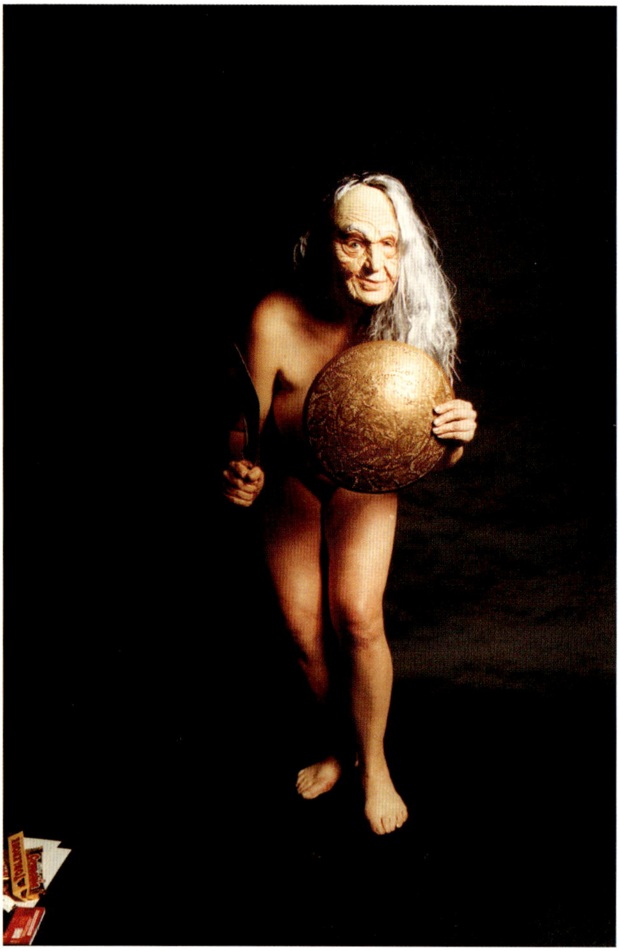

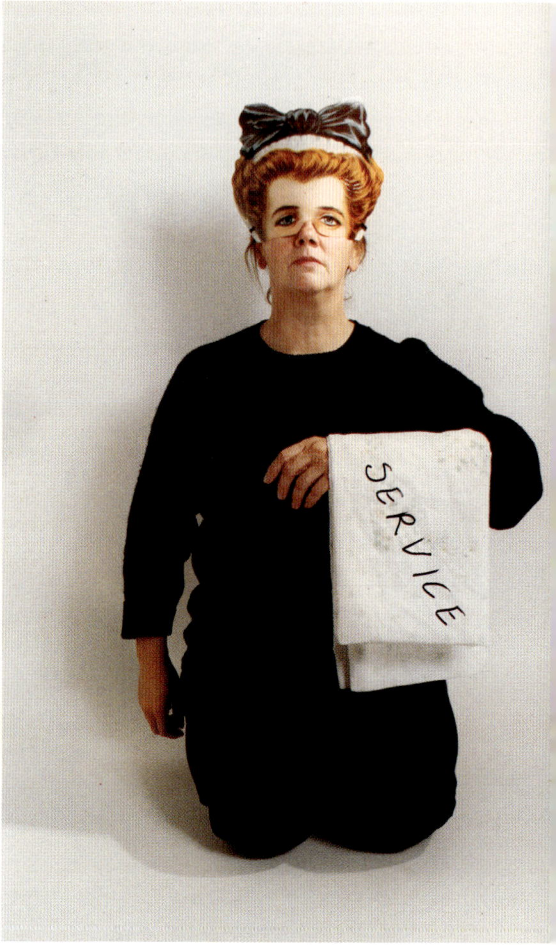

20 Jo Spence/Dr Tim Sheard, 1988
Untitled, from the fifth triptych of 'Triple Somersaults'

21 Jo Spence/Ya'acov Kahn, 1989
Service
Where are our role models as women coming from a working-class background? In a mask workshop I symbolically re-enact my grandmother's life and discover the thread which attaches me to her, thereby identifying certain structures of feeling (and economic relations) within the discourse of cultural production.

22 *opposite* Jo Spence/Ya'acov Kahn, 1989
Yesterday's Face (from the 'Triple Somersaults' series)
'You are today where your thoughts have brought you/You will be today where your thoughts take you.'

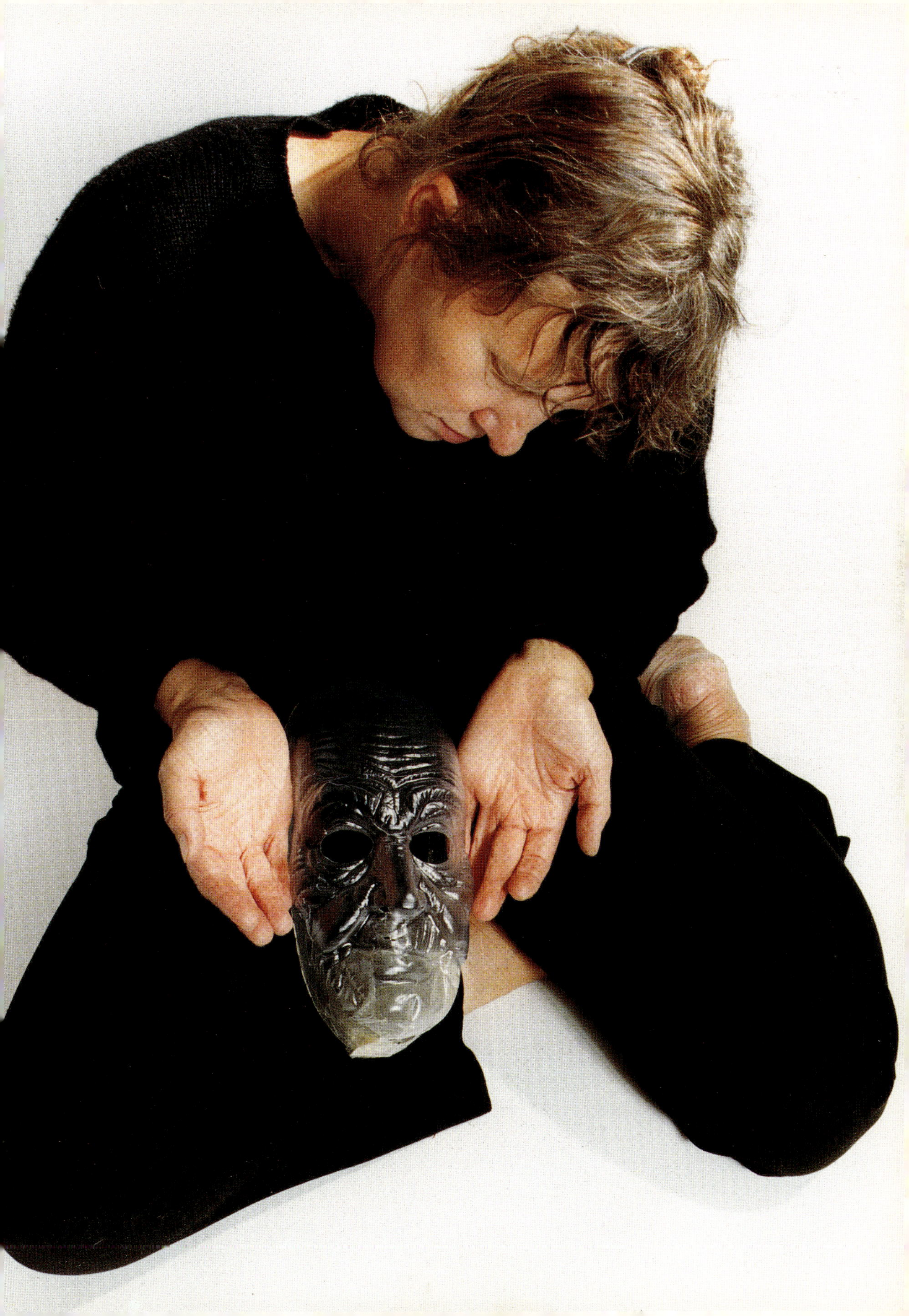

images', but often entails the working through and going beyond the idealized parents or family histories which have been produced by our defence system. Sometimes it means revisiting the childhood scenarios of the 'family romance' – the fantasy that we did not belong to our actual families in the first place but come from a 'better' background. This work also has immense implications for examining and contradicting the often unarticulated conflict of wishing to belong to another class or race, or the desire for validation for differing sexualities. . . .

The richness and complexity of this visual cornucopia has to be seen to be believed and stands in total contradiction to the poverty of the imagery of the 'family album'. All this then becomes raw material for further work.

20 · PHOTOTHERAPY
The potential for a benevolent and healing eye?

This paper was given to the Psychoanalytic Conference at the Institute of Contemporary Arts, London, on 6 December 1987.

First, an anecdote: when I was a studio photographer I spent many hours with clients whilst they scanned dozens of proof prints of photographs I had taken. They were looking for the ideal image [and in that process created many 'rejected proofs'].

INTRODUCTION

Phototherapy – what is it? It would perhaps help to situate it by describing it as existing in the context of continuing debates on cultural studies, and various theories of subjectivity and identity. As my own path through theory has a very specific focus it also relates to some aspects of feminism and to Marxism.

It should also be seen as one strand among many of the ongoing results of the theory/practice debate within photographic discourse. In some senses it was born of a continuing frustration at the refusal of theoreticians within the visual arts and cultural and media studies to engage in any practical way with the most central of all photographic practices: that carried out by and within the family itself. But then presumably it never felt safe enough for people who are too powerfully language-based to be seen to be that vulnerable.

Speaking autobiographically, it also comes out of the frustrations and cumulative criticisms of the inadequacies of my own various practices as a photographer endeavouring to represent the unrepresentable.

In short it is a marriage of photography and therapy, most particularly

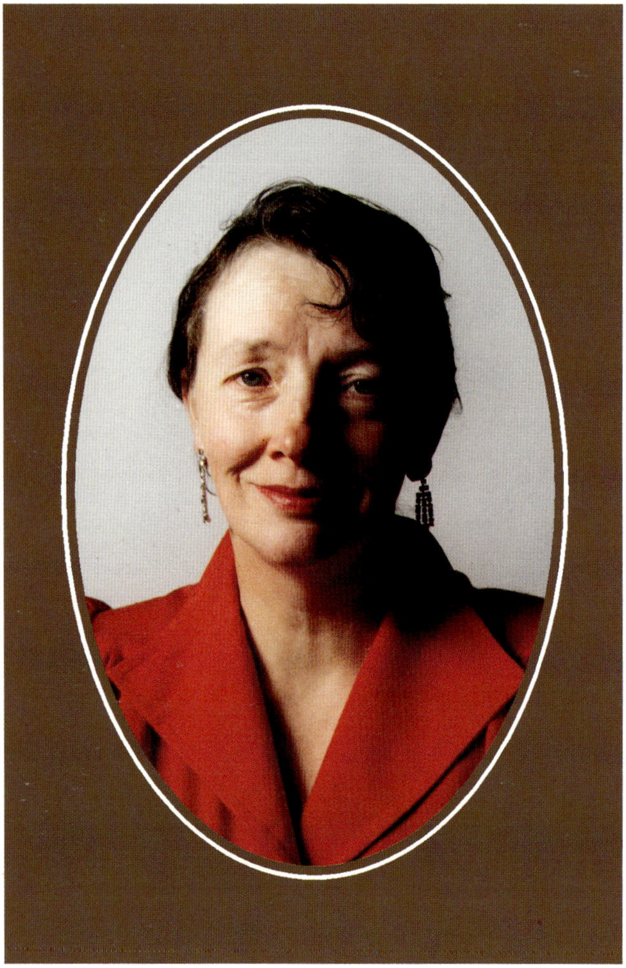

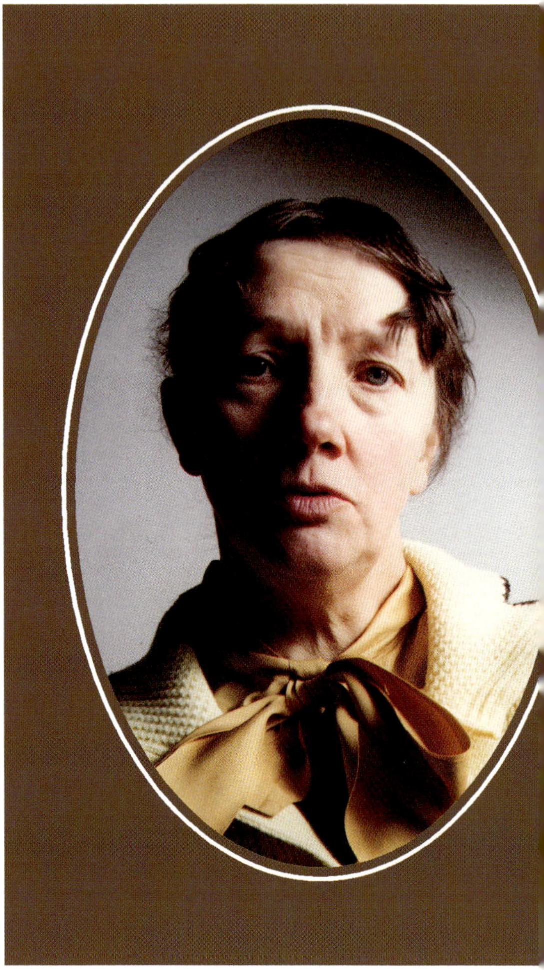

23 Jo Spence/Rosy Martin, 1985
My Mother, Gladys Clode, c. 1938
Going beyond the family album when working on family history.

24 Jo Spence/Rosy Martin, 1985
My Mother, c. 1952
Going beyond the family album when working on family history.

25–26 *opposite* Jo Spence/Rosy Martin, 1986
Daddy's Good Little Girl c. 1943 (from 'The Minefield of Memory')
Part work on the 'shadow side' of my life. I start by being 'Daddy's little girl' and very soon another image comes to mind from the same period: myself as a 'class victim' from a poor family.

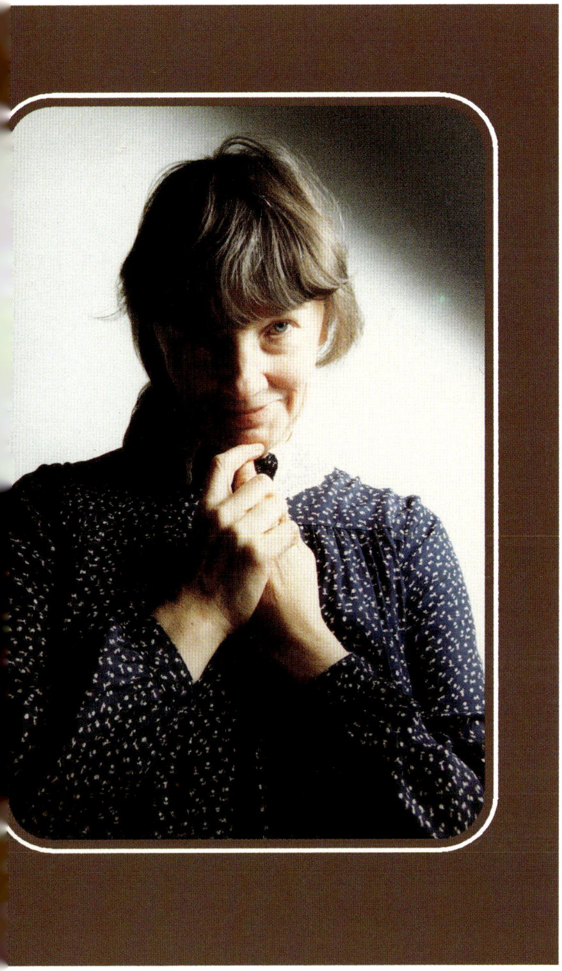

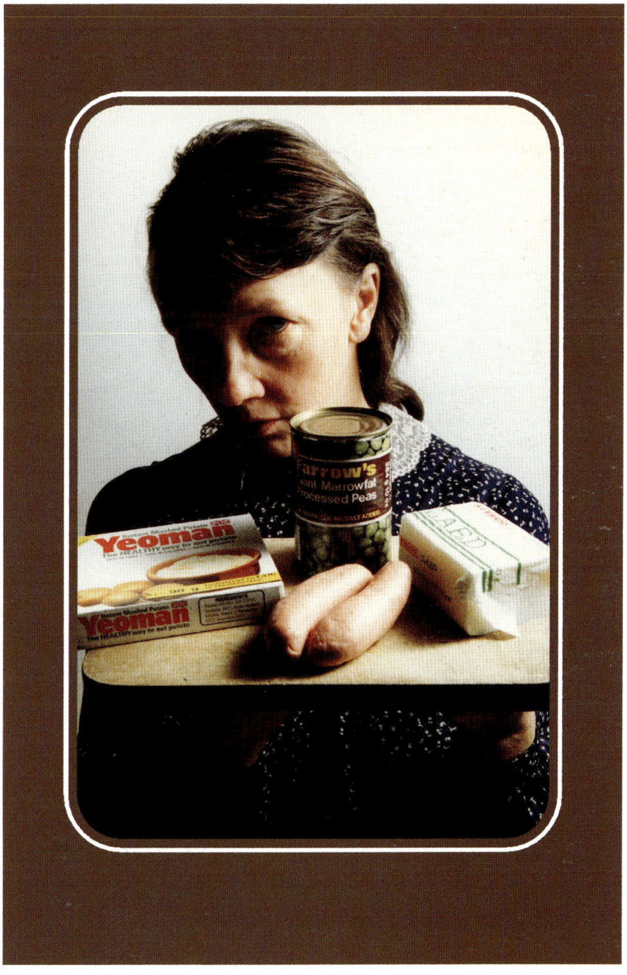
Instant Mashed Potato
Yeoman
The HEALTHY way to eat potato
Instant Mashed Potato
Yeoman
The HEALTHY way to eat potato

using the activity skills of co-counselling, psychodrama and gestalt. Drawing specifically upon the theoretical framework of Alice Miller (of which more later),[1] one is then at liberty to float with a camera, non-evaluatively, within the personal archetypes of the inner worlds of clients. What they portray to me in the course of a session will result in a set of pictures which are totally for themselves and over which they have complete control.

I do not earn my living as a phototherapist, but consider myself to be in training, which is a matter of synthesizing from different disciplines, and drawing upon my own resources as a photographer. I only tend to work with people who are themselves already in a therapeutic or supportive counselling situation as I do not consider myself adequately trained to be able to deal with all the various theoretical frameworks which my clients are coming from. However, in carrying out a session, my approach to somebody working with a Freudian therapist might be very different from my approach to someone working with a Transpersonal or, say, a Reichian therapist. Each of these systems would bring with it a particular (though not exclusively so) system of picturing and representing the self.

Many of my clients are themselves therapists. For those who are merely clients in therapy, the sessions I conduct with them (which might take all day – extensive and free-wheeling talking comes before photography) have at least three stages. First comes the planning and carrying out of a session (and this might involve them going away and getting props). In this initial situation they will hopefully experience the benevolent gaze of the phototherapist, and I would say that this might be likened to a revisit to Winnicott's idea of mother as mirror. However, to extend that metaphor, it is important that mother-as-mirror be understood, eventually, as any representation of power or authority which might need to be worked through. In the course of any single session we would be working towards a laying out or displaying process which can in itself be very healing. This is accompanied by a gradual transformation of the feelings which have lain hidden or buried behind any hitherto screened memories.

The second stage is one of catharsis and reconnections made when the actual prints arrive in the privacy of the clients' homes. Privacy is absolutely essential as this stage seems to be one of self-reflexivity as a variety of moods, thoughts and further memories flood to the surface. My own experience was that I would lay prints out on the floor and timelessly gaze at them. Later I would start to use them as a form of photo-montage, moving elements around.

A third stage is the sharing of photographs with the therapist and their use as further jumping-off points. The whole cycle would then start again with the next session which might be weeks or months later. I must say that I have found it impossible to work with people who are politically aware of the needs of others, but not aware of their own needs and the depth to which these have been denied or unmet in the past. This is the situation I myself was in for many years, resisting the idea that I might be seen to be less than politically perfect by admitting to my 'neurotic' needs for therapy.

In phototherapy I have been both in the position of phototherapist to others, and also in the client/director position (all the developmental work on phototherapy was done by Rosy Martin and me on a reciprocal basis). Throughout my own therapy, photography has been an invaluable addition in retelling my stories, making new connections about memories of myself and the power relationships I have had with significant others in my life. Most especially I have been able to see the connection between certain types of narcissism and powerlessness. The sessions Rosy and I had together consisted for both of us of the (often painful) self re-enactment of memories/fantasies, often starting with single images which we opened out into mini-narratives. These then became starting points for asking new questions. Most especially we investigated our childhood and adolescence and much of this work has been given a public profile in galleries (though, with hindsight, I feel this was perhaps not the best place to have displayed or used our work).

It became clear during the production of this large body of work that we were dealing with our own internalized shame (what could perhaps be described theoretically as the cultural imposition of a negative self-image), and the working through of the 'family romance' – an over-idealization of parents, and the conflict of wishing we belonged to another class. We also retravelled the path of our own heterosexualization and class social mobility, with all the pleasure, pain and humiliation this involved.

For Rosy and me, our material was always dealing with our 'inner child', though our starting points were usually within the individual traumas and desires of our adult lives and in social and political relationships. This meant quite simply that long before one reaches that inner sanctum which appears to house the painful and forgotten memories of childhood it may be necessary to work through other, more recent, experiences. In doing this, the ribbons of memory which connect one to the other begin to be laid bare. Sophie, for example, needed to work on the psychic and body trauma of abortion, then the ongoing saga of diabetes and her relationship to her mother through her own body, only then moving with safety into dredging up and talking about childhood sexuality.

All phototherapy is process-based: the products (i.e. the photographs produced) are always raw materials, with no fixed meanings. This is in contradistinction to the commonsense use of snapshots over which we tend to tell the same old stories (unless they are used as a basis for psychotherapy or oral history). Phototherapy is essentially a private practice, and such raw materials, if shared with others outside a therapeutic framework, may spark off very different memories for viewers, be seen as banal, pornographic, upsetting; they can provoke joy, hostility, laughter or anger as they engage with the unconsciously repressed memories of the viewer. Sometimes they are dismissed as meaningless.

Sharing the work at all has only been possible because, having dealt with the traumas inherent in the reworking of many memories, the work no longer has the power to upset, shock or move me. Instead of seeing myself as shameful, inferior, wrong, ugly, unloved, I now see the work and myself with different eyes. Eventually the many hundreds of images and mini-narratives that go towards an archaeological matrix within therapy can individually be disposed of. As the work progresses it becomes impossible to fulfil the expectation of narrative closure and we begin to understand that we are in the presence of an irreconcilably fragmented self.

The production of hundreds of small prints could perhaps best be described as using them as highly valued transitional objects which can enable us to take a visual representation of a chosen aspect of a fantasized past with us whilst we try to move forward into the future. Eventually we are enabled to let go – particularly of imagos of our parents – and to move on. In that much of the work also encourages us to take up different psychic positions within the scenarios we work upon, we are in the presence of multi-realities. Once a client has acknowledged that a parent also has a viewpoint, or a history, the process of defetishizing the self as the work progresses becomes clearer. Eventually we find that we are not involved in parent blaming but rather in the unstitching of a series of interpellations which transcend the individual self or family.

PHOTOGRAPHIC PRACTICES

Within the dominant spheres of photography itself, phototherapy relates initially to the fairly rigid conventions of the family album, to high street photography and to certain strands of popular photography. Aspects of some of these genres have hardly changed in a hundred years. Certainly the power relationship between photographer and sitter in the high street portraiture situation has remained static as have the overall aesthetics of the various genres. (The most notable change has been in the proliferation of 'pornographic' snapshotting, since the processing and printing of such films became legal.)

Sometimes it has been useful to use existing family imagery as starting points for sessions; we can then pleasurably destroy and let go of it before moving into the absences and silences which such 'agendas' set up. Given that our earliest photographs in family archives have been taken by adults who are themselves caught up within a set of aesthetic expectations, and who also have a vested interest in what is represented and what is not, it is hardly surprising that the stories about ourselves which we can commonsensically construct from family albums probably say more about the history of photography than they do about the history of the family.

As a high street photographer for seven years, and lifetime amateur, I can now see with hindsight that images of the family (whilst containing many clues to the struggle for power and a social identity within the family) should perhaps be viewed more readily as visual indexes of the unconscious desires of our parents to provide evidence of their own 'good parenting': 'It was in your interests' . . . 'We did the best we could' . . . 'Look, what a happy family we were.'

Except in unusual circumstances, family snaps hardly give any real indication of the contradictions and power struggles inherent at all levels of family life, or at the intersection of that life with the wider institutions and structures which go to make up a patriarchal society with a sexual, racial and class division of labour.

On the other hand, viewed as a genre, family albums if viewed collectively contain valuable resource material for *social* historians who are retrospectively compiling dissenting histories of oppressed or minority groups. The work of Stuart Hall bears witness to this. When the various histories of childhood come to be written perhaps family albums will prove to be useful tools.

In phototherapy the power relationship between photographer and sitter, and the types of narrative fragments constructed, together, completely redefine and reinvent the family album. If the work is done on a reciprocal basis there is full power sharing. If not, then as phototherapist it is up to me to make sure that I share the decision making with my clients, and that they have the potential to go in any direction they wish, or to stop, at any time.

THE WORK OF ALICE MILLER

In phototherapy it seems we are dealing with what Alice Miller has termed the 'inner child'. As such, she suggests, we become the child's advocate. We are also dealing with the agenda of the 'poisonous pedagogy of childrearing'. For those of you who are not so familiar with her work, I would like to draw briefly upon points made in an unpublished paper by Liz Whiting, called 'Aspects of the advocate'.[2] Liz has drawn out three major threads of the role of the therapist: those of advocate/witness, advocate/protester, and advocate/nurturer.

The *advocate/witness* allows it to be safe enough for clients to remember, and ultimately to reframe, or see differently, the poisonous practices involved in their own upbringing as children. This safety can allow one to see these practices for what they are, and to stop censoring oneself through internalized authority (self-censoring). This arena also coincides with what some people have termed 'child abuse' in all its psychic and physical manifestations. Through the skills of the phototherapist as witness, and provider of a very precise means of visual communication, it also becomes possible to see the cultural, class, gender and racial *specificities* of this pedagogy. In the case of my own memories of childhood this eventually enabled me to connect to the social and political dimensions of family life. It then became possible to validate other aspects of my history as a female working-class child, having identifications with particular groups. However, before I could do this (and even though I had intellectual knowledge of these connections) I first had to allow myself to get incredibly angry with an internalized repressed imago of this early mother.

I was very upset as this work emerged to realize how deeply I had internalized a total image of myself, my gender, my family, and this (imaginary) social group as *inferior*. In therapy I eventually came to realize that there was nothing wrong with me! Or the groups with which I was identified.

Liz Whiting has pointed out that the second role of the *advocate/therapist* is to help the person (having witnessed his or her own history) to begin to protest about what has happened. The encouragement to show indignation or anger is very important here. It is not that people are required to repress anger or hurtful feelings but that they *should not even have these feelings in the first place*. This can be a rehearsal for a more politicized and collective anger, as in my own work on powerlessness as a breast cancer patient in relation to the medical orthodoxy. Such work is tantamount to assertiveness training and as such leaves one transformed, with reduced feelings of powerlessness.

Whilst it may be very healing to be allowed to be angry, it is also useful to have photographs afterwards as evidence to yourself that you went on the journey, that you survived and that it was OK to do so. Otherwise, to quote Liz again, 'the child's voice of protest may be repressed and may continue to be persecuted by the internalized parent ... which is not dead but remains in the unconscious'.

The function of the therapist as *advocate/protester* is to work with and support this voice, which is now becoming a visual voice, until such time as it is freed and able to articulate spontaneously the person's objection to, and protest against, attitudes which deny or distort her/his own reality. It is here that phototherapy can intersect with 'issue-based' photography (for example the work I did with Sophie on abortion).

The other aspect of Alice Miller's work is, again to quote Liz, the role of the therapist/advocate as finally having 'the opportunity to work with the person's own internal nurturer, which has been repressed in the unconscious'. For me this meant quite simply learning to accept my both 'good' and 'bad' internalized parents, and beginning to learn to *parent myself* according to my perceived needs. Beyond that arises the question of how to have the knowledge to get these needs met, but that is outside the scope of this paper.

NARCISSIM

Perhaps it would be useful, in conclusion, to discuss how we can engage with aspects of a powerless self in relation to what has been termed narcissism. The definition of narcissism which has made the most sense to me was the idea of the narcissistic searching for the self in the mirror as being of ourself as an 'as-if personality', or a self-representation constructed out of the views and attributions of others.

If we add Alice Miller's perspective we can then see that the self in the mirror is also constructed out of the unmet narcissistic needs of the parents, which is itself linked to the wider cultural structures of any given society. As a simple example of this I offer images of myself re-enacted as a 5-year-old, already aware that I can be 'daddy's little girl', and 'mummy's little girl' – and that these require the projection of very different aspects of myself. In the same session I also re-enacted a composite visual icon of how I felt during the same period in terms of being a member of a particular class (always scraping to make ends meet), and a victim of war (part of my perception of the ongoing saga of abandonment which litters my life).

Phototherapy allows us to visualize these selves and to begin to prise apart the two images (of the mirror and internally experienced self), which have been condensed into one. One is made out of the views, desires and needs of others; the other, those fragments of inner selves which have remained silent until now in order to survive at all. This emergent composite is not a 'true self' but is at least one which is linked to our entire history.

I found, though, as my therapy progressed, that these two images, which constitute a primary split in the self, are themselves made up of a myriad fragments of imagined selves which can be presented to the camera. These internalized images are all inflected with our interaction with myths, fairy tales, Hollywood, the media generally, as well as people we have known directly. . . . All then becomes raw material for an understanding of a split self.

21 · REWORKING THE FAMILY ALBUM

This appeared in *Media Education*, no. 12, 1990. It was a reworking of a number of projects on family album work (including the 1979 'Beyond the Family Album' exhibition) which Jo had intended to extend into a whole book on the topic. It foundered because her co-editor left Britain, though some of the ideas found expression in the Virago anthology Jo and Patricia Holland co-edited, *Family Snaps*.

The focus of this article is on some potential uses of the family album as a starting point for work within formal education. Working with adults, both as a teacher and as a therapist, making use of the family album within both discourses, I felt it might be useful to share some of my insights and to foreground problems. Such work may be most useful to teachers who are willing to use existing snapshots to explore their own memories and history in private. Details of suggested projects for this are given below. By investigating our own family representations of ourselves it can sometimes be very productive to experience our resistance to remembering: not all memories are celebratory. In this way we may be able to understand some of the ways in which we have been taught to be self-censoring. We will then find it easier to grasp the problems and reticence often experienced by students when they are expected to work on identity projects. In the process it is also possible to discern the overlap between what we normally call 'reality' and 'fantasy'. An example of this is some of the work I did in phototherapy, in revisiting and restaging aspects of my own adolescence. In doing this I discovered that a predominant way of playing out my sexuality was through my fantasized and stereotyped memories of Hollywood (a denial of my own internalized ugliness), which I then later juxtaposed with another set of more realist memories. . . .

OPPOSITIONAL PRACTICES?

There have been many progressive, educational or socially useful ways in which family albums and snapshots have been used and created by people in the recent past. To give some examples: oral historians and artworkers often use them in working with people on collective or cumulative storytelling; social workers create 'life story books' with children who are being fostered or adopted; some people in psychiatric care are being encouraged to use snapshots or to take new photographs containing clues about their lives which are then shared and opened up in group discussions; family photographs are often used by people as the basis for talking about their relationships when visiting a counsellor or therapist; people in institutions often use pictures for what has been called 'reminiscence work'. Such a range of uses is usually carried out under the guidance of a psychologist, social historian or therapist – all of whom have received specialized training in ways to help provide group safety with non-invasive forms of social interaction between themselves and their clients. . . .

If as teachers we are interested to provide 'enablement' or 'empowerment' facilities for student-centred work (as well as curriculum-centred work), then I would argue that we need to begin to be conversant with some therapeutic techniques which might be contradictory to most of our existing teaching practices. Primarily I am talking about the difference between the 'process' of storytelling (which should be done in private), and 'products' (which can be made available for public or educational scrutiny). Working on family albums and snapshots is also a way of looking at a particular genre of photography and being aware of its conventions and limitations.[1] In doing this work I eventually needed to find ways of contradicting categories and labels which I felt I inhabited (and with which I had colluded) and of making new fragmentary narratives about how my subjectivity was formed. . . .

CONTRADICTIONS?

In my many years of research into the production, meaning and uses of family albums I was never shown a single picture of an unclad human body, except for births (now fashionable) and jokey bum-flashers. I am forced to ask then what happens to all the body pictures which we know are taken. Are they part of our unofficial histories of our bodies and our sexuality which we are unable to share with most people? Similarly, whilst the media are saturated with stories of victims, unhappy families, disasters, the family records we keep for ourselves seem to be decidedly lacking anything more than celebrations. Why is this so?

The reasons are surely more profound than the fact that the advertising of companies like Kodak encourages us to have very limited types of snapshotting practices.... Maybe people just haven't grasped the uncomfortable fact that photography can be used in so many ways beyond the present agendas.

Whilst such limited documentation of our private lives obviously gives us a lot of pleasure, it means that whole areas of our lives go by without being recorded in any way. For instance, a large part of our lives is spent working, yet the conflict, oppression, exploitation, power dynamics and achievements of this world are seldom recorded.... If, as has been argued elsewhere, we are on the brink of an overarching theory of representation, linking media, film and cultural studies to art history, we must now begin to take seriously the signs and symbols that people choose to make and keep to represent themselves and their everyday lives. If this is to be addressed within formal education, then there are many questions we need to formulate about the power relationships between students and teachers. I would argue that the potential for family album work, for a kind of radicalized re-remembering, could be very profound but the nature of the type of disclosures which might be invited might not be in the self- (or group) interest of many students. Clearly teachers are not therapists or social historians, and working on family albums (if one is to get beyond the tip of the ideological and emotional iceberg) requires a great deal of skill in evoking safety and trust on the part of those doing the work. But in teaching we need to remember that our students are often in the presence of members of another class, or another race, or of another sexuality, which is not usually conducive to such safety....

SOME PRACTICAL WORK FOR YOU, THE READER, TO DO

1 Get together all the pictures of yourself which you can find. Also look through other people's collections in the family. Handle them very carefully because they are precious. Now find a quiet space and several hours to yourself to give them your undivided attention. Lay them all out on the floor and sort them out into piles with a separate one for each year. Now sort out one single picture for each year of your life and then lay them out in a line on the floor, starting with the earliest year. Play about with them until you are satisfied that you have the ones which mean the most to you. Lay the chosen pictures out onto a long piece of white paper and write down the approximate date of each photograph. This will probably be enough for the first session and it is emotionally draining to do this work for too long at one go. At the next session, try to remember key *emotional* events in your own life which link up to the years you are dealing with and write them down. In another session start to

work with another set of key events, but this time concentrate on those which are *social* or *economic*. Try to separate these two life matrices out from each other. Any painful memories are more likely to come from within your emotional matrix which can then be contexted within socio/economic memories. Key events like births or deaths, moving home, starting school, changes of jobs by parents, divorce, all take on greater significance if recalled, written down and worked upon in this systematic way.

Now add another layer of comments underneath by trying to remember who took the photographs of you, writing down your relationship to them, adding any comments which seem relevant. When you are satisfied that you have stopped changing your mind and have written down all you can remember onto the spaces underneath your line of photographs, firmly tack the photographs onto the paper so that they form a semi-permanent record. If there is space, then put the whole thing onto your wall with masking tape.

2 Take one or two photographs from your 'self-history' and find a quiet space to do some more detailed work on them. It is vital that you are not interrupted or overheard in this work as the flow is easily broken. This aspect of the work can either take the form of talking into a tape recorder (always start by giving the current date, followed by a brief description of the snapshot under scrutiny), or be done through writing in a scrapbook or 'creative journal'.[2] Write down everything you can think of about the photograph and the events surrounding it. Be prepared to be distressed at some of the things you remember. Pause to give yourself time to think and to feel – don't get up and make a cup of tea or have a biscuit. Work in a methodical way; this time is just for yourself.

If you have a close friend you could work together, perhaps asking her/him to 'interview' you about what was going on in the pictures. Interviewing should take the form of just asking relevant questions and prompting if you get stuck. Similarly it might be possible to use techniques from co-counselling but this requires some commitment to basic training.[3] Recall work should not be done as a conversation or as nostalgic reminiscing. The person you are working with should not comment upon what you say or ask for amplification, but be there as a prompter. Think of this as a pleasurable piece of work which might help you to understand your own history more, including all the bits which you'd rather forget. In my experience working with somebody from one's own class background or of one's own sexual orientation or racial group can be a great asset in establishing safety. Once you have done enough of this stage of the work, then go back to your original 'self-history' and start to think about what is missing from it. Make notes about pictures which might have been taken but never were, or things that you regret not being recorded, or that it would have been impossible to represent. (Think of how, for instance, you might attempt to photograph Christmas in your family, then think of how such images could be related to the commercial world of Christmas.) I suggest that all stages of this work be kept totally private; it is a time and space just for yourself.[4]

3 Start to think about how you might photograph a day in your own life. Notice what your patterns are, what gets repeated day after day, what seems trivial, what seems important. If you live with someone, ask them to comment upon (or get involved in) such a task. They might be able to notice things that you take for granted and therefore discount altogether. Then when you are in the mood put a special film into your camera and record the day as you go along. Forget about aesthetic conventions: this is a form of self-documentation which can be the basis for further journal work or storytelling into a tape recorder. Decide if you want to photograph what *you* see, as opposed to having yourself *included*. Send the film/s off to be processed at a bulk processors, making notes of what you have done plus any relevant difficulties about what you would have liked to photograph and couldn't think how to, or didn't dare. Don't restrict yourself to taking pictures of people but also think of how you could perhaps use just parts of rooms, or objects symbolically arranged, to say something about yourself.

4 Make a close-up photographic self-portrait or one of somebody in your family, a friend or a living partner. Concentrate on making yourself or them as idealized as possible. Then restage it to show them at work, or doing something active. Think about the differences between the pictures and what they do and don't show. If coming this far has interested you, then I suggest you think seriously about keeping a photo-diary in future. This is a book into which you could write not only your private thoughts, but also stick pictures of things which are important to you. Don't take pictures which repeat what the words say, but try to think of the pictures as another level of communication with yourself. A photo-diary is also a good place to play about, for example by adding speech balloons to pictures or writing underneath a sequence of pictures rather like a photo story. Occasionally it might be interesting to take a snapshot and write a few paragraphs about it as if you were a stranger looking at the picture, describing what you see and forgetting what you think you know. In my own photo-diaries I often include images of myself in home-made paper masks with words written on the face, expressing my 'mood of the moment'.

In having myself done all the above work, over the years of intermittent photo activity I have come to accept the way I am, understanding some of the ways in which my subjectivity was constructed as very contradictory and fragmented. I have long since ceased to look for idealized images of myself, accepting the spectrum and variety the camera has offered. I see also that there is no single, coherent self, but a multiplicity of selves which are positioned in the world in a variety of ways, within a range of power dynamics. I have also been able to generalize from my understanding of myself that nothing is fixed, natural or unchangeable. Out of such raw beginnings come new forms of creativity and thinking.

22 · THE DAUGHTER'S GAZE
Blaming, shaming, renaming and letting go

Extracts from this (apparently unpublished) text were used as catalogue notes for the 'Mothers' exhibition, at the Ikon Gallery, Birmingham, 1990.

In recent years there have been shattering shifts in how we view 'autobiographical' or 'self-portrait' work in photography. Emergent theories of subjectivity and identity seem to have rendered obsolete any idea of a single unitary self made visible by an interpretation of surface appearances and the capturing of 'essence'. By extension, perhaps we can conclude that the notion of the conventional portrait is in tatters ... but we don't yet know it. Instead, the term 'the construction of subjectivity' has emerged: 'Who is this "I" who I seem to be?' 'How do I know that?' 'How did I become her?' 'Is she fact or fiction?' By extension other questions can then be formulated: 'Who are other people?' 'By what set of processes do I know that?' Finally it is feasible to ask 'To which groups do I choose to be allied rather than assigned?' This subjectivity is neither ahistorical nor universal. Rather, it is specific, a web of psychic processes, uneven, split, contradictory and potentially antagonistic to itself, formed and articulated within specific historical moments and contexts, in which I oscillate between being the object of others' discourses and the uneasy subject of my own. Nor can my subjectivity be unproblematically represented through other conventional codes and genres of photography, though it is grounded in them.

Identities are acknowledged and experienced now as fractured and multiple, mobile and discontinuous, changing over time. And though we are identified through the fragmenting and dividing identifications of religion, race, ethnicity, sexuality, social and economic class, just as important is how we inhabited and struggled against ways in which our identities were also constructed for us within various discourses such as education, medicine and law:

discourses which help to set in place potential matrices of disempowerment for countless millions. Other aspects of identity under fresh scrutiny have been the ways in which we are addressed through the media. Here we are hailed or interpellated through visual and verbal signs in such a way that we feel that somebody knows 'I' actually exist (rather than, as is the case, being the hypothesized psychological constructs of a bewildering variety of commercial organizations to which we are target audiences for various forms of consumption). Similarly, within radical political theory identity has shifted from simple notions of class being fixed, moving from a theorization of the 'labour force' and 'point of production' into complexities of identities and subcultures constructed through 'consumption', and the ways in which we are caught up in discourses of desire. New militant identities and groupings have also emerged in recent years, for example around disability, sexual orientations, different cultural histories, feminism(s) and peace movements. In the work offered here, at the tip of this vast theoretical mountain of representation lie tiny human beings caught up in webs of shifting identities and identifications.

Whilst this is only the beginning of an even larger map of ways of conceiving the self within psychoanalytic theory, I want to concentrate here on something quite specific: the primary tie between my mother and myself – how we related and became bonded (I might almost say psychically chained) together and how this interaction between us shaped my conscious and unconscious identity. Put another way, I have ventured into the domain of how my psychic inner reality collided with, and was formed through, the impact of hers in the social and economic world. Turning this on its head, through cultural activity and the making of artworks, I have begun to represent the daughter's gaze (my own) towards my mother, and also to enact fantasies of myself as seen through (my projection of) her gaze to me. Although the ways in which I have come to represent this dichotomy are still embryonic I nonetheless offer aspects of them here in *Libido Uprising* which is a transformative narrative fragment. Here I have re-inhabited, re-remembered, re-enacted, re-staged aspects of my subjectivity through a series of personal metaphors which allow me to speak at last from the position of rebellious loving daughter rather than mother-blaming victim, shifting between the two terms of mother/daughter, until they merge, then finally separate.

For artists, moving into explicit areas of working on subjectivity has opened up a hornet's nest about whether we are dealing with conscious or unconscious processes when we refer to the 'self'. A whole series of questions arises: whether we are to work 'spontaneously' or 'theoretically' (for myself a symbiosis between feelings and intellect is invaluable); will 'creativity' be destroyed through becoming 'too theoretical'? Should the work be 'private' or 'public', become part of a public performance, a political act, or merely an activity grounded in a desire for better self- and societal knowledge? Perhaps a mixture of all these? . . .

I have begun to witness myself as an 'I' who first came into being through the structuring psychic processes of specific absences and losses, pleasures and unpleasures, through the stating of division and difference, and to experience an oscillation between being powerful and powerless. In this theatre of the self, as well as reinhabiting and reinventing the fantasies of my childhood and my sexuality,[1] as the child of working-class parents, my work has also helped me to understand how the ever-shifting everyday economic and ideological interplay between social classes also helped to construct my subjectivity. The work is currently now moving beyond *Libido Uprising* into the more dangerous territory of seeing myself as Other, as Monstrous, as potentially powerful through a display of my vulnerability and my wounds. I see this as a shamanistic act of sharing my journey rather than speaking from a pinnacle of academic knowledge.[2] . . .

In order to produce *Libido Uprising*, four separate photo sessions involved the *process* of making hundreds of images which I later saw as overlapping elements in my interior dialogues: these were then reduced down to the *product* of the final fourteen images. Before the work moved into the final stages (and much work remains totally private) I needed to be sure that I had already become separated from the specific memories/fantasies which lay behind it. Only at that stage could I feel safe enough to share the work.

Although the work is autobiographical I do not assume that it speaks to all people. Just as there are no universal subjectivities it must follow that there are no universal viewers. There may also be an unevenness of the individual viewer's ability to comprehend, or face up to, ways in which I have both clinically and emotionally scrutinized and taken apart my own history (leaving aesthetic debris littered everywhere). Much of the previous work has been described as in 'bad taste', 'unsuitable for galleries', 'revolting', 'ugly', 'narcissistic' and 'obsessive': pejorative and dismissive words, presumably spoken because of the thwarted expectations of the viewer/critic who might prefer to continue to consume the female body, or to dwell only in fantasies of idealization of self and others, rather than be encouraged to ask critical questions. . . .

27 Jo Spence/Rosy Martin, 1989
Libido Uprising – Extract from Part 1, c. 1948
As part of our Mother and Daughter work I map out my continuing desire, as an adolescent, to be loved by my mother. Alongside this I place my perceived view of her at that time, *c.* 1948.

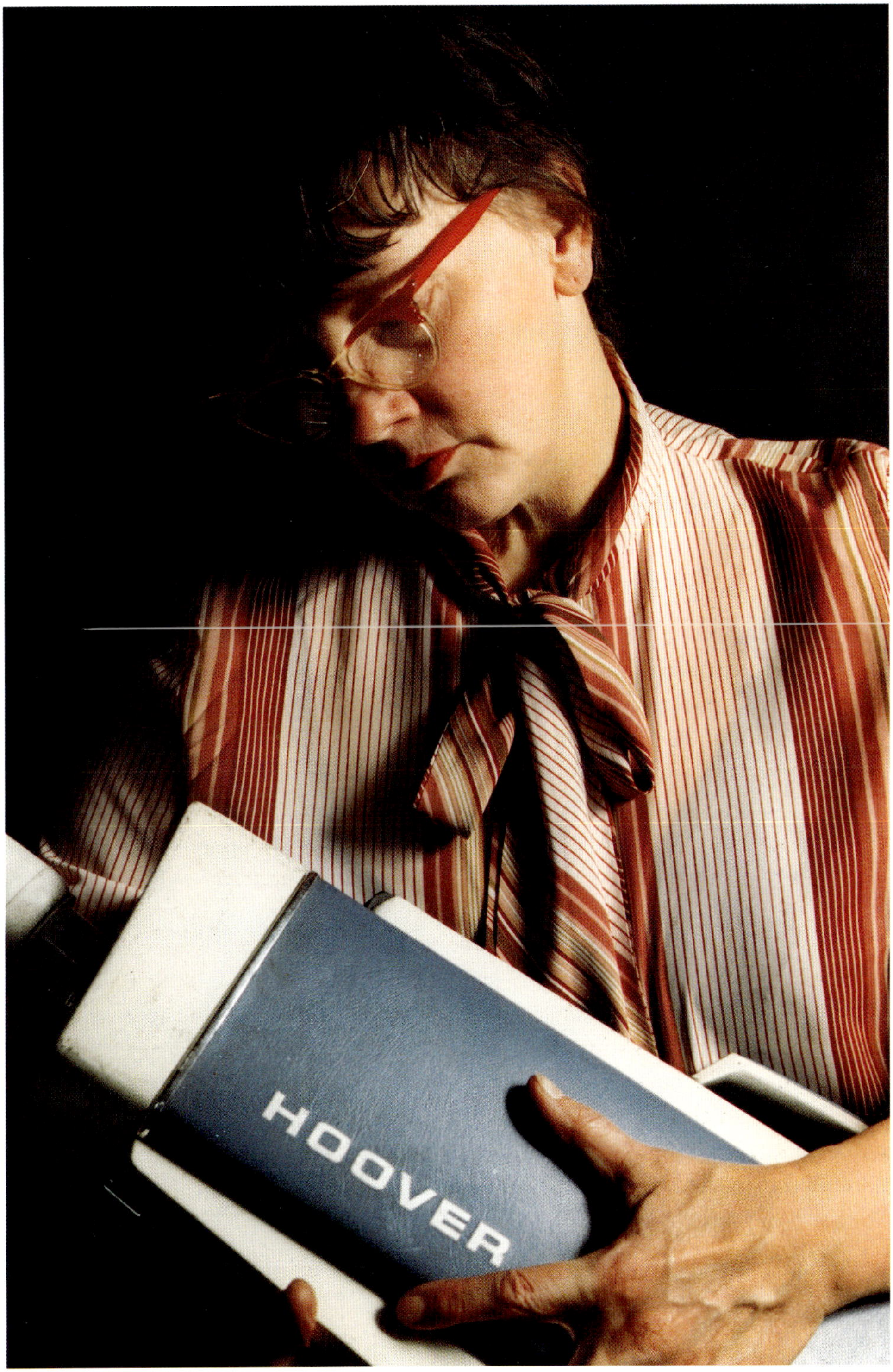
HOOVER

The emotional trajectory of my work during the past fifteen years has been: first, to shift away from the suppressed rage of injuries done to my 'inner child' (embodied photographically in an image of myself as 'the good fairy'/'the good daughter' – taken at my fiftieth birthday party) via an intellectual 'understanding' of my family history; then to move through my resistance to expressing the rage I still felt towards my mother and thence into a grieving for, and acceptance of, her loss. Finally came a letting go of resentment towards her for all her fantasized 'wrongs', thence into forgiveness of myself and an acceptance of who *she* was. In an integration of all these transformed feelings I then symbolically said goodbye in a ritual made seventeen years after her physical death. In the wake of the rebirth of my libido has come a creative anger which continues to inform my life, my work and my study. Most of the work remains private to me, but I have chosen to share some which I feel may resonate with the experience of some viewers (particularly women), flashing up before them like a no longer imprisoned memory. I am not seeking sympathy but rather am indicating the interplay between being 'victim' or 'heroine' (and the final abandonment of such deeply internalized and disempowering definitions of self). The work is offered more as a 'case study', as tools for exploration, play and analysis than as prescription, dogma or as an illustration of theory. . . .

In collaboration with Rosy Martin since 1983, our work has become an intervention into the fields of health and education, since it engages with the institutionalized mind and body split of western culture.

In *Libido Uprising* I have endeavoured to enact interior metaphors for my conflict between the domestic and the erotic, between my imago of my non-sexual mother and that part of myself which is still coming into being. At the beginning of each session with Rosy I had very little idea what I was trying to tell myself, but by the time the interaction between myself and my collaboration became a series of visual narrative fragments I had a much clearer idea of what I was saying, and then seeing. In the making of the pictures and the telling of the story I often became aware that 'that is not what I meant' . . . and the whole process started again. Sometimes I have been amazed at how much I have unmasked in the making of the work; at other times it has been a jumping-off point for going deeper, or moving sideways into new fragments of memory. Once repressed memories and disavowed fantasies have become visible they begin to ebb away, no long being dragged around as dead weight.

'Individualistic psychotherapy focusses not on the global struggles between imperialism and subjected peoples, but on the microcosm of marriage and the family within which those global forces are transformed as intra- and inter-psychic relations.... A comprehensive therapy must include not only a recalling of repressed, "rejected" part-objects and part "self-representations", but also "conscientisation" (as Paulo Freire calls it) concerning people's own historical roots through which, for instance, a mother's failing and rejection can be understood in its political and economic context.'[3]

23 · CLASS CONFUSION OR CULTURAL SOLIDARITY?

This appeared in *FAN, Feminist Art News*, in an edition called 'Working-class women working it out!', vol. 3, no. 6, 1991. Jo had been one of those who pushed for an edition on that theme. Finally she was too unwell to be at the launch at the Institute of Contemporary Arts, London, but got reports of it from Julia Tant, Valerie Walkerdine and me. One of the guest co-editors, Gabrielle Humphreys-Power, had attended Jo's workshop on class, gender and identity at the Photo Co-op, May 1990.

How are splintered subjectivities represented within cultural production? Where is it possible to begin to speak of such confusion?

In my family we had little connection to 'art' except perhaps my dad's exquisitely funny poetry (rather more limerick than lyric), and a reproduction of Franz Hals's *Laughing Cavalier*, proudly framed in black oak with gold inlay to match the table and chairs. Given this as a background, it is hardly surprising that it took me until the age of 55 to finally say that 'Yes, perhaps sometimes my work *is* Art'. By what criteria has it been judged up to now? Why the silence around artworks that try to deal with class/power relationships? Or use humour? Why do some of us still have to plead to be taken seriously as working-class artists? In view of our histories of exclusion or Otherness, many of us feel (yet again) that we just don't exist. What role models exist for working-class women to become artists or cultural workers? Even more important, given the post-structuralist climate, what hope for us to be able to get validation from curators, critics and theoreticians whilst still wishing to identify ourselves with (and being understood by) our own class?

Class and education ... as a working-class artist I feel I have an obligation to offer something back to my own group; to help other women (and men) to seek and find the resources they need for an art education which suits their particular class/ethnic/racial/sexual needs (something I never located within higher education). My work within education has always been class identified and linked to political consciousness, but it was not until the late 1980s that the question of my class *un*consciousness became relevant. I then moved rapidly away from social or socialist realism and began to develop the concept of psychic realism along with Rosy Martin, taking techniques from psychotherapy and merging them with photography into a 'theatre of the self'. Such work remains grounded in humorous, ironic and paradoxical cultural forms with which I grew up as a working-class child, playing with puns and contradictions as it represents subjectivity-in-process. Here I am beginning to unravel the knots of the psychic, social, economic and ideological processes which constructed the 'me' who struggles in and out of consciousness. A large component of this work has begun to devolve around shame, to make visible my apparent shifting between classes, masquerading as 'someone else', my self-silencing and my intermittently repressed rage which often manifested itself as sarcasm. . . .

People like me, who became fragmented, splintered, hybridized across differing (and contradictory) class positions by entering further (then higher) education, operate a kind of double consciousness, having a split use of language. Now I have become aware of this I see it as a strength, no longer wasting my energy 'passing' as 'middle class' (I neither come from the middle class, nor have I experienced any of its wealth or power, nor do I work as a professional or manifest managerial skills to control others). Instead I use my energy to encourage others to 'come out', drop the mask and get in touch with their creative anger. But as none of us can do much on our own, so work on class subjectivity must, of necessity, begin eventually to move beyond the split subjectivity of 'I' and into the solidarity of 'we'.

24 · CULTURAL SNIPER: PASSING/OUT

Thoughts on split class subjectivity (Jo Spence in conversation with John Taylor)

This was published in *Ten. 8*, vol. 2, no. 1, 1991. The first reference to her practice as cultural sniping had appeared a year earlier in *Variant* (see Chapter 18 of this volume). During this period, despite now knowing she had leukaemia, Jo relished going round meetings and parties announcing her new self-definition: 'I'm a cultural sniper.'

I've found in looking back that for a lot of my life I've had to pretend that I was somebody I wasn't. I had to pass myself off. I've been able to cross between groups very easily, but never belong to them. I'm talking about coming from a working-class background and 'becoming' middle-class. My subjectivity is very split up between my early life and my later life. This became very clear to me after five years in therapy where it seemed to me that I still wasn't able to talk about class with any safety. I then realized that I hadn't been able to talk about it with any safety in lots of other places, most particularly within higher education unless I happened to be somewhere where there were Marxists. Certainly, within the developing discourses of photographic theory I haven't seen a strong thread emerge which made it safe to speak.

But if your history is one of class conflict, it will not go away. In my work around phototherapy and self-portraiture, class has begun to be foregrounded much more. I have a verbal language, but not a visual one yet. . . .

As a photographer I don't think my work is going to reach a peak until I am in a safe space with other people from a similar background who may want to do very different types of work, but who want to focus on *class* and *power*. My experience in the women's movement is that I haven't felt very safe most of the time because the movement has been dominated by middle-class women, whether people like to admit it or not. Working with people like Rosy Martin has allowed an amazing amount of joy for me because she comes from the same background as I do, as do Terry Dennett and my husband David. From moving around the country and talking to different people I think that we are beginning to assert our class consciousness, especially in relation to how our subjectivities were formed. Many of us now know each other in different parts of the country and speaking for myself that gives me a degree of safety that I didn't have before. I am really talking also about how we can use the theories of Foucault and Althusser, for instance, and *some* psychoanalytical theory, to talk about class in ways that don't just position us as victims, or don't just come up with utopian impossibilities.

There are still a lot of people in cultural circles today who don't want to understand that there is such a thing as class identity because they only see the world in terms of labour and consumption. But that isn't my experience of travelling the country. For me, class consciousness is made from several different matrices: there's the economic matrix, the political, and the cultural matrix in which I see myself as having different sub-identities. To that I would add an ideological matrix: an understanding of how I got to be who I am, and which envelops all the other matrices.

I took my initial identity from my parents, and then rejected it. I've now reclaimed and reinvented it. I've reclaimed a mythological history because when I go back to my roots (beyond books on economics) there's no evidence it even existed. My whole family is broken up, scattered or dead. The factories they worked in have gone. The housing estate that we lived on is now yuppified. It's like it never happened. The only evidence I have is in my head, and because my brother still works in a factory. With him I can discuss a set of relationships that are invisible and don't appear to exist for anybody else. Still, though, there are places on the housing estate where I found privacy for my sex life. I went back and photographed them all recently and my overwhelming feeling is one of total sadness at the sordidness of the whole thing. I shared a partitioned bedroom with my brother until I was 25, and then I left home. My sex life was mostly conducted (and for sex life read 'groping') in the cemetery. So I've been back and photographed the trees I used to get groped against, round the garages, round the back of the dance hall and down by my brother's shed. Anywhere but in the family home. Now those incidents were as formative to me as anything that ever happened to me. But my desire, my excitement, that all had to be held in check because I didn't want to be a 'slag' or whatever the term was at the time. I

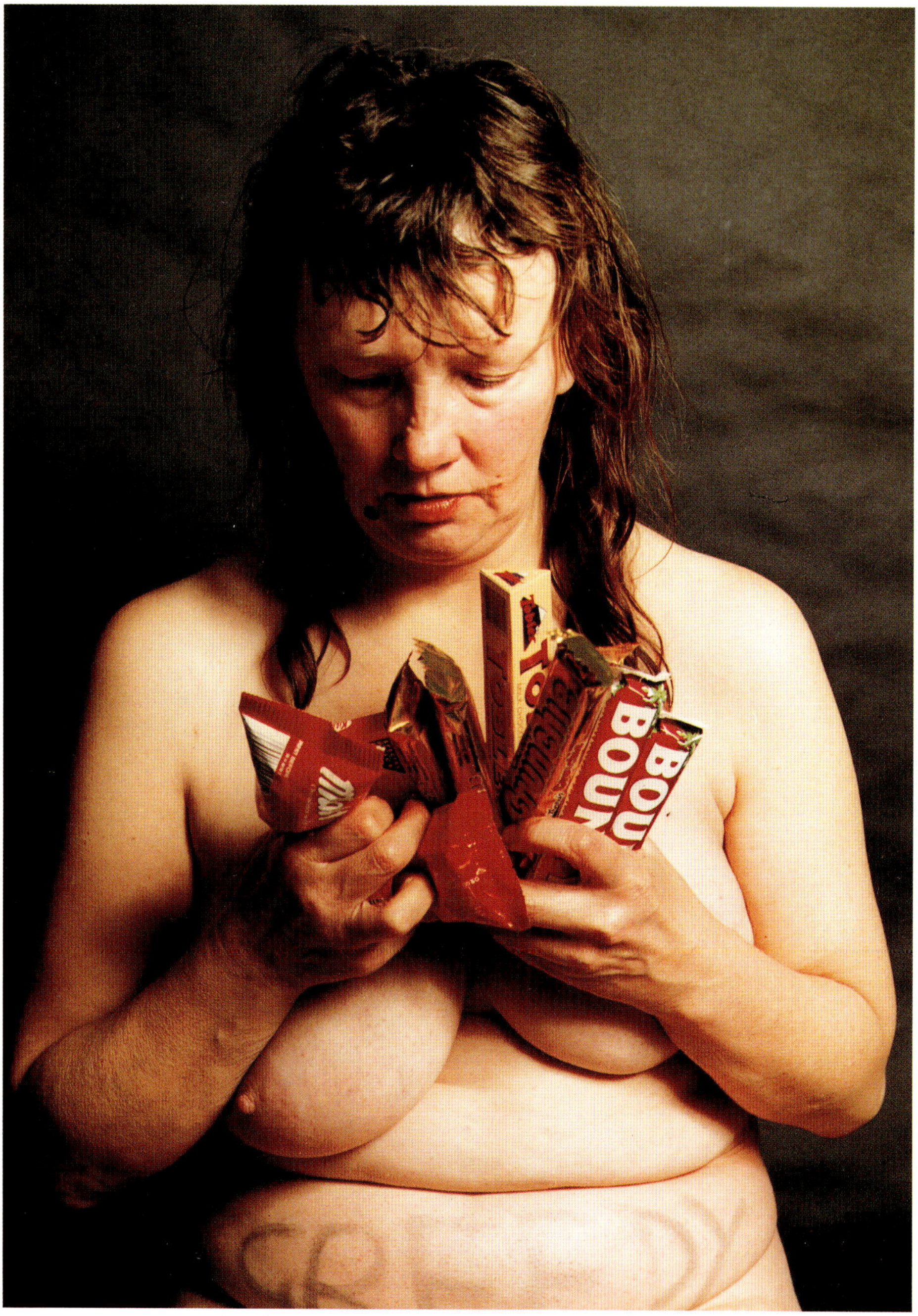

28 Jo Spence/Dr Tim Sheard, 1989
Greedy
I recreate my journey into emotional eating, a rebellion against parental disapproval.

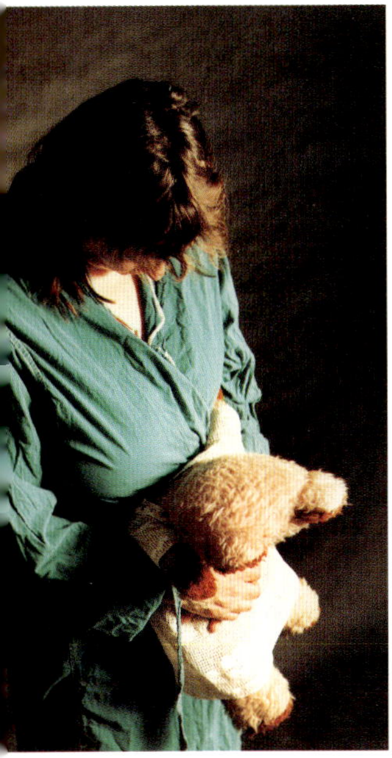

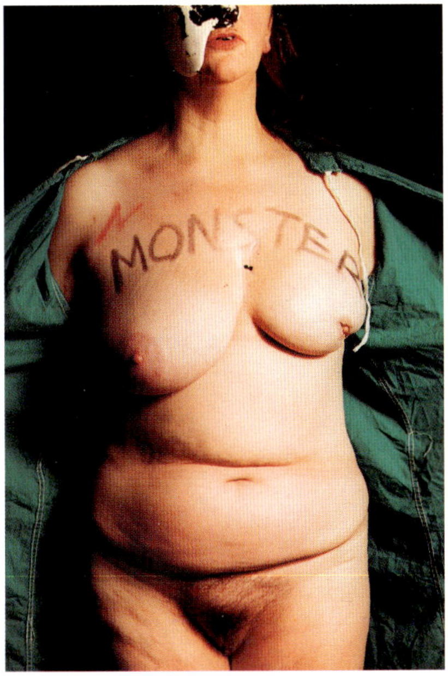

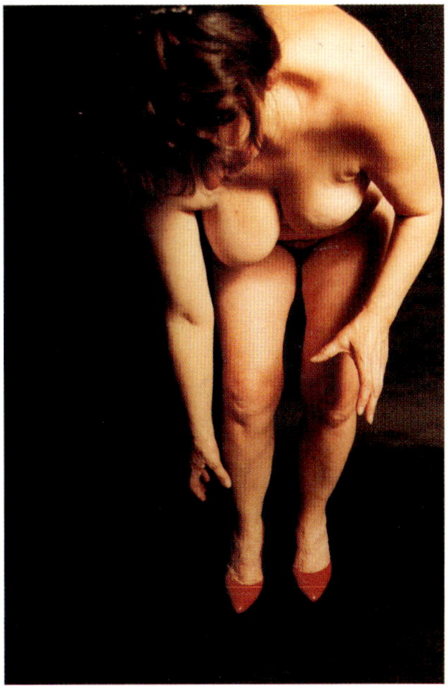

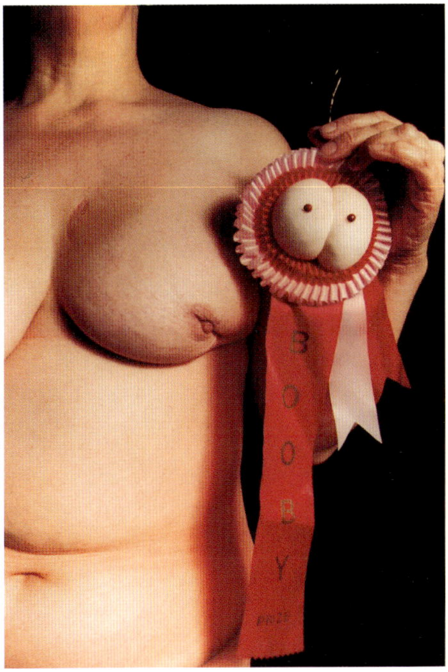

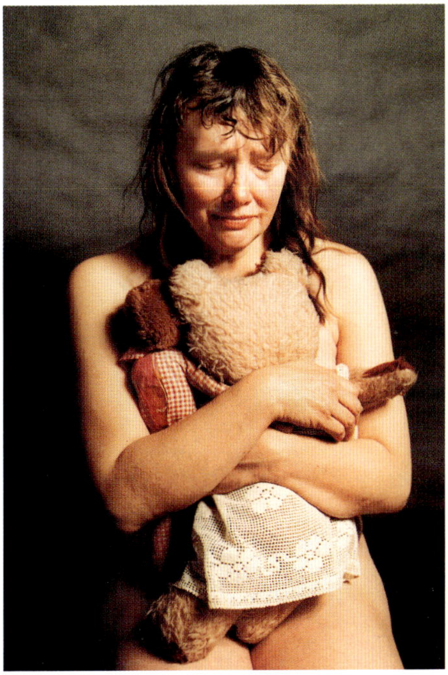

29–33 Jo Spence/Dr Tim Sheard, undated
Narratives of Dis-ease
29 *Excised* 30 *Exiled* 31 *Expected*
32 *Expunged* 33 *Included*

couldn't go 'too far' because I might get pregnant and I would be disgraced. I had no snapshots or representations of any of that. Photographing those sites of my adult libidinal beginnings has been really amazing. Interestingly, in the cemetery just behind the tree is a grave that says 'In Memory'.

Nothing remains of my family except the family album and conversations with my brother over the telephone to Devon. That's about it. What we have in the album is so poverty-stricken and so highly prescriptive of what we *ought* to have in it that I just want to howl my eyes out when I go through it now. Both my brother and I started taking photographs when we were in our teens. We went off in two totally different directions. I went into picturing the classic 'model girl' look of 1948. I didn't want anything to do with my parents: I didn't want to show I had a background. My brother, on the other hand, went into the other side of what I call 'working-class photography', which was to set up a whole series of jokey icons of my father pretending to kill my mother, and my father being shocked at reading *Lady Chatterley's Lover*. When I look at those photographs I think there is far more going on in psychoanalytic terms than anything I ever attempted to do. Mine are about class displacement and disavowal. In his, through a set of jokes, a lot of unconscious sexually repressed things are coming through. When they died, I didn't inherit much. In fact I don't even know what happened to my mother's wedding ring. The fact of them dying and possessing nothing in a sense wipes out your history and the quicker you forget it the better. I had to go into therapy to reclaim my history and begin to understand my parents' history and therefore to value them.

I believe that what happened to me after I left my family is of a different order from what happened to me when I was under the roof of my father. I left home at about 25 but it seems that most of the trauma and the conflict in my life was set up in my early childhood. Most of the patterns that I am caught up in come from that, including class and power relationship patterns.... Since I have been in therapy, and also began to connect to the historical component that was missing from my subjective experience, I now have a compassion for my family which I didn't have before. But this feeling hasn't come from the therapy so much as from politics: putting the two together has actually allowed me a place back in my own history and my own family. Yet it hasn't given me any peace, because you can't get rid of class conflict through therapy. What therapy has done is make me strong enough to understand that I can speak about that conflict: not in order to privilege it, but to do work that illuminates the process, so you can survive the conflict and try to change things.

Going into higher education was the most amazing thing that ever happened to me, but it was also one of the most painful because it couldn't deal with the conflict that I wanted to theorize, which was class. It gave me some amazing tools, though, which I'll always have, but I felt very much like the woman in the film *Educating Rita* who says she feels like an intellectual 'half-caste'. I've had neither a good education nor a thorough education, nor have I had *no* education. I have crossed boundaries and I am in limbo land. I'm sorry to talk in parables but I think the story of the ugly duckling is very important because it ties up to the story of Cinderella. If I was going to do the Cinderella work again I would concentrate on the ugly sisters. The point about the ugly duckling story is that you have to know who you can relate to, who are *your* group. In class terms, crossing social barriers, my greatest pleasure in life would be to understand what group I belong to. But at least now I understand that I never assimilated, I only masqueraded.

As a cultural worker I am producing materials that are about history and memory, and I am using myself as a case study, so when a curator of a show says virtually, 'Fuck the process, let's have a look at the products in the shop', my history vanishes immediately. What they are doing is fitting what they choose to see from my work into their own preconceived ideas of what will make a show. You have no control at all. I was approached by somebody to turn into a television series all the work I'd done on the family album, and we worked on script outlines. I was allowed to put what I liked into the script outlines. I thought they were quite exciting. Channel 4 thought they were exciting, the production company thought they were exciting. However, when it came to making the programmes, what I had put in gradually disappeared and I was told: 'You don't know how to make television.' But what disappeared was my class history and my class knowledge. I'm not saying the programmes were bad but they were nothing to do with what I had conceived of as programmes on the family album. I literally felt like killing because they had used my name to raise the money and I was in a very strange situation there: my name, my outline, and then I was gradually argued out of it to the point that finally I had such a bad asthma attack I was hospitalized and I had to pull out. What I was involved with was a class clash which was very subtly disguised. I don't think I am incapable of conceiving of how something would translate onto television. They didn't want to hear what I had to say.

I have also begun to see aspects of class manifested in the work some students are doing on their own history, their parents' history, the history of the organizations their mothers and fathers are involved in. I'm not talking about work on 'style' or 'subculture'. I'm actually talking about work on a larger idea of what history is. It might be very problematic to use the term 'history' but what I mean is that the people who come from the fishing industry or from the coal-mining industry, or whatever, perceive of themselves as part of a larger history than they are part of at the moment as de-classed photographers. In their work they are trying to make visible that history they feel is invisible but there is nowhere to go with it at the moment. They are getting good degrees and then they are coming out of college and floundering as far as I can see because there is no platform to speak from.[1]

Outside the unions, I have no notion where speaking of class consciousness could take place except perhaps in therapeutic spaces – dirty words to working-class people because 'therapy' is a very problematic term. Most people in our culture don't go for therapy unless they are from the middle classes. Instead, for 'social or psychic disturbances', most people are given drug therapy. That's why I made the work on cancer visible through the 'Picture of Health?' which could then go out onto the health circuit and self-help groups, as well as being a critique of the 'cancer industry'. It included family album photographs which made me look very bland and happy but, with my medical history alongside it, there was a clear contradiction. Sites within the social services are also being colonized by cultural workers of different types. Playleaders, theatre and education groups, movement people, people doing photography, artists and so on are going into spaces where communities or people are falling to bits and they are offering their skills as enabling tools. That's not the same as saying you can use your photographs to construct a new history of yourself or to deconstruct the old history but I think they are all part of a spectrum.

Given my belief that class is a dominant feature in our lives, that is where I choose now to put the bulk of my work. That might take the form of how to be 'difficult' within any given discourse. For instance, how could you challenge the discourse of medicine? What I bring to my work on discourse theory is my subjectivity as a working-class woman, brought up at a particular moment in a particular family, where we were labelled through our economic status. That helped to shape my consciousness and, I would argue, my unconsciousness. Those are the basic tools that I bring to discourse theory. When I am working on how I am treated as a cancer patient, I am very aware from my own knowledge that people who have had a better education than me, who are more able to mobilize resources for themselves, might have a very different position from mine within that discourse, even though they might still be merely patients. So again class would come into it for me, particularly as illness has become one of my major themes of work.

Demographically speaking, working-class people invariably kill themselves through the work they do. More middle-class people are likely to be doctors and obviously more patients are likely to be classified economically as working-class. As a cultural worker I feel that I can contribute as a dissident patient who represents the power relationships. I think of it as a form of civil disobedience. . . .

I am working now with a cancer doctor who last year said he would like to do some photography with me because I am also an asthmatic and in his opinion I suffer from inhibited anger. He did a session with me in which I was able to be angry for the first time, letting the real hatred out. We did a joint session on aggression. Part of that revolved around him as a doctor and me as a patient. I said: 'I want to show you what I think happens to a cancer patient when they go into hospital.' I displayed to him how I felt – literally I was a tearful child holding her teddy bear. He understood very well, and stood on a chair and photographed me from the dominating position of the doctor. I have a hospital gown which I stole from hospital because I needed it as a prop. I have used it in this piece of work. I then opened the gown and wrote 'monster' across my chest, because that's how I experienced myself as a cancer patient: monstrous to other people: 'How dare you talk about it. I can't bear to hear your pain. I might get cancer.' This is the unspoken material of people who are terrified of cancer. I wanted to make tools to make visible ways to talk of power and shame. . . .[2]

Most documentary photography is about victimization in which there is an appeal for somebody else to listen and change something for you. An outside agency makes the appeal on your behalf, a bit like an advocate would in a court. I've learnt to be my own advocate so I'm willing to go into the lion's den with my slide show. . . .

Now that I am moving on to work on ageing, the breast has taken on a completely different set of meanings for me. Last year I had a tragic love affair with a bloke (tragic in that it didn't work out). I was rejected because of my age, because I don't look 'beautiful'. He didn't want this clapped-out working-class woman who has a spirit and intellect but also a badly scarred breast and is overweight. These other structuring presences of male desire are there, however much you love and respect your body or your class background for having got you to this stage in your life. I still would like to look like a 25-year-old. I feel a bit daft even saying it.

25 · THE ARTIST AND ILLNESS
Cultural burn-out/holistic health! (interview with Jan Zita Grover)

This appeared in *Artpaper*, USA, 1991, and was originally titled 'The artist and illness'. Jo developed great respect and fondness for Jan Zita Grover and spoke a lot about a long car drive they had made in the US, conversing non-stop.

THE NATURAL HISTORY OF MY ILLNESSES

JAN ZITA GROVER You've addressed illness in your artwork for close to a decade now. How did you get started with this project?

JO SPENCE I've had three major illnesses, so perhaps I ought to mention them all. From the age of 12, I've had chronic asthma, but it would never have occurred to me in a million years to make it the subject of any artwork. I learned that it was something that people didn't want to know about, and I hid it. I simply naturalized and normalized the illness and never gave it a thought. . . .

I see now that the difference between how I think about representing my present illness, which is leukaemia, and my breast cancer ten years ago is that in 1982 I was very closely linked to a political model of photography and I hadn't been in therapy. I thought immediately about *how to be useful* – how to turn my illness into something useful. I think to some extent I abused myself: I was so anxious to be useful that I exploited myself in some ways.

Taking those photographs affected the rest of my life, actually. I had never before understood that I was a victim of anything. I had been so assertive all my life and I so rebelliously, full-heartedly pursued my own ends. When I recognized myself as a victim of breast cancer I realized that I hadn't been assertive – I had been aggressive. I needed to find other ways of getting myself heard, getting what I needed. That had been the situation in the hospital: I had won the confrontation with the surgeon by refusing his treatment – a mastectomy – but I didn't yet have anywhere else to go. I didn't know how to have a dialogue.

Now the third time around, with leukaemia, I asked totally different questions and came away in a different frame of mind because of the rehearsals, if you like.

ART OUT OF ILLNESS

J.Z.G. How did your breast cancer affect your artmaking and vice versa?

J.S. I don't think I've ever been so lonely in my entire life as I was after I'd refused traditional allopathic treatment for breast cancer – the mastectomy and radiotherapy.

Nearly everybody I knew thought I was mad. This loneliness was terrible.

I asked Maggie to take photographs of my alternative treatment as a confirmation that I had made the right choice. I could see from the photographs that I was clearly doing things to heal myself: juicing juices and mixing up herbs and doing exercise. In some way, these photographs were like my advocate's eye saying I needed to do these things to become well. I placed these images around me and looked at them a lot. I think I was beginning to learn to love myself. They gave me a lot of information about how gentle I was being with myself – a major shift from the steroids and antibiotics I had taken all my life as an asthmatic.

Being ill affected me as an artist in a very disastrous way. I already had quite a good profile as a cultural worker when I fell ill from breast cancer. I had worked for years in community politics and issue-based politics and as a gallery artist trying to problematize representations of the female nude. To leap suddenly into something as taboo as breast cancer was like facing a void. Maggie asked me to put some photographs into a juried show, and I found myself feeling very diffident about doing it. As an artist, I had used my own body to make statements about the history of the nude. But that was totally different – the body I had put up on the wall then was not diseased and scarred. Those nudes had been about ideological things. Cancer was about my own history. So taking this step was profoundly difficult for mc.

I put up these photographs of my illness and progress and I got no feedback from *anyone*. I went to the opening of the show and nobody spoke about my photographs to me all evening except for one woman, who came up and said, 'Where did you get the green card they were on?' – she quite liked the green card. I felt as if I were in a madhouse. I thought, 'Don't you understand that

I might be *dying* – that I've put up this work on the wall to help other people see that there are other ways to think about this illness?' And additionally, 'This isn't just an art work. This is an actual body that someone inhabits.'

Afterwards I felt I had blundered into the biggest minefield of silence I had ever been in in my entire life. I'd blundered through quite a few, working on class and gender and sexuality. But cancer – I had no way of knowing where I was going or what I was doing because nobody would speak to me. This may sound like an exaggeration today; so much work has been done on illness recently, but it hadn't been done then. I didn't know Frida Kahlo's work, which is brilliant on body trauma and childbirth and illness.

I began to get the feeling that I wasn't there, despite the fact I'd been given money by the British Arts Council to make the work, which they felt was right-on political work. The fact of the matter is, nobody knew what to do with it.

I had a retrospective: 'Jo Spence: Review of Work' in 1985. For that show, I did an information piece on breast cancer, 'The Picture of Health?', that went alongside the nudes and all sorts of other work. It was then that I realized nobody was going to speak to me unless they were in the health world. I began to understand that there were different audiences – the art world, the health world – but I didn't quite understand how to reach them.

Art audiences didn't then have a vocabulary to talk about identity work, which is what my new work was. Everybody is quite glib about it now – we've got a vocabulary for talking about identity work. When doing work on identity, I now see with hindsight, I needed to be clear of the trauma I'm representing before going public with it. If a trauma I'm representing is fresh and I haven't had a catharsis or any kind of insight or resolution from the trauma, I am literally putting my trauma on the wall. It isn't an interpretation: it's the trauma itself or an extension of it.

The situation for dissident cancer patients is not the same as it is for people with AIDS. There is no groundswell of loving dissidents surrounding cancer patients. In this country, the groundswell to change anything has come from the medical profession and holistic practitioners. People with cancer are so scattered among social classes and economic makeup, so isolated, that each of us belongs to a cluster of family helpers or at most a small self-help group, but tends not to know many other people with cancer. . . .

I'm addressing people within the disability movement as well as within the art world. Artists working on disability are few and far between in England. It seems to me that photography in relation to disability, or art in relation to disability, has been a Cinderella until recently. People went through art therapy or they were photographed as cripples or as people in wheelchairs. But suddenly, people like David Hevey, who is part of the disability arts lobby as well as an artist working on disability, and I are addressing disability in a completely different way. We're inhabiting the images ourselves and inviting others to do that for themselves.

For me, the arena of the art world has been very much more nurturing than the theoretical world of photography that spawned me. But I didn't choose to work in a vacuum any more than I chose to have cancer. Nonetheless, that vacuum exists: the representation and politics of cancer simply do not get debated in the world of politicized photography in Britain, whereas people who do cultural work on AIDS have available the language and theory developed around the politics of homosexuality.

ART ABOUT ILLNESS

J.Z.G. How have your identity and practices as an artist affected the way you've dealt with your recently diagnosed leukaemia?

J.S. I thought having cancer was lonely, but it was nothing to having leukaemia. Leukaemia is seen as a killer disease. There is no cure for it. If you deviate one iota from the path of chemotherapy, everybody, literally everybody, thinks you're stark raving mad. This time my witness, my advocate's eye, is a hundred times keener than it was before, and I'm now using my camera as a notebook. I keep a diary. I'm watching, and I know there is no easy answer.

How do you make leukaemia visible? Well how do you? It's an impossibility. It's what I went through before – a crisis of representation. I actually haven't got very much to say at the moment. I'm dealing with an illness that is almost impossible to represent. I have not the faintest idea how to represent leukaemia except for how I feel about it.

I didn't have the faintest idea when I first had cancer how to represent to myself what was happening. Finally I found a language for it. Now that I have leukaemia, the language that worked with breast cancer doesn't seem applicable. This time around, I'm looking at it ecologically and globally and I have a totally different attitude to my body, my illness.

J.Z.G. So how do you now see your identity in relation to art and illness?

J.S. Now I see it in psychoanalytic terms; it was a bit like the silenced child who keeps tugging at its mother's apron strings, saying, 'Listen to me!' and when the mother won't listen, the child sets fire to the house or manifests asthma or throws its younger sibling out the window. Looking back, I'd say that the more silence there was, the more I upped the ante, the more I was determined to be heard. The problem was that I split myself across the art world, the photography world, the health world. So I had to do the job three times over. I ended up burning myself out, something not unknown in the world of radical health politics. Activists get ill, and decide to campaign around the radical politics of healthcare, and finally burn themselves out by becoming ill again. This is what happened to me with breast cancer. It's worse this time.

The art world didn't drive me on; it selected me. That's the interesting part about it. My work got seen because I write about it a lot. If your work goes into print, curators see it and ask you to contribute to shows. When I gave lectures, people would say, 'Oh, it's Jo Spence, the artist.' I would think, 'Who are they talking about? I've been making work for years.' But Jo Spence the photographer didn't seem to have the same resonance – and Jo Spence the cultural worker didn't have any resonance at all. Something to do with the magical word, 'artist'.

In the world of art colleges, the independent artist is the radical cutting edge. By coming in and giving a dangerous talk, I help the radical cutting edge emerge from the students. Anybody coming in from outside can provide enough energy for that radical cutting edge to emerge. It's very lonely, exciting, exhausting work. I did it for five years before I fell ill this time. I loved covering that tremendous territory of theory, making the bridge between body politics in terms of aesthetics and the politics of representation of health and disease. That's a tremendous bridge to work on building.

I began to take on harder and harder tasks. 'Yes, oh yes of course, I'll go to Australia, oh yes of course, I'll go to France, of course I'll go to America.' They all seemed like the next obvious steps. But I wish there had been more people to do the work. There was no shortage of people to talk about the politics of representation, but there was practically no one in this country to talk about cancer and the politics of cancer. That's the lonely path I continued to walk until I collapsed with leukaemia.

When I was told I had leukaemia, I sank into a suicidal depression overnight. As I began to come out of that, I saw that my illness was a sign, though I didn't know what it was a sign of. This time around, I'm spending my time trying to decide what story my illness is telling *me* rather than trying to impose a narrative onto other people that I still don't even understand myself. That was what I did with breast cancer, as I now see it. So it is possible I will never be a photographer or an artist again.

It is such a stressful world. Artists are incredibly badly paid and under-validated. I've done my stint as a cultural worker over many years of working in groups, but there are no groups around the politics of leukaemia or cancer. And so I've taken up tapestry and gardening because that's the only way I know how to have any peace in my life. It seems to me that choosing to go like an Amazon into the lion's den over and over again in order to be politically useful is just too energy-consuming and too conflictual. In the end it didn't seem to me to serve any function at all, so it feels at this point as if I will never do anything again except look after myself. The task of looking after myself with leukaemia is like having a newborn baby to look after; the amount of things daily that I have to do to nurture myself, which is what I've never been able to do before! Somebody in Australia called me Mother Courage – you know, from the Brecht play: I go around dragging my wares behind me, trying to make a penny and be useful.

Who wants to be a Mother Courage? If there was a movement to belong to it would be a different matter, but I don't see one. Of course I belong to a peer group, in the global sense of a politics of representation, but my struggle is now with a particular illness.

In terms of representation, I spend a lot of time writing letters back to people who've written to me from all over the world encouraging me to go on working. When I say to people I'm retiring, they say, 'Yes, but you'll get better', and I say 'Yes, but I won't want to do the same work.'

I don't know what that work will be. I take my snapshots. I've been keeping a visual diary about the crisis of representation that I'm passing through. I will probably write about it one day.

But I feel at age 57 it's my time for a rest. It's time to stop being a mother to the world and instead turn my energies inward for the first time. Yet I still feel the need to be politically useful. I wonder in psychoanalytic terms what that's all about – if I still have some unresolved trauma that drives me to prove myself over and over again. My guardian angel and my advocate and my nurturing selves are all saying, 'No, that's not where it's at – let's concentrate on the good things in life. Even if the Gulf War continues, even if the whole of the Soviet Union has fallen to pieces, even if whatever . . .'

I can't really watch the news. I used to be a political self linked to issues of class and poverty and childcare, gender definitions. But now I'm much more focused on disability and illness and suffering. What I notice all the time now is people being disabled: disabled by unemployment, disabled by state policies, disabled by soldiers coming into their village. I really am beginning to understand why people enjoy *Cinderella* and fantasy films. When you're as badly damaged as I am, you just want to have nice things around you. I don't really want to have to think about the *politics* of leukaemia . . .

26 · 'THE CRISIS PROJECT: Scenes of the Crime' (with Terry Dennett)

Subtitled 'Collaborative Work on the Theme of Public and Private Crisis', this photographic project was Jo's work in progress. She and Terry were collaborating on it at the time of her death in June 1992. A version of this article has since appeared in the Danish magazine *Katawa* and in the exhibition 'Real Stories' which opened in Denmark in July 1992, a few days after her death. It is scheduled to tour for four years. 'Scenes of the Crime' is part of the Crisis Project, as is 'Real Stories'.

This is the last article Jo wrote. However, she authored her own funeral, which was conducted in accordance with written instructions she left with David Roberts. The event was thoroughly photographed.

Crisis: A turning point in the progress of anything; a state of affairs in which a decisive change for better or worse is imminent.... The point in the progress of a disease when a change takes place which is decisive of recovery or death....

(*Oxford English Dictionary*)

The study of crisis as a subject in its own right has occupied us practically and personally for many years now. Our initial starting point was the important question of economics, and the problems of how to represent it. At an everyday level the work was also the result of having to confront a life-threatening illness and encountering the many taboos which surround the cancer patient. These twin poles then brought about a double 'crisis of representation' which we as photographers have continually tried to address. Thus, our 'Crisis Project' does not simply stem from theory, nor is it an attempt at 'correct positionism'; rather, we have tried to amalgamate our lived experiences in crisis management with diverse theories of the visual.

In concept, this current work is perhaps nearest to the one project that most people participate in at some time in their lives – that of making a family album or scrapbook. Such enterprises traditionally concern themselves with the documentation of private and ritualistic celebratory events, but in a reworking of the genre, ours has slowly acquired a wider scope. Not only does it celebrate, but it also mourns, accuses and attempts to heal.[1] It also draws upon a history of the documenting of street life, particularly the model offered to us by the worker photographer movement.[2] The 'Real Lives' shown in this work take as their starting points the fragmentary records which are part of our ongoing and separate personal archives. In combining material from these archives we have tried to bring about a new reality by juxtaposing the social with the psychic. These then become the building blocks and component parts in making the work. This technique is based upon a rereading of the Vertovian principle of 'Factography',[3] which we frequently supplement with 'photo theatre',[4] re-enactments and subjective/fantasy observations of 'part selves',[5] done in phototherapy sessions. To these we finally add a text which challenges the assumptions of the viewer.

Exhibiting such private material in a public space allows our images and text to connect with other people's transitory memories, fantasies and lived experience. In short, we try to offer our images as motivational (and contradictory) starting points, as working tools and methods, for others to produce similar documents of their own lives-in-context. In this respect our exhibitions are much more of a pedagogical exercise than consumerist fine art. Such interventions from below are politically essential at this time for it is our belief that global economic crises cannot be separated from so-called personal crises. They need to be debated in tandem. Nor can the need to nourish and nurture the self be divided off from the need to nourish and nurture the world.

The work is drawn from a larger project which has grown into two 'Crisis Archives' – one on economics,[6] the other on physical and mental health – both taking their basic methods and theory from several places in addition to photography. With such archives and diverse theoretical back-up, 'Real Stories', which have previously been repressed, can thus begin to be envisaged.

In our work, we have no ready-made scripts but rather use storytelling modes, allowing fragments to emerge in the course of the work. This is often facilitated through the application of psychodramatic techniques[7] which allow memories and fantasies to surface and be re-enacted (using the therapist/

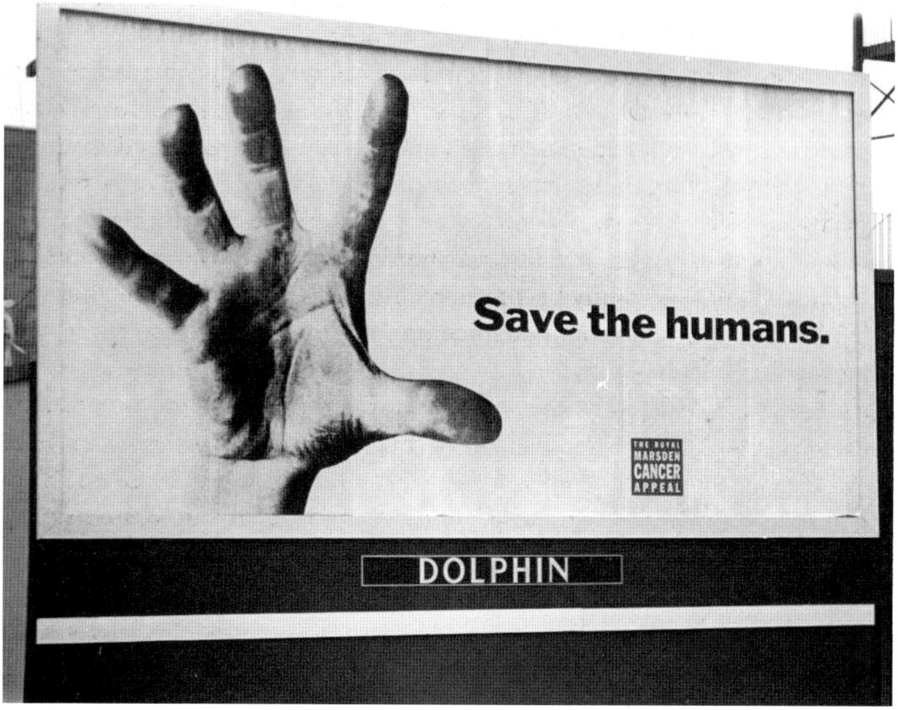
Save the humans.
THE ROYAL
MARSDEN
CANCER
APPEAL
DOLPHIN

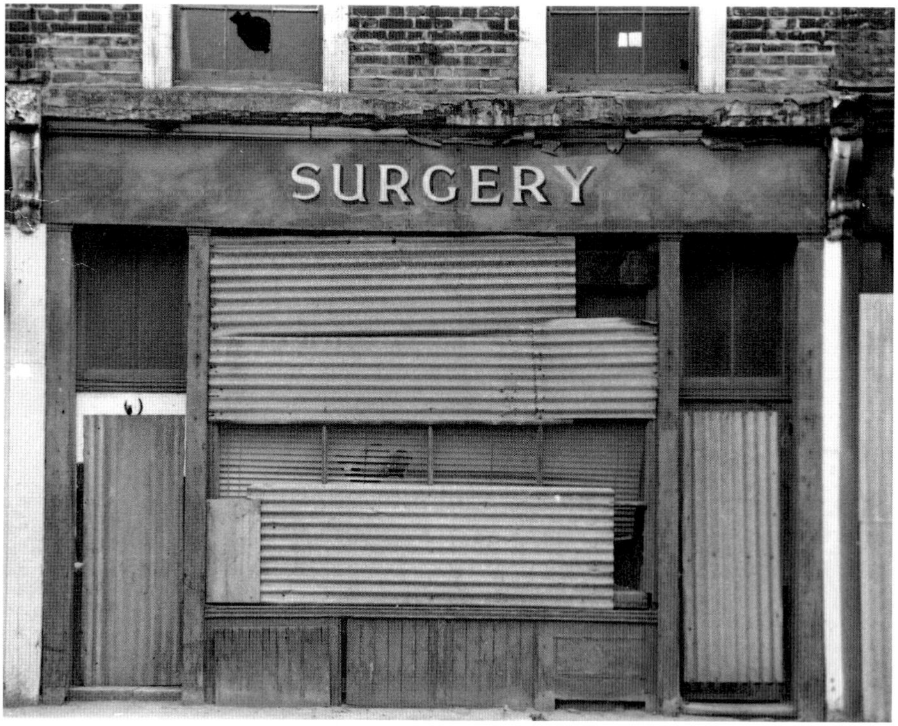
SURGERY

photographer as advocate), and then be photographed. In such sessions what emerges is a provocatively visible form of psychohistory.

In planning and undertaking 'The Crisis Project' we have proceeded as if we had been given a 'historical commission' for a future government to produce visual material for a criminal trial against those who have presided over the despoliation and pollution of today's society. Technically of course this is fantasy but in fact the archives we are building up using this 'historical imagination' approach will, if they survive, be truly transported forward to the future and the project will then almost certainly become a reality. 'Scenes of the Crime' uses two genres: legal record photography (documentation of the scenes of the crime) and staged photography.

Through the application of such methods which produce new connections and new visual possibilities (by a form of 'lateral imaging' analogous to 'lateral thinking') it becomes possible to map out many 'private' internalized conflicts which are otherwise difficult to highlight with traditional photographic approaches and are thus seldom documented and rarely acknowledged in the visual history of many individuals.

'The Crisis Project' is conceived principally as an archive documentary project. Central to its evolution was the notion that the documentary photography of our time must reorientate itself and look at the world from within the photographer's daily life experiences. Through inhabiting our own history, which is also the history of our class or group, and becoming aware of it in everyday life, we can begin to make visible that which has been 'overlooked' or is too painful to acknowledge and to develop a historical imagination about past, present and future.

Our overall aim is to use photography to open up for discussion the social, political, institutional and subjective spaces which we occupy daily. In fact ordinary daily life becomes the starting point for our projects, much in the tradition of the worker photographers who were trained to photograph everything that concerned them as workers: the ordinary as well as the extraordinary.

34–35 Jo Spence/Terry Dennett, 1991
'The Crisis Project: Scenes of the Crime'
(from 'Real Stories' exhibition)

Notes on 'The Final Project: A Photofantasy and Phototherapeutic Exploration of Life and Death' Jo Spence and Terry Dennett, 1991–2 (unfinished)

'The Final Project' was one of the two major collaborative pieces of work that Jo Spence was involved with during her last heroic struggle to overcome leukaemia. It was initially conceived as 'Final' only in the sense that work on her illness was the last photography she wished to do: it was her 'retirement project' after which she intended to try to catch up on all the things she had been unable to do when she was rushing from pillar to post giving lectures, helping students and organizing exhibitions.

However, being a realist as well as an optimist she reasoned that, if this was to be her last work it must be carried out properly as it was autobiographically important. The original outline envisaged a two-element project: an ongoing photo documentation with David Roberts of her health and survival treatments, and, dependent on her energy levels, photo theatre and phototherapy sessions around areas connected with death and death culture, backed up by a study of approaches to death in different cultures.

As she researched into the clinical aspects of leukaemia it became clear, however, that the condition was, for her, potentially more debilitating than the breast cancer that she had so successfully stabilized naturopathically for eight years. Its characteristic feature, a proliferation of immature white cells and a reduction in the red cell count, would progressively reduce the supply of oxygen to her brain, slowing down its functions, eventually robbing her of her most prized possessions, her sharp wit and critical power of thought and, above all, making her less mobile and sapping her energy.

Two photographic sessions in a cemetery made her realize that her health was no longer good enough for her to engage directly in photography. Out of frustration and necessity, she decided instead to use the existing material from her archive to create the kind of pictures she would have taken. Experimenting in the periods she had between her health treatments she began projecting images onto photographs and sandwiching slides together, a return to the techniques that she used with children during the Photography Workshop Mobile Darkroom Project of the 1970s. These 'post reality' superimpositions she called photofantasy she included as a major element of the project. In parallel with this she directed the setting up of a series of still life and constructed pieces as explorations of morality. The therapeutic intention of this work was to 'get to know death' so as to reduce the fear of the subject, but she realized that the methods that she had started to evolve also had important implications for photography.

Unfortunately she did not live to explore these new paths; that is left for those who follow her.

Terry Dennett, Jo Spence Memorial Archive, August 1994

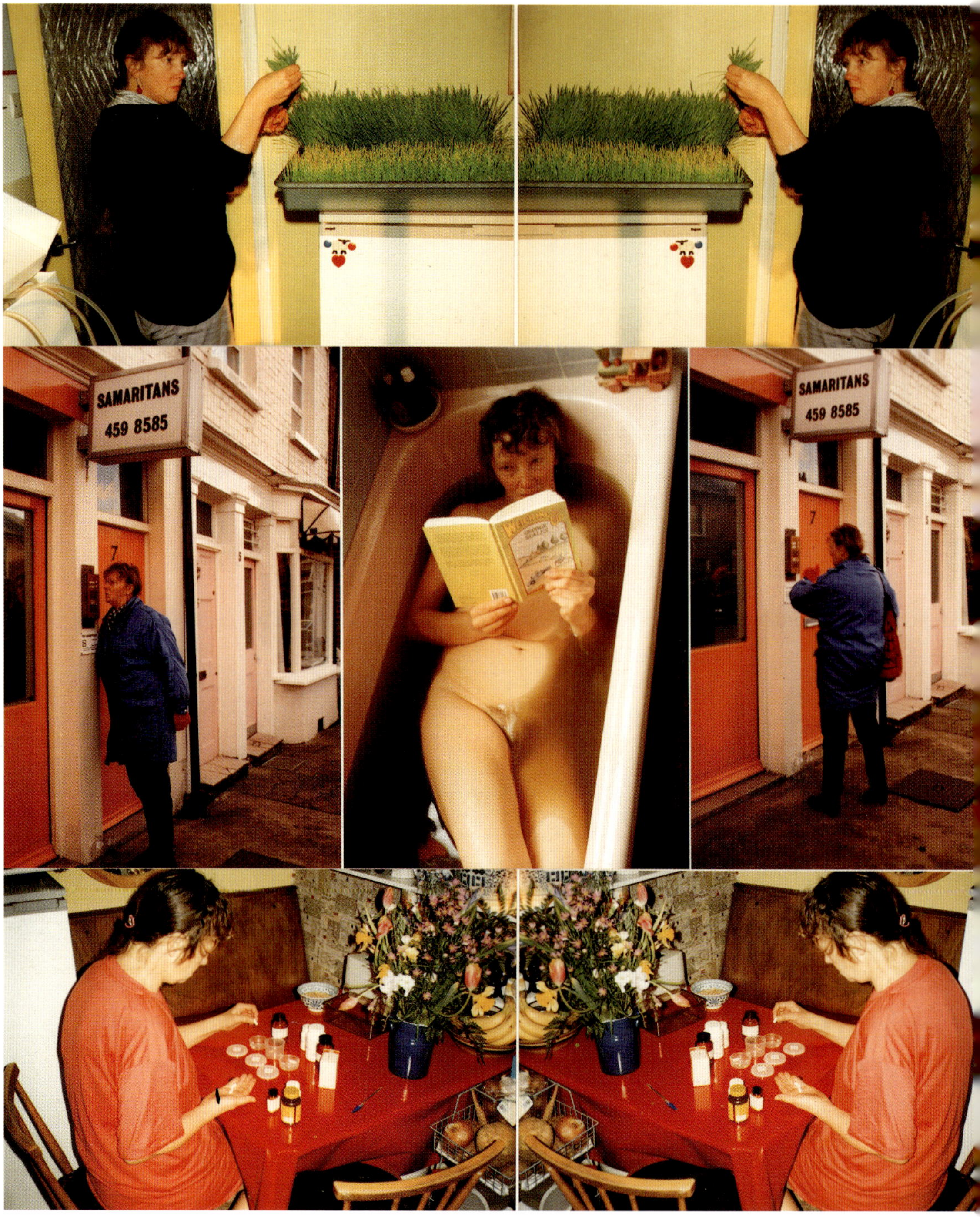

36 Jo Spence/David Roberts, 1991–2
Epic Journey (from the *Leukaemia Diary* series)
A page from Jo's on-going documentation of her survival programme.

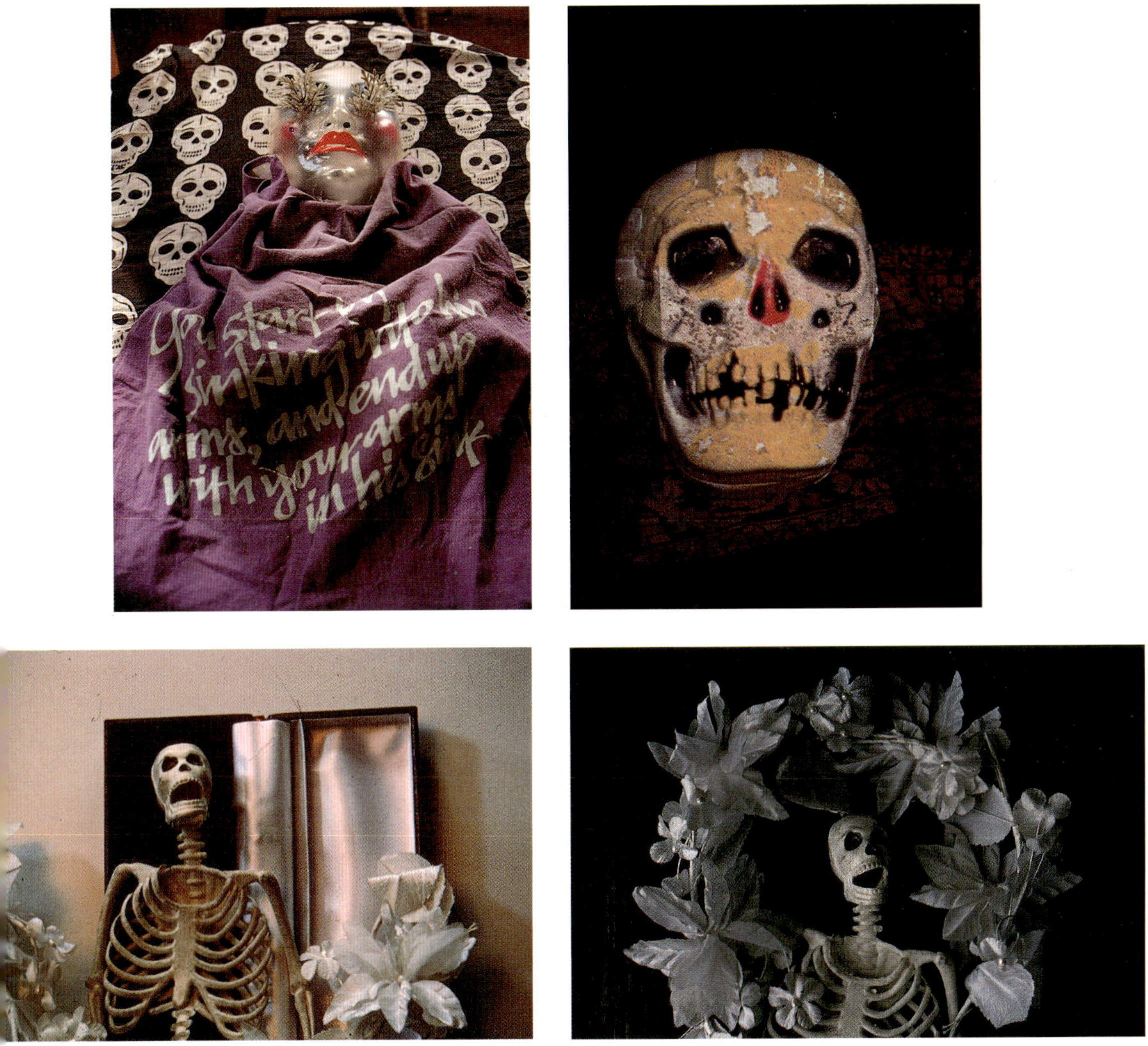

37a–d Jo Spence/Terry Dennett, 1991–2
'The Final Project' (unfinished)
(from the *Death Rituals* and *Return to Nature* series)

(a) Jo as a symbolic person passing from death to new life as the minerals in her body feed and nurture new plant growth. Based upon ideas from fertility cults and ancient Egyptian rites. The shroud is a 1970s feminist table cloth with the inscription, 'you start by sinking into his arms, and end up with your arms in his sink'.

(b)–(d) Tableau inspired by the death and mortality rituals of different cultures, but mainly based upon ideas from the Mexican *Dia de Muertos* (Day of the Dead) celebration.

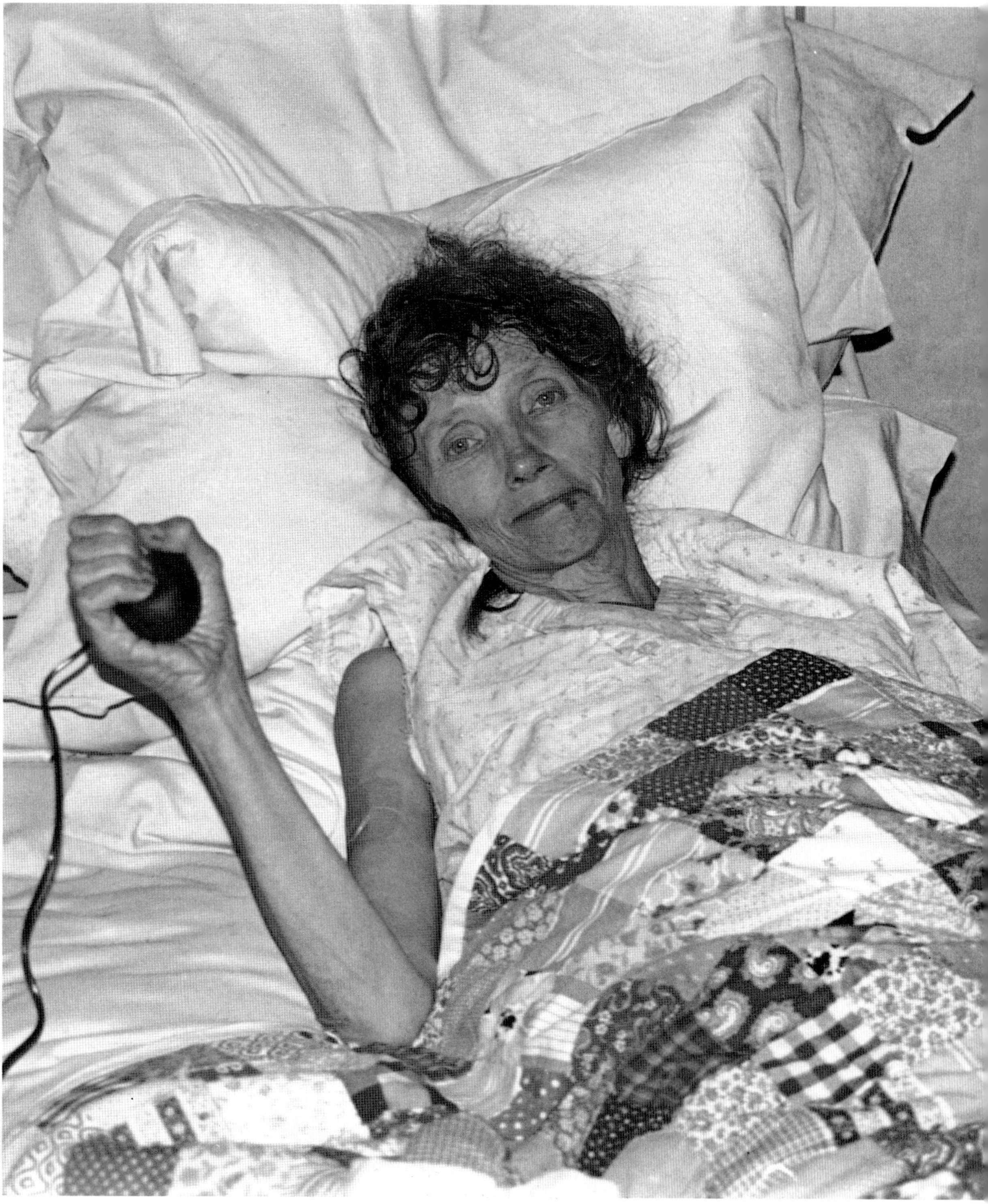

38 Terry Dennett, 1992
Untitled
Jo Spence on a 'good day' shortly before her death, photographing visitors to her room at the Marie Curie Hospice, Hampstead.

NOTES TO PART THREE

17 THE POLITICS OF TRANSFORMATION: THE FEMALE GAZE

1 Edward Adamson, *Art as Healing*, Coverture, 1986.
2 Especially relevant here is an article by Laura Mulvey, 'Visual pleasure and narrative cinema', *Screen*, vol. 16, no. 3, 1975.
3 See, in particular, Judith Williamson, 'Family, education and photography', *Ten. 8*, no. 14, issue on control and consent. See also Jo Spence/Photography Workshop exhibition, 'Beyond the Family Album', 1979, and the catalogue of 'Three Perspectives on Photography', London, Arts Council of Great Britain, 1979.
4 See in particular David Krauss, 'A summary of characteristics of photographs which make them useful in counselling and therapy', *Camera Lucida*, vol. 1, no. 2, 1980. See also Judy Weiser's 'Phototherapy – becoming visually literate about ourself', *Phototherapy Journal*, vol. 2, no. 4, 1984.
5 The most useful available book on this topic is *Phototherapy in Mental Health*, edited by David A. Krauss and Jerry L. Fryrear, Charles C. Thomas, Springfield, Ill., 1983. It has a huge and invaluable bibliography. *Phototherapy Journal* discontinued publication in the late 1980s. Back copies do not seem to be available anywhere in Britain. Its editor was Jerry Fryrear, UH-Clear Lake Box 127, 2700 Bay Area Boulevard, Houston, Texas. See also Resources list on p. 239 and Recommended reading on p. 231 of this book.
6 Edward Adamson, *Art as Healing*, Coverture, 1986.
7 Editor's note: Works on visual autobiography which are relevant here include two exhibitions by Jo Spence and others: 'Beyond the Family Album', and 'The Picture of Health?', plus Jo's work on fairy tales and photography. See Exhibitions list on p. 237.
8 See especially Richard Bandler and John Grinder, *Frogs into Princes: Neuro-Linguistic Programming*, Moab, Utah, 1979, and Richard Bandler, *Using Your Brain – for a Change, NLP*, 1985. Both published by Real People Press, Moab, Utah.
9 See exhibitions by Rosy Martin and Jo Spence: 'Don't Say Cheese, Say Lesbian' and 'Double Exposure – the Minefield of Memory'.
10 J. Spence, *Putting Myself in the Picture*, London, Camden Press, 1986.

Also see S. Kent and J. Moreau (eds) *Women's Images of Men*, London, Writers and Readers, 1985.

18 'COULD DO BETTER' . . . TOWARDS A PERSONAL AND POLITICAL THEATRE OF THE SELF?

1 See touring exhibition '*The Picture of Health? New approaches to breast cancer*' by Jo Spence, Jessica Evans, Maggie Murray, Rosy Martin and Yana Stajno.

19 PHOTOTHERAPY: PSYCHIC REALISM AS HEALING ART?

1 Sheila Ernst and Lucy Goodison, *In Our Own Hands, a Book of Self-help Therapy*, London, Women's Press, 1991.
2 D.W. Winnicott, *Playing and Reality*, London, Tavistock, 1971.
3 See Chris Weedon, *Feminist Practice and Post-structuralist Theory*, London, Basil Blackwell, 1987.
4 Patrick Casement, *Learning from the Patient*, London, Tavistock, 1985.
5 Liz Whiting, 'Alice Miller, making practical use of her work', *Journal of the Institute of Self-Analysis*, vol. 2, no. 1, 1988. The institute is based at 12 Nassington Road, London NW3. See also Alice Miller's books in Recommended reading, p. 231.

6 R. Assaglioli, *Psychosynthesis*, London, Turnstone Books, 1975; see also J. Spence, *Putting Myself in the Picture*, London, Camden Press, 1986.
7 See Ernst and Goodison, op. cit.

Rosy Martin and Jo Spence both thank Annette Kuhn for her helpful comments on our first draft of this article.

Further reading

Blatner, H., *Acting-in, Practical Applications of Pyschodramatic Methods*, New York, Springer, 1973.
Coward, Ros, *Female Desire*, London, Paladin, 1984.
Kovel, Joel, *A Complete Guide to Therapy*, London, Penguin, 1976.
Evison, R. and Horobin, R.W., *How to Change Yourself and Your World*, New York, Co-Counselling Phoenix, 1985.
Jackins, Harvey, *Fundamentals of Co-Counselling*, Seattle, Rational Island Publishers, 1981.
Perls, Fritz, Hefferline, R. and Goodman, P., *Gestalt Therapy*, London, Penguin, 1973.
Rowan, John, and Dryden, Windy, *Innovative Therapy in Britain*, Milton Keynes, Open University Press, 1988.

20 PHOTOTHERAPY: THE POTENTIAL FOR A BENEVOLENT AND HEALING EYE?

1 For information on Alice Miller's work see Recommended reading, p. 231 of this volume.
2 Now published as Liz Whiting, 'Aspects of the advocate', *Journal of the Institute of Self-Analysis, no. 2, London, April 1988.*

21 REWORKING THE FAMILY ALBUM

1 See the touring exhibition 'Beyond the Family Album'.
2 For a detailed account of phototherapy in relation to uses of the family album, see Chapter 19, 'Phototherapy: psychic realism as healing art?' by Jo Spence and Rosy Martin, on p. 164 of this volume. See also 'Memory factory', *Ten. 8* magazine, no. 34, autumn 1989, which is also about the family album and popular photography; see especially Jeremy Seabrook, 'My life is in that box: photographs and popular consciousness'; Gaby Porter, 'The economy of truth: photography in museums'.
3 Much has been written about co-counselling. It can be tracked down in your local progressive bookshop or in the Karnac bookshops in London.

> Co-counselling is based on the belief that human beings are born with tremendous intellectual potential, natural zest and lovingness, but that these qualities have been blocked and obscured as result of accumulated distressing experiences which begin in early life . . . people trained in co-counselling usually aim to assist each other in this process.
>
> (Jill Rakusen, *The New Our Bodies, Our Selves*, London, Penguin, 1989)

4 A useful account of various types of journal or diary keeping can be found in Tristine Rainer, *The New Diary*, London, Angus & Robertson, 1980.

22 THE DAUGHTER'S GAZE: BLAMING, SHAMING, RENAMING AND LETTING GO

1 See exhibition 'Double Exposure – the Minefield of Memory', by Rosy Martin and Jo Spence.
2 See exhibition, 'Narratives of Dis-ease' by Jo Spence with Tim Sheard, 1990. This was commissioned for the 'Great British Art Show', Glasgow, 1990, but now forms Part II of the exhibition 'The Picture of Health?'
3 Barry Richards, *Capitalism and infancy*, London, Free Association Press, 1988.

24 CULTURAL SNIPER: PASSING/OUT (THOUGHTS ON SPLIT CLASS SUBJECTIVITY)

1 As an attempt to bring about an inter-class dialogue between photographers, I recently ran a weekend workshop, Class, Gender and Identity, through the London Photo Co-op. I wanted to be in touch and work with people like myself who are now 'post-education working-class', to examine how the splitting of our identities had affected our lives and our cultural practices.

2 See Chapter 18, 'Could do better' . . . towards a personal and political theatre of the self?' on p. 156 of this volume.

26 'THE CRISIS PROJECT: SCENES OF THE CRIME'

1 This is especially profound when the use of techniques from phototherapy allow significant absences to be represented. It draws in particular on Alice Miller's ideas. The work of James Baldwin has also been germane to the emergence of phototherapy, particularly his insights into victimization, for example his idea that 'The victim who is able to articulate the situation of the victim is no longer a victim. He or she is a threat.'

2 This model for social and political action through the use of the personal camera has been adopted by Terry within his crisis project. For background reading, see 'Left photography between the wars: the international Worker Photographer movement', *Photography/Politics: One*, London, Photography Workshop, 1979. See also T. Dennett, 'Popular photography and labour albums', in J. Spence and P. Holland, *Family Snaps, the Meaning of Domestic Photography*, London, Virago, 1991, with particular reference to the camera in the service of the working-class ten-hour beginners' courses of the Arbeiter Foto Group, 1929.

3 Factography: the production and collection of unstaged photographs of ordinary life to provide an archive of images to draw on for montage and juxtaposition. Soviet filmmaker Dziga Vertov, in his proposal 'The factory of facts', emphasizes an inventory of possibilities for documentary by 'filming facts, sorting facts, disseminating facts, agitation with facts'. Such 'facts' also include all the material relevant to any given subject including ephemera, documents and images.

4 Of use here have been radical theories of dramatology. See in particular Dennis Brisset and Charles Edgeley (eds) *Life as Theatre: A Dramaturgical Sourcebook*, New York, Aldine de Gruyter, 1990; Erving Goffman, *Strategic Interaction*, Oxford, Blackwell, 1969; Augusto Boal, *Theatre of the Oppressed*, London, Pluto Press, 1974.

5 This term is borrowed from psychosynthesis, which is a humanistic way of reaching and giving tangible form to inner parts of the self which have been previously repressed or unidentified. This allows for a dialogue between such parts and problematizes the notion of a unified self. As 'part selves', we become more knowledgeable and participatory actors in the drama of 'life as theatre'.

6 In relation to economics we have drawn upon the systems of technical and financial analyses used in the stock market, especially in Elliot Wave theory, notably Glenn Neely, *Mastering Elliott Wave*, USA, Windsor Books, 1990, and Weiss Research's *Timing the Market*, USA, Probus Publishing, 1986; also Robert Beckman's seminal book, *The Down Wave*, USA, Milestone Publications, 1985.

7 In relation to psychodrama see especially H. Blatner, *Acting-in: Practical Applications of Pyschodynamic Methods*, New York, Springer, 1983.

Acknowledgements and thanks to Rosy Martin, David Roberts and Tim Sheard for their collaborative work in phototherapy.

RECOMMENDED READING

This bibliography includes various reading lists that Jo Spence gave out to people doing her workshops and books recommended in articles which are not published in this anthology. Other titles can be seen in the notes at the end of each of the three parts of this book. About twenty further titles, by people we think she would have liked to include, have been added posthumously.

Akeret, Robert U., *Photo-analysis: How to Interpret the Hidden Psychological Meaning of Personal Photographs*, New York, Fireside Book by Simon & Schuster, 1973.

Barthes, Roland, *Camera Lucida*, Cape, London, 1981.

Belsey, Catherine, *Critical Practice*, London, Routledge, 1980.

Berger, John, *About Looking*, London, Writers and Readers, 1980.

Betterton, Rosemary (ed.) *Looking On: Images of Femininity in the Visual Arts and Media*, London, Pandora, 1987.

Bly, Robert, *A Little Book on the Human Shadow*, San Francisco, Harper & Row, 1988.

Boal, Augusto, *Theatre of the Oppressed*, London, Pluto Press, 1974.

Bourdieu, Pierre, *The Logic of Practice*, London, Polity, 1990.

Brisset, Denis and Edgeley, Charles (eds) *Life as Theater: a Dramaturgical Source Book*, New York, Aldine de Gruyter, 1990.

Buck-Morss, Susan, *The Dialectic of Seeing: Walter Benjamin and the Arcades Project*, Cambridge, Mass., Massachusetts Institute of Technology Press, 1989.

Burgin, Victor (ed.) *Thinking Photography*, London, Macmillan, 1982.

Chapman, Rowena and Rutherford, Jonathan (eds) *Male Order: Unwrapping Masculinity*, London, Lawrence & Wishart, 1988.

Coe, Brian and Gates, Paul, *The Snapshot Photograph: the Rise of Popular Photography 1888–1939*, London, Ash & Grant, 1977.

Davies, Thomas L., *Shoots: a Guide to your Family's Photographic Heritage*, London, Travelling Light, 1978.

Dewdney, Andrew and Lister, Martin, *Youth, Culture and Photography*, London, Macmillan, 1988.

Dickson, Anne, *A Woman in Your Own Right: Assertiveness and You*, London, Quartet, 1982.

Ernst, Sheila and Goodison, Lucy, *In Our Own Hands: a Book of Self-help Therapy*,

London, Women's Press, 1981.

Ernst, Sheila and Maguire, Marie, *Living with the Sphinx: Papers from the Women's Therapy Centre*, London, Women's Press, 1987.

Faucan, Bernard, *Summer Camp*, New York, Xavier Moreau Inc., 1980.

Fraser, Ronald, *In Search of a Past*, London, Verso, 1984.

Goss, Larry, Katz, John Stuart and Ruby, Jay (eds) *Image Ethics*, Oxford, Oxford University Press, 1988.

Hall, Marny, *The Lavender Couch (a Consumer Guide to Psychotherapy for Lesbians and Gay Men*, Boston, Mass., Alyson Publications, 1985.

Hill, John, *Approaching Photography*, London, Focal Press, 1982.

Hirsch, Julia, *Family Photographs: Content, Meaning and Effect*, Oxford, Oxford University Press, 1981.

Holland, Patricia, Spence, Jo and Watney, Simon, *Photography/Politics: Two*, London, Comedia/Methuen, 1987.

Isherwood, Sue, *The Family Album*, London, Channel Four Publications, 1982.

Jhayham, Jasmine and Walton, Kamina, *As Easy as ABC, an Introduction to Photography and Language Work in the Primary Classroom*, London, Blackfriars Photography Project, n.d.

Kent, S. and Morreau, S., *Women's Images of Men*, London, Writers and Readers, 1985.

King, Graham, *Say 'Cheese'*, London, Collins, 1986.

Krauss, David A. and Fryrear, Jerry L. (eds) *Phototherapy in Mental Health*, Springfield, Ill., Charles C. Thomas, 1983.

Krzowski, Sue and Land, Pat (eds) *In our Experience: Workshops at the Women's Therapy Centre*, London, Women's Press, 1988.

Lesy, Michael, *Time Frames: the Meaning of Family Pictures*, New York, Pantheon Books, 1980.

Metcalf, Andy and Humphries, Martin (eds) *The Sexuality of Men*, London, Pluto Press, 1985.

Miller, Alice, *Thou Shalt Not Be Aware: Society's Betrayal of the Child*, London, Pluto Press, 1981.

——— *Pictures of Childhood*, New York, Farrar, Strauss & Giroux, 1986.

——— *The Drama of Being a Child*, London, Virago, 1987.

Milner, et al (eds) *Post-modern Conditions*, Berg, 1990.

Olivier, Christiane, *Jocasta's Children: the Imprint of the Mother*, London, Routledge & Kegan Paul, 1989.

Progoff, Ira, *At a Journal Workshop: the Basic Text and Guide for Use of the Intensive Journal Process*, New York, Dialogue House Library, 1975.

Rainer, Tristine, *The New Journal: How to Use a Journal for Self-guidance and Expanded Creativity*, London, Angus & Robertson, 1980.

Saunders, Gill, *The Nude – a New Perspective*, London, The Herbert Press, 1989.

Sekula, Allan, *Photography against the Grain: Essays and Photo Works 1973–83*, Canada, The Press of the Nova Scotia College of Art and Design, 1984.

Skynner, Robin and Cleese, John, *Families and How to Survive Them*, London, Methuen, 1983.

Sontag, Susan, *On Photography*, London, Fontana, 1984.

Spence, Jo and Dennett, Terry et al (eds) *Photography/Politics: One*, London, Photography Workshop, 1982.

Steedman, Carolyn, *Landscape for a Good Woman: A Story of Two Lives*, London, Virago, 1986.

Tagg, John, *The Burden of Representation: Essays on Photographies and Histories*, London, Macmillan Education, 1988.

Vaneigem, Raoul, *The Revolution of Every Day Life*, Vaneigem, 1983.

Walkerdine, Valerie, *Schoolgirl Fictions*, London, Pluto Press, 1990.

Walkerdine, Valerie and Lucey, Helen, *Democracy in the Kitchen: Regulating Mothers and Socialising Daughters*, London, Virago, 1989.

Weiser, Judy, *The Secret Lives of Snapshots and Albums: an Introduction to Phototherapy Techniques*, Canada, forthcoming.

Williams, Val, *The Other Observers: Women Photographers 1900 to the Present*, London, Virago, 1986.

Zipes, Jack, *Breaking the Magic Spell: Radical Theories of Folk and Fairy Tales*, London, Heinemann, 1979.

——— *Fairy Tales and the Art of Subversion: the Classical Genre for Children and the Process of Civilisation*, London, Heinemann, 1983.

PUBLICATIONS BY JO SPENCE

BOOKS

Dennett, Terry, Evans, David, Gohl, Sylvia and Spence, Jo, *Photography/Politics: One*, London, Photography Workshop, 1979.

Greenhill, Richard, Murray, Maggie and Spence, Jo, *Photography Guidelines*, London, MacDonald, 1978.

Holland, Patricia, Spence, Jo, and Watney, Simon, *Photography/Politics: Two*, London, Comedia/Photography Workshop, 1986.

Solomon, Joan and Spence, Jo, *What Can a Woman Do with a Camera?*, London, Scarlet Press, 1995.

Spence, Jo, *Putting Myself in the Picture*, London, Camden Press, 1986.

Spence, Jo and Holland, Patricia, *Family Snaps: the meanings of domestic photography*, London, Virago, 1990.

PUBLISHED ARTICLES

These are articles that are known. Readers are invited to send copies of/information on any other articles by and about Jo Spence to her Memorial Archive, address on p. 239.

As sole writer

'The politics of photography', *Camerawork*, no. 1, 1976, and *British Journal of Photography*, 26 March 1976.

'What did you do in the war, mummy? Class and gender in the images of women', in Dennett, Terry, Evans, David, Gohl, Sylvia and Spence, Jo (eds) *Photography/ Politics: One*, London, Photography Workshop, 1979.

'What do people do all day? Class and gender in images of women', *Screen Education*, no. 29, Winter 1978/9.

'Beyond the Family Album', *Ten.8*, no. 4, Spring 1980.

'Self-portraits', *Ten.8*, 1980.

'Confronting cancer', *City Limits*, 22 July 1983.

'Getting better', *Family Welfare Association Newsletter*, 1983.

'What is a political photograph?', *Camerawork*, 1984.

'The documentary forum', a contribution by Jo Spence, *Creative Camera*, February 1986.

'The sign as a site of class struggle: reflections on the work of John Heartfield', *Block*,

1982. An amended version of the original was published in Holland, Patricia, Spence, Jo and Watney, Simon, *Photography/Politics Two*, London, Comedia/ Photography Workshop, 1986.

'The picture of health?', *Spare Rib*, February and April 1986.

'Body beautiful or body in crisis', *Open Mind*, April 1986.

'Putting yourself in the picture', *Women Live*, 1987.

'No, I can't do that. My consultant wouldn't like it', in Mark Kidel (ed.) *The Meaning of Illness*, London, Routledge, 1988.

'Identity and cultural production or, on deciding to become the subject of our own histories rather than the object of somebody else's', *Views*, Summer 1990.

'Disrupting the silence: the daughter's story', *Women Artists Slide Library Journal*, 1989, and *Oral History*, 1989.

'"Could do better" . . . towards a personal and political theatre of the self?' *Practice*, 1990, and *Variant*, no. 8, 1990.

'Shame work: thoughts on family snaps and fractured identities', *Family Snaps*, London, Virago, 1990.

'Soap, family album work, and hope . . .', *Family Snaps*, London, Virago, 1990.

'Reworking the family album', *Media Education*, no. 12, 1990.

'The daughter's gaze: blaming, shaming, renaming ... and letting go', catalogue notes from 'Mothers' exhibition, Ikon Gallery, Birmingham, 1990.

'Class, gender and society', *Photo Co-op Newsletter*, 1990.

'Class confusion or cultural solidarity?', *Feminist Art News*, no. 6, 1991.

'Unbecoming mothers', catalogue notes from 'A Daughter's View', Bristol Watershed, 1991.

Written with others

With Ed Barber

'Public images, private functions', Ed Barber talks to Jo Spence, *Ten.8*, no. 13, Winter 1983/4.

With Ros Coward

'Body talk', a dialogue, in Holland, Patricia, Spence, Jo and Watney, Simon, *Photography/Politics: Two*, London, Comedia/Photography Workshop, 1986.

With Terry Dennett

'Photography, ideology and education', *Screen Education*, 1977.

'The unpolitical photograph?', *Camerawork*, no.7, 1978.

'Remodelling photo-history: an afterword on a recent exhibition', *Screen*, vol. 23, no. 1, 1983.

'Remodelling photo-history – a collaboration between two photographers', *Ten.8*, no. 9, 1982, republished in *Incite*, 1982.

'Ten years of Photography Workshop', in *Photographic Practices: Towards a Different Image*, London, Comedia, 1986.

'The Crisis Project: Scenes of the Crime', *Katawa*, Denmark, 1992.

With Jan Zita Grover

'Cultural burn-out/holistic health?', an interview with Jan Zita Grover, *Artpaper*, USA, 1991.

With David Hevey

'Cancer and the marks of struggle', interview with David Hevey, in David Hevey, *The Creatures that Time Forgot: Photography and Disability Imagery*, London, Routledge, 1992.

With Amanda Hopkinson

Interview in *Creative Camera*, 1987.

With Rosy Martin

'New portraits for old – the use of the camera in therapy', *Feminist Review*, no. 19, Spring 1985.

'Double exposure – the minefield of memory', *Photographers Gallery catalogue*, 1987; anthologized in Rosemary Betterton (ed.) *Looking on – Images of Femininity in the Visual Arts and Media*, London, Pandora, 1987.

'What do lesbians look like?', *Ten.8*, no. 25, June 1987.

'Phototherapy: psychic realism as healing art?', *Ten.8*, no. 30, 1988.

With David Roberts

'Things my father never taught me: a dialogue between lovers', *Ten.8*, no. 25, June 1987.

With John Taylor

'Cultural sniper: passing/out (thoughts on split class subjectivity)', Jo Spence in conversation with John Taylor, *Ten.8*, vol. 2, no. 1, 1991.

With Simon Watney

'An *Omnibus* dossier', by Jo Spence with introduction and afterword by Simon Watney, *Screen*, 1983.

With others

Spence, Jo, Brackx, Annie and Margolis, Laura, 'Facing up to myself', *Spare Rib*, no. 68, March 1978.

EXHIBITIONS BY JO SPENCE

1979
'Women and Work in Hackney' and 'Who's Holding the Baby', with Hackney Flashers.

'Beyond the Family Album', Hayward Gallery, London, and touring.

1982
'Family, Fantasy, Photography, with Polysnappers.

'The Picture of Health?', with Jessica Evans, Rosy Martin, Maggie Murray and Yana Stajno. Various versions created and exhibited since.

1985
'Review of Work: 1950–1985, Jo Spence, Camerawork Gallery, then touring internationally. A separate exhibition emerged from a section of it.

'The Phototherapy Road Show', with Rosy Martin.

1986
'Don't Say Cheese, Say Lesbian', with Rosy Martin, touring.

1987
'Double Exposure – the Minefield of Memory', with Rosy Martin, Photographers' Gallery, then touring.

'Body Politics', Photographers' Gallery.

'Transforming the Suit – What Do Lesbians Look Like?', with Rosy Martin. Plus 'Tales My Father Never Taught Me', with David Roberts, Photographers' Gallery.

1989
'Great Expectations', with Rosy Martin at Islington Libraries.

1990
'Jo Spence – Collaborative Works', touring Australia and US.

1991
'Missing Persons/Damaged Lives', with others, Leeds City Art Gallery, then touring.

'A Daughter's View', with others, Watershed Gallery, Bristol.

1992–3
'The Crisis Project: Scenes of the Crime' in 'Real Stories', Museet for Fotokunst, Odense, Denmark, and touring.

'Jo Spence; Photographs', Derby Photography Festival.

'Class Shame Projects' in 'Re Negotiations', Norfolk Gallery, and touring.

1994

'The Cancer Project', in 'Public Domain', Gallery de Art Santa Monica, Barcelona.

'Jo Spence: Matters of Concern', collaborative images 1982–92, Royal Festival Hall (Level 2), London, and Impressions Gallery, York.

'Our Bodies, Ourselves', selection from 'The Cancer Project', Nottingham Castle.

'Photographs from the Archive by Women', Museum Folkwang, Essen, Germany.

1995

'The Cancer Project', Melkweg Gallery, Amsterdam.

Forthcoming

'Alter Ego', Rotterdam.

'Freedom', Working title.

'In Memoriam': a exhibition of works to the memory of the late Jo Spence, Jo Spence Memorial Archive, London.

'The Final Project: a Photofantasy and Phototherapeutic Exploration of Life and Death', Jo Spence Memorial Archive, London.

'The Jo Spence Archive Installation'.

RESOURCES LIST

Jo Spence Memorial Archive, 152 Upper Street (rear entrance), London N1 1RA.
Tel: 0171 359 9064. *Contact*: Terry Dennett

For all pictures, exhibitions, articles, enquiries about Jo Spence. Also welcomes contact with people who worked with Jo. Delighted to accept any donations of photos of her in action, correspondence with her, items of her work, and stories/comments about her practice and life. Please enclose SAE for reply.

Rosy Martin, 31 Grimthorpe House, Percival Street, London EC1V 0BS
Fax: 0171 250 3477

For workshops and talks on phototherapy ideas worked out with Jo Spence. Also contact about joint exhibitions with Jo Spence.

Joan Solomon, 41 Cotham Road, Bristol BS6 6DG

For workshops and talks on topics worked out in collaboration with Jo Spence: contexting the self, autobiography, photography, creative writing.

Photo-therapy Centre, 1107 Homer Street, Suite 304, Vancouver, British Columbia, V6B 2Y1, Canada
Tel: (604) 689 9709 Fax: (604) 689 0854 *Contact*: Judy Weiser

For information about workshops, annual training institute courses each summer, books, articles, consultations.

INDEX